ASSASSINATION
IN ALGIERS

ASSASSINATION IN ALGIERS

Churchill, Roosevelt, de Gaulle,
and the Murder of Admiral Darlan

ANTHONY VERRIER

W · W · NORTON & COMPANY
New York   London

Printed in the United States of America.

The text of this book is composed in Lino Walbaum,
with display type set in Bodoni.
Composition and manufacturing by
The Maple-Vail Book Manufacturing Group.
Book design by Jacques Chazaud

First Edition

Library of Congress Cataloging-in-Publication Data

Verrier, Anthony.
Assassination in Algiers : North Africa and France, 1940–1942
by Anthony Verrier.
p. cm.
Includes bibliographical references.
1. Operation Torch.   2. World War, 1939–1945—Campaigns—Africa,
North.   3. World War, 1939–1945—Diplomatic history.   4. World War,
1939–1945—France.   I. Title.
D766.82.V45   1990
940.54′23—dc20   89-36578

ISBN 0-393-02828-3

W. W. Norton & Company, Inc.
500 Fifth Avenue, New York, N.Y. 10110

W. W. Norton & Company Ltd.,
10 Coptic Street, London WC1A 1PU

1 2 3 4 5 6 7 8 9 0

A Tous Les Français

and for F.S.—to whom more is
owed than can ever be expressed.

Ideological wars are revolutionary wars,
easily transcending national boundaries,
and always, at least in intention, and in
the imagination of the men involved in them,
total wars.

GARRETT MATTINGLY,
The Defeat of the Spanish Armada

Contents

———

Acknowledgments

I am most grateful to the late Lord Stockton; the late Barley Alison; Sir Brooks Richards; Sir Douglas Dodds-Parker; Rear Admiral Royer Dick; Lieutenant General Sir Ian Jacob; Sir Robin Brook; John Charmley; Robin Edmonds; and, in a very special sense, Alexander Elkin and Donal McCarthy, for crucial information, revealing material, sound advice, and unflagging support. Comparable assistance, occasionally spiced with mordant comment, was provided by French respondents, whose recollections, strongly supported by certain written reminiscences and papers, amply compensate for lack of officially available documentary material.

Christophe Campos, Directeur of the Institut Britannique de Paris, and François Bedarida, Directeur of the Institut d'Histoire du Temps Présent, ensured that the themes which are tackled in the following pages were subject to searching analysis, and not only from a French viewpoint. A particularly stimulating—and moving—*Table Ronde* was held in Paris during September 1988, where Historiens and Témoins shared discussion compounded about equally of goodwill and controversy. Clio demands arguments from her disciples.

My debt to C. M. Woods (SOE adviser for most of the period of research and writing) cannot easily be repaid. Through his good offices I was not only able to appreciate the SOE roles in North Africa, but the resentment and alarm expressed in London by Eden and others as the real purpose of American dealings with Darlan became plain. That real purpose was conveyed to London from British officials and soldiers in Algiers, amongst whom the representatives of SOE were not the least vocal. As always, the staffs of the Public Record Office; the National Archives in Washington (notably Sally Marks and John Taylor); the London Library; and the Royal United Services Institute were unfailing in support. The New York Public Library provided useful clues. Mrs. Nicole Gallimore and her colleagues in the Library of the Royal Institute of International Affairs were forbearing at all times, never more so than when boxes of papers were left in their care. I am also grateful for assistance given by the staffs of the British Library (Cunningham Papers); the Guildhall Library; the Imperial War Museum; the French Institute in London; the British Film Institute; and Mrs. Angela Radford, of the Suffolk County Library. Colonel J. A. Aylmer, and the Archivist of the Middle East Centre at St. Anthony's College Oxford (Miss Gillian Grant), kindly gave me permission to examine the papers of Sir Edward Spears—a crucial source for understanding the depth of Churchill's commitment to de Gaulle. I am also grateful to the Librarian of the Royal Archives and the Clerk of the Journals of the House of Commons for helpful letters.

In several ways, I am grateful for advice and support from Murray Pollinger and Michelle Lapautre, my agents in London and Paris. Eric Swenson, of W.W. Norton, proved to be friend and mentor during editorial collaboration in the wholly sympathetic atmosphere of the New York Yacht Club. Joan Barber typed the manuscript with her habitual accuracy and watchful eye for blemishes. Mr. J. M. Studd, Manager of Barclays Bank, Southwold, supported my endeavours with something more than a banker's understanding of a writer's task.

I would also wish to thank: Professeur José Aboulker; Major General R. H. Barry; the late J. G. Beevor; Martin Blumenson; Jean Borotra; McGeorge Bundy; Peter Calvocoressi; William Colby; Sir William Deakin; Arnaud de Chanterac; the late Sir John Colville; Baron Geoffroy de Courcel; Jacques Delarue; Colonel A. Dewavrin; Mario Faivre; Professor M. R. D. Foot; Professor Arthur Layton Funk; Louis-Dominique Girard; Lord Gladwyn; Olivier Guichard; Charles Hargrove; General Sir Charles Harington; Lady Selina Hastings; David Irving; Captain N. L. A. Jewell, R.N.; Dr. H. R. Kedward; C. G. Keightley; Lord Lansdowne; the late General Lyman Lemnitzer; the late Drew Middleton; Pierre Ordioni; Sir Michael Palliser; the Comte de Paris; G. H. M. Paulson; Bernard Pauphilet; Jean Planchais; Forrest Pogue; Anthony Powell; Philippe Ragueneau; Pierre Raynaud; Sir Patrick Reilly; Dr. Henri Rosencher; Brigadier-General Charles Saltzman; Lord Sherfield; the late Major General M. Z. Rygor Slowikowski; Dennys Sutton; Lord Thomas of Swynnerton; Professor Christopher Thorne; Group Captain Hugh Verity; H. Wharton-Tigar; Sir Peter Wilkinson; and Admiral Jerrauld Wright, U.S.N.

Preface

————

The Introduction which follows seeks truth about the events that are narrated in the text as a whole. The central issue may be simply defined: Anglo-American forces invaded French North Africa (Operation TORCH) during November 1942 in order to establish a base for offensive operations against the Axis in Europe. Franklin D. Roosevelt believed that such operations could be conducted within the framework of a strategy designed not only to liberate France and Western Europe, but also to prevent the emergence of revolutionary movements or the establishment of left-wing governments. Roosevelt, therefore, supported the Vichy government of Marshal Philippe Pétain. Roosevelt also believed in asserting the newfound power of the United States in the settlement of postwar European affairs. Winston Churchill shared Roosevelt's opposition to revolutionary movements and the left, but being committed to Charles de Gaulle and the Free French movement, opposed the Vichy government with all the force and vigor he could command. In the process, Churchill found himself in direct, and ultimately violent opposition to Roosevelt.

The complex, fluctuating relationships between Churchill and Roosevelt, Churchill and de Gaulle dominate much of the narrative. There is still a school of history which argues that Churchill frequently considered abandoning de Gaulle—and not only in deference to Roosevelt. The narrative rebuts this argument. Rebuttal is based on strong evidence, but is, doubtless, sustained in the last resort by personal recollection of June 1940 and the months that followed. What happened then forged a bond—if never an alliance—between Churchill and de Gaulle which time, adversity, and disagreement only strengthened. De Gaulle was excluded from participation in TORCH, mainly at Roosevelt's insistence, but partly because nothing remotely definable as "Gaullism"—or even sustained resistance to the Vichy administration—existed in the North Africa of November 1942. Yet the record shows that Churchill's support for de Gaulle—and French resistance to Adolf Hitler, and Vichy— was sustained throughout this testing period.

Churchill never forgot the early months, when the bond was forged. Defiance of Hitler and his evil deeds was the note struck by both leaders from the outset of their long, complex, ultimately triumphant relationship. It may not be generally known that in planning his state funeral, Churchill expressly desired that the president of France should be chief among foreign dignitaries. And so it fell out, and the tall figure of one who found refuge in Britain during French defeat and betrayal was first to follow the Queen, the Churchill family, and assorted royalties into St. Paul's Cathedral. Of course, Churchill could not foresee that de Gaulle would be president of France at the time of his death. But time works its way to the fitness of things.

Nor did de Gaulle, in his latter years, forget. On 7 April

1960, in Westminster Hall, after fifteen years' absence from the country of his exile, and in the presence of his old comrade in arms, now hunched and bowed, the "Constable of France" said, " in dipassionate but moving tones," the liberation of Europe invested Winston Churchill with the immortal glory of having been the leader and inspiration not only of Britain in the sternest test she has ever known, but also of many others." When de Gaulle had finished speaking, "none could be unaware of the surge of emotion that passed through Westminster Hall. He came down the stone steps, at once an exalted and rather mystical figure."

The years pass. And yet, the mold of history cannot easily be broken. When Churchill died, de Gaulle said: "I see in the passing away of this very great man the death of my war companion and friend." To the Queen—whose parents in 1940 had been among the first to visit de Gaulle and his few compatriots—he wrote of Churchill: "In the great drama he was the greatest of all." And there is the signed photograph of de Gaulle at Chartwell: beneath—"*A mon compagnon.*" What else is there is to say?

But memory, not less than history, requires reminders. During luncheon at Ten Downing Street some years ago an unmistakable voice sharply queried a guest: "Who is he? I don't know him." To which her guest of honor, President François Mitterand, replied: "That, Madame Prime Minister, is one of the Englishmen who helped to liberate my country." Mitterand remembered Robin Brook, once head of all French sections in the Special Operations Executive, that secret wartime organization which did, indeed, play a notable part in the liberation of France.

All errors—and omissions—are the author's. Whatever merit may be found in the story is due to others, one above all.

Introduction

—————

At 1500 on 24 December 1942, a cold but sunny day in Algiers, two shots were fired from a 7.65-caliber pistol into the stomach of Jean-François Darlan, Pétain's former deputy, yet Roosevelt's collaborator in maintaining the Vichy administration of North Africa in full, repressive force. Two hours later Darlan died, on the operating table. The future of France had been decided. Six months later de Gaulle was virtual master of "a French Government in exile."

Nearly fifty years later, few remember Darlan, Churchill's "odious Quisling," George Patton's "little red-faced pig," Robert Aron's "great enigma of the war." It was Darlan's ambition, however, that put Roosevelt, Churchill, and de Gaulle into conflict about France. Darlan's death at the hands of the twenty-year-old Fernand Bonnier did not end the conflict, but imposed on Churchill the task of accepting, and backing, what the United States embassy in London called "de Gaulle's political primacy."

Darlan, commander-in-chief of the French Navy in June 1940, was thereafter both a potent and a mistrusted figure of the Vichy regime. He represented a France that preferred defeat to defiance, collaboration with Hitler to fighting the "universal war" against fascism in which, as de Gaulle said in his first broadcast from London on 18 June 1940, "all must engage." The gulf between Darlan and de Gaulle, between Vichy and Fighting France, was absolute: France, prisoner of Hitler's will, or France defiant, one day to be liberated.

Pearl Harbor on 7 December 1941 had driven Roosevelt into a global war neither of his making nor seeking. Once imposed, however, it was a war capable only of being waged against the Axis with the full wealth and resources of "the arsenal of democracy"—the United States of America. Roosevelt did not want to arbitrate Europe's—or the world's—affairs. Being forced to do so, however, he was determined to brook no opposition. So far as France was concerned, a Vichy government that collaborated with Hitler might be induced to collaborate with the United States, one satellite role being exchanged for another. Darlan became the hinge of France's fate as a result because, at the time when TORCH was mounted, he appeared to be the one Frenchman who could collaborate effectively with American interests—while serving his own.

Robert Sherwood, a wartime associate of Roosevelt's, stated in 1948:

> The Vichy policy had been formulated long before [1942] and was adhered to unswervingly until the time of the invasion of North Africa. It never was and never became a policy that we thought we could rely on. Quite the contrary, it was a day-to-day, hand-to-mouth policy all the way through. No one in the State Department liked the Vichy regime or had any desire to appease it. We kept up the connection with Vichy simply because it provided us

with valuable intelligence sources and because it was felt that American influence might prevail to the extent of deterring Darlan and his associates from selling out completely to the Germans.

Whatever one's interpretation of this statement, evidence is abundant that Roosevelt's policy was much more positive than Sherwood indicates. Interpretation of Roosevelt's foreign policy is, however, difficult because he was rarely explicit, in speech or in his brief, occasional, written instructions and comments. Moreover, as Robert Sherwood has also said, Roosevelt had "a heavily forested interior," which few penetrated.

Nevertheless Roosevelt is on record as favoring dismemberment of the French Empire; reducing the size of Metropolitan France; denying it membership in the United Nations or any role in a peace settlement and the postwar occupation of Germany. In order to attain these objectives, a complaisant Frenchman had to be found, who would be offered political leadership, of a kind, in postwar France. Darlan filled the bill. Anthony Eden, who was both consistent and articulate in his opposition to Roosevelt's Vichy policy, wrote in his memoirs: "It seemed to me that Roosevelt wanted to hold the strings of France's future in his hands so that he could decide that country's fate." Darlan's assassination wrecked Roosevelt's policy of actively collaborating with Vichy or a successor to it, but did not remove opposition to de Gaulle. A Foreign Office note of 4 April 1943 concerning United States policy argued: "Their whole policy culminating in the Darlan experiment only makes sense on the assumption that they have believed it possible to create a sort of American party in France to form the basis of a future Government."

Churchill and his cabinet differed widely about de Gaulle, supporting his defiance of Hitler, and Vichy, mistrusting his poorly disguised ambition to become ruler of a liberated France. Relations between Churchill and de Gaulle were close in 1940, strained throughout 1941 because of violent differences about

British and French interests in Syria and Lebanon. During much of 1942 the relationship became increasingly complex, as Roosevelt's emergence onto the world stage drove Churchill to accept Britain's subordinate role in the Anglo-American alliance. Intermittent British submission to American dictates reflected Roosevelt's distrust of and hostility to de Gaulle and all his works. De Gaulle, passionate champion of a liberated, independent, sovereign France, stood in direct opposition to Roosevelt's postwar objectives for a Europe whose affairs would be arbitrated between the United States and the Soviet Union.

Churchill, torn between his support for de Gaulle's nationalist beliefs and his dependence on the United States, faced both ways as TORCH was planned and executed. During 1941, as Roosevelt coped with an isolationist Congress and a public hostile to American involvement in "foreign wars," Churchill was forced to propitiate him in all ways short of actually abandoning his own policies, strategies, and beliefs. The bases-for-destroyers deal in late 1940 and the passage of lend-lease in early 1941 had ruffled many British feathers. But, as Churchill said, "our needs were clamant." Roosevelt's Vichy policy ruffled many more British feathers, especially as the Royal Navy's attack on the French fleet at Mers el-Kébir on 3 July 1940 had "drawn a line of blood" between Britain and Vichy, which subsequent hostile actions—Dakar, Syria, Madagascar—only widened and deepened.

Nevertheless, by 5 June 1941, Churchill had written, "We must do as they tell us in these small ways." But the "ways" were rarely small, and Roosevelt knew it. Indeed, much was at stake when Churchill wrote with apparent resignation. The U.S. secretary of state, Cordell Hull, had said that if the British government continued to protest against American economic support for Vichy, lend-lease aid for Britain would be curtailed. Britain did continue to protest, but the tone was muted. The Royal Navy continued its blockade of Vichy at home and overseas, but increasingly resorted to covert methods.

Increasing British support for a struggling French Résistance throughout 1941—entirely a matter of covert, clandestine warfare—received little attention in Washington. But the reports of Admiral William Leahy, U.S. ambassador to Vichy—and one of Roosevelt's few confidants—stated unequivocally that the French people supported Pétain and opposed de Gaulle. By extension, France was not about to become a nation of résistants. Churchill's vigorous attitude to Vichy was not so much ignored as dismissed. Roosevelt was opposed to the British invasion of Vichy-governed Madagascar in May 1942—all the more so as Churchill asked for his support, yet made it clear that a Gaullist administration would eventually be installed in the territory—but appeared convinced that his Vichy policy was bound to prevail over all others.

The genesis and evolution of TORCH certainly offered a basis for Roosevelt's conviction. The ARCADIA Conference in December 1941, when Roosevelt and Churchill made their first concerted attempt to agree on an Anglo-American strategy for prosecuting the war, was followed in January 1942 by a meeting of the embryonic Combined Chiefs of Staff. This meeting ended with a strategic prescription: "The main object [for 1942] will be to strengthen this ring [around Germany] and close the gaps in it, by sustaining the Russian front, by arming and supporting Turkey, by increasing our strength in the Middle East, and by gaining possession of the whole North African coast." This prescription followed Churchill's strategic arguments, as deployed at ARCADIA, almost word for word. Roosevelt was not particularly enamored of the arguments, and his advisers were strongly opposed to them. But with American eyes focused on the Pacific at a time when Stalin was already urging an Anglo-American "Second Front," Churchill's strategy was adopted by default.

A price was to be paid: Roosevelt was determined to back an Anglo-American invasion of French North Africa in order to prosecute his Vichy policy. Robert Murphy, Roosevelt's emissary in North Africa, had been instructed early in 1941 to foment a conspiracy among the civil administration and armed forces in the three French territories which would enable any American-dominated invasion to be a virtually bloodless affair.

Thus, in Roosevelt's view, TORCH was less a strategic option than the first stage whereby his Vichy policy would be consolidated. The second stage would be the "Liberation" of France, but in terms fundamentally different from de Gaulle's revolutionary Résistance. Roosevelt was convinced that Churchill would be prepared, under pressure, to abandon de Gaulle as the price for the adoption of a strategy that he urged not only in the Allied but specifically in the British, and imperial, interest. "Closing the ring" would not only return the Mediterranean to the undisputed control of the Royal Navy, but would also preserve Britain's interests in the Middle East, and beyond. Roosevelt, no friend to the British Empire, reckoned that if he was prepared to humor Churchill's whims—as he saw them— the latter would do as he was told once TORCH evolved into a political campaign, whose strategic element would progressively be abandoned.

Roosevelt did have a concern for strategic factors—naturally enough, in the American interest. TORCH, once concluded, would remove a prospective Axis threat to North, and West, Africa. Prospective Axis acquisition of French naval facilities at Casablanca and Dakar threatened American maritime interests in the North and South Atlantic, and on a scale compelling Roosevelt and his advisers to divert naval resources from the Pacific. This threat had been considered seriously in Washington well before the United States was forced into war. Although Roosevelt lacked Churchill's obsession with the fate of the French fleet, he was certainly enough of a strategist to grasp the significance to Allied fortunes as a whole encapsulated in the phrase "gaining possession of the whole North African coast."

The evolution of TORCH appeared to strengthen all Roosevelt's convictions. Churchill kept quiet, and agreed to the exclusion of de Gaulle and the Free French movement from the operation. Churchill, apparently, accepted a subordinate role as Roosevelt's "First Lieutenant." British formations earmarked for TORCH were designated "supporting forces," despite the fact that the overall contribution from the Royal Navy, Royal Air Force, and Army was substantially larger than that from their American counterparts. Much went on behind the scenes—as the reader will discover—which, if Roosevelt had known might have shaken his convictions. This point, however, is debatable: Roosevelt was a hard man to shift.

What is not debatable is Churchill's apparent acquiescence in Roosevelt's policy toward Vichy and in the machinations of his agent, Robert Murphy. In fact, however, Churchill not only maintained a close relationship with de Gaulle but also, in doing so, gave tacit support to the British Chiefs of Staff, the Foreign Office, and SOE. By the time TORCH was finally mounted on 8 November 1942 these executive and operational branches of the British government had put together plans for installing an *anti*-Vichy administration in North Africa. These plans were forestalled by Murphy's collaboration with Darlan, and by resort to conspiracy, sometimes farcical, occasionally tragic, but in every way a reflection of the fundamental difference between American and British policies.

Within days of the invasion, British representatives in North Africa began a series of protests about American collaboration with Darlan which increased in force and intensity until the fatal event of 24 December. With the exception of Admiral Sir Andrew Cunningham, British representatives were excluded from American collaboration with Darlan. Exclusion bred frustration, and protests. These protests are notable for vigor of expression and stark simplicity of viewpoint: collaboration with Darlan was a prescription for civil war in North Africa and France; such collaboration had produced "a blasting and withering effect" among the British-supported French Résistance.

The conclusions were equally stark: Darlan must be "eliminated." Reaction in London, especially among the Chiefs of Staff, the Foreign Office, and SOE was swift and positive.

Once it became clear that diplomatic protests by the British government to Washington fell on deaf ears, the reaction moved from alarm to consideration of action. Churchill and Eden failed with protests as comprehensively as their subordinates. By 17 November Eden had noted: "It's a question of Darlan or de Gaulle." By 12 December Churchill had learned that Roosevelt intended "to work with Admiral Darlan for a very long time . . . at least until the end of the war in Europe." Less than two weeks later Darlan was dead.

The invasion of North Africa thus introduced a new element into the whole course and pattern of the war, widening the rift between Churchill and Roosevelt in consequence. A former member of SOE who fought in North Africa and France supporting just those values espoused by democratic Europeans reflected: "We waged in North Africa and in France an ideological war, increasingly a clandestine war." Two years were to elapse before the truth struck home that ideological commitment was an inevitable reaction to the fall of France. The truth struck home in North Africa, reaching its dramatic moment with Darlan's assassination. Thereafter, the British commitment to de Gaulle and, by June 1943, the Committee of National Liberation, was unequivocal; Roosevelt's support for de Gaulle's quondam rival General Henri Giraud was hesitant and ineffectual.

De Gaulle's utter rejection of Pétain's capitulation to German arms in June 1940 was not, by itself, ideological. But an ideology was thereby imposed on those who supported de Gaulle. From June 1940 the British, as that expert commentator Edward R. Murrow noted, "were living a life, not an apology." Neither Churchill, nor any other British adherent of de Gaulle, could be immune from this fact, although for so long the stress of war and de Gaulle's instinctive—and essential—intransigence enabled equivocation about political principle to be maintained. Neither Churchill nor his advisers were moved by de Gaulle's rhetoric—except in 1940. De Gaulle's invocation of Bernard Shaw's St. Joan—"France is alone; and God is alone; and what is my loneliness before the loneliness of my country and my God?"—had little appeal for Churchill, less for his advisers. Yet, by January 1943, a month after Darlan's assassination, Churchill could not but approve a more down-to-earth de Gaulle: "I represent the French people who cannot represent themselves."

Sir Edward Spears, who brought de Gaulle to England for his long years of defiance and exile, was to turn against him, from wounded pride and unsatisfied ambition. But Spears realized, as did few others, that Vichy, in presaging civil war, imposed an ideology on the Fighting French, and its supporters. None has expressed better than Spears, or with more tragic insight, the nature of that ideological conflict. Accompanying de Gaulle on the ill-fated expedition to Dakar in September 1940, Spears wrote of the enforced contact between Free French and Vichy officers: "Both groups hated each other with a bitter hatred, yet having been at the Naval School, the *Bordat*, together could not help using the familiar 'tu' to each other. They reviled each other intimately." The ideological conflict was one rooted in beliefs and attitudes that transcended—or descended below—political convictions as such.

Many Americans were as sensitive to moral issues as their British compatriots. But whereas "Vichy did confront the British with a genuine moral dilemma," many Americans were able to plead a privileged geographical or historical position to escape from de Gaulle's *"chose morale."* Nowhere is this escape route better indicated than in the observations of Roosevelt's ambassador to London, John Winant, when the former's collaboration with Darlan became generally known.

> What did the Mother in Ohio know about de Gaulle? What did she know about Darlan? All she felt was that it would be terrible if her boy died fighting the French. It [collaboration between Roosevelt and Darlan] was worth it.

Such an escape route was simply not possible for those in Britain who, whether supporting or opposing de Gaulle, opposed Vichy.

We are left, however, with a fundamental question: Was there an alternative to Roosevelt's Vichy policy? The question, although fundamental, becomes, in a sense, academic with time. Arguably, Roosevelt's policy succeeded: TORCH, in itself, was a relatively bloodless affair. Undoubtedly, the policy failed thereafter: Darlan entrenched himself in power, only to fall, almost by his own hand. (As it happens, the landings were relatively bloodless because Vichy forces could see the size of the Allied armada. But that is by the way.) The question has an importance nonetheless, which derives from any consideration of how war at the top is actually conducted. There was no "movement" in North Africa between 1940 and 1942 that was prepared either to replace the Vichy administration or, alternatively, to support de Gaulle. There was not even a movement committed to working with the United States, overtly and covertly, for the maintenance of a Vichy administration that would, at the critical moment, support Allied forces—and oppose the Axis. Roosevelt, as advised by Robert Murphy, his man on the spot, believed in the existence of—or the potential for—such a conspiracy. Other Americans working in the field did not so believe.

The British, by and large, were skeptical about this, or any other conspiracy. What the British came to believe in, however—by mid-1942—was the existence in North Africa of a group of "mostly Jewish and left-wing young men and women." These, it was perceived, would prove decisive saboteurs at the moment of maximum danger for TORCH—when the assault parties landed—thus giving the hazardous enterprise some chance of success. But the British in question believed that these young men and women expected rewards for their courage: an *anti*-Vichy administration throughout North Africa. Indeed the necessity for such an anti-Vichy—not necessarily Gaullist—administration formed part of the wider British thinking and planning in relation to the eventual liberation of France. Unfortunately—if one regards Roosevelt's policies as unfortunate, to say the least—neither the saboteurs' roles nor their expected rewards received attention at the crucial level below Churchill, and Roosevelt: the Combined Chiefs of Staff.

We can say that there was an alternative to Roosevelt's Vichy policy, specifically in its North African context, and particularly in relation to TORCH. But setting aside Roosevelt's power to get what he wanted by such means as he thought fit, the alternative was never seriously considered—at the top. Those directly committed to planning and executing TORCH discussed the question, the alternative, the whys and wherefores. But these frequently harassed soldiers were provided with conflicting intelligence—when provided with it at all. The priority tactical objective for TORCH was to establish bridgeheads before Vichy forces riposted—or Axis troops arrived in North Africa. Political issues were subordinated to what could be discussed from professional knowledge and on the basis of reliable, prosaic intelligence about numbers—men, landing craft, airfields.

But even such professional discussions took place in an atmosphere of improvisation, and confusion. Lieutenant General Eisenhower, as commander-in-chief of the "Allied Expeditionary Force," was less like a soldier commanding an army than the newly appointed managing director of a business operating from recently acquired premises, troubled by inadequate communications and conflicting orders from the chairman. To his credit, as we shall see, Eisenhower, not much of a soldier's soldier but a man others increasingly came to respect and follow, rose above these difficulties. But when immersed in them, neither Eisenhower nor his staff came to grips with fundamental questions. In such a situation, Roosevelt's Vichy policy went by default.

All Roosevelt's design, every strand of Darlan's ambition, was ended by the assassin's bullets. But this fatal act had its origin in causes, beliefs, circumstances, mutual incomprehensions, and recriminations. These varied elements proved stronger than definable objectives and deliberate intention. Roosevelt comprehensively failed to establish a satellite France, or Western Europe. In retrospect, we can say that Roosevelt could not impose his will on Allies beyond a certain point. Churchill as comprehensively failed to make his will prevail at Moscow, Teheran, Yalta. De Gaulle, in a sense, was alone triumphant. The triumph, nevertheless, owed much to men and women, British, French—and, eventually, American—on whom war had imposed an ideology that could not be denied.

PART ONE

1940–1942 Background to Conflict

1

———◆———

1940
The Fall of France

I

T he armistice that was signed between France and Germany at Compiègne on 22 June 1940 did more than mark the collapse of French armies in the face of blitzkreig. Nominally the armistice was signed by the plenipotentiaries of sovereign powers. In reality, however, it was a case of terms being imposed by a new German imperium on a French state that political conflict and military defeat had reduced to the level of a vassal.

The armistice can be defended—or, at least, explained—as the inevitable result of outright and overwhelming military defeat. Nevertheless, the French government that accepted Hitler's terms was, to a degree rarely acknowledged in France, both sympathetic and subservient to the New Order that he had established, and intended to extend elsewhere in Europe.

Anti-Semitic legislation was passed by the Daladier government in July 1939, and thereafter the large number of both
native and foreign Jews in France was subjected to increasing
humiliation and denial of basic rights. Among this large foreign community the Poles were most prominent. The contribution of these heroic exiles to the Résistance—in France, and
North Africa—sufficiently indicates the degree of persecution
from which they suffered.

Because Hitler understood so well that the French government was broadly sympathetic to his aims, above all
regarding Jewry, he was able to offer terms at Compiègne that
did more than indicate the relationship of emperor to vassal.
The armistice provided for a limited, and geographically well-
defined, German occupation of French metropolitan territory,
within which the French government would continue to exercise normal administrative control. Elsewhere in France, Vichy
would govern without even the appearance of German control.
French ground and air forces would be reduced in size and, in
France itself, rendered virtually nonoperational. But the French
fleet would remain very much "a fleet in being." Hitler opposed
the German naval staff by conceding the French fleet's "neutralization"; it would remain in port, but entirely under French,
not German, control. This fleet was formidable in size and
quality, the morale of officers and men far superior to their
unhappy compatriots in the French Army and Air Force. This
fleet, with which the Royal Navy had enjoyed close if difficult
relations, was the creation, paradoxically, of a bitter Anglophobe, Jean-François Darlan.

The French Empire would in no obvious sense be affected
by the armistice, nor would diplomatic missions cease to function. France, in short, would also remain in being to the world
at large, a fact that the United States—and the Soviet Union—
were prompt to acknowledge in diplomatic terms. French
colonial governors and the like would continue to administer
in the name of France, and their remit from the French government would not be considered invalid because the latter

had transferred itself from Paris to Vichy. In particular, Hitler showed no disposition to exploit his military defeat of France by considering occupation of French North Africa. A "Mixed Armistice Commission" was established for the three North African territories, on which Italy, always ambitious concerning Tunisia, was happy to serve. But the commission was established mainly in order to acquire political and economic intelligence, not as a fifth column for later aggression. Although so close to the scene of Mediterranean—and Atlantic—conflict, North Africa was, apparently, unaffected by the fall of France. The French armed forces stationed in the three territories retained their internal security and garrison roles, and would remain considerable in size if questionable in quality.

Given the factors summarized above, it is hardly surprising that Roosevelt was convinced that most French citizens, at home and overseas, welcomed the Compiègne Armistice and accepted the legitimacy of Pétain's government. In consequence, and governed also by American isolationism and the constitutional limitations on his powers to make or conduct foreign policy, Roosevelt acknowledged Vichy as a legitimate French government with which the United States might usefully engage in diplomatic negotiation, economic relations, and, prospectively, political bargains. The political and constitutional inhibitions on Roosevelt's freedom of action throughout 1940, and most particularly until his return for a third term in November, had led him to turn a deaf ear to pleas from Churchill and Paul Reynaud during the last, agonizing days of French defeat. Messages of sympathy were sent, but couched in language that left the recipients in little doubt that Roosevelt could not, or would not, either appeal to Hitler or threaten him. Whether Roosevelt's messages persuaded either Churchill or Reynaud into the belief that the United States would not "recognize" a French government that negotiated under duress must remain a matter of speculation. Roosevelt was particularly ambiguous

on this point. But the only material factor is that in giving diplomatic recognition to Vichy, he left Churchill in doubt whether
the United States would regard Pétain as a free agent or not.

The doubt was strongest concerning the future of the
French fleet, and it is in this context that Darlan's actions during and immediately after the fall of France sowed the worst
suspicions in Churchill's mind. Darlan's subsequent collaboration with Hitler only deepened Churchill's suspicions, and
personal loathing, to a stage where he was seen as an outright
enemy of Britain and British interests, however and wherever
represented. Some of these suspicions may have been
unfounded. Even during Darlan's closest collaboration with
Hitler, when he was at his most powerful position in Vichy (the
summer of 1941), he was careful to avoid complete commitment—and to keep one eye on the United States. But Churchill's attitude to Darlan was consistent; he was an enemy of
Britain, an ally of Hitler. In short, even in 1940, "it was a question of Darlan *or* de Gaulle." Churchill certainly recognized
de Gaulle as *"L'homme du destin"* from the moment he first
met him in May—a temporary brigadier general transmogri-
fied into a junior minister in Reynaud's palsied government.

Churchill acted on that recognition as panic succeeded
palsy, welcoming de Gaulle the exile in London on 17 June
with "a smile that was very warm and friendly." De Gaulle was
friendless and virtually penniless: Churchill's immediate support, above all, in allowing him to broadcast twice to France in
language both moving and defiant, ensured that "Free France"
would have a chance to rise from a challenge to a triumph.
Despite virtual rejection of de Gaulle in France and by French
servicemen in Britain, Churchill put out his hand to one who
said during those tragic days, "Keep your Royal Air Force in
Britain: it is needed here"—not in a France whose military
defeat had to be recognized in all its bitter detail.

But, all that said, Churchill's fears for the French fleet
once the Compiègne Armistice was signed governed his attitude to Darlan, and to Roosevelt. De Gaulle and his nascent

Free French movement was a potential ally, but Darlan represented an immediate threat—which might be partly count-
ered by diplomatic and material support from the United States.
Well before the French defeat, Churchill had appealed to
Roosevelt. On 15 May, virtually initiating their wartime correspondence, Churchill pleaded: "Help us with everything short
of actually engaging armed forces . . . the loan of forty or fifty
of your older destroyers . . . several hundred of the latest types
of aircraft . . . anti-aircraft equipment and ammunition . . ."
Churchill also suggested a more active role for the U.S. Navy
in the Pacific "to keep that Japanese dog quiet . . ." Churchill's
list of pleas and proposals was a reflection not so much of the
immediate situation as of a strong, natural need to shock Roosevelt into a realization of what was happening in Europe, and
to the world.

Roosevelt's response the following day was noncommittal,
and deeply disappointing to Churchill. "The best of luck to
you" would neither keep German armies from the Channel
ports nor encourage a French Navy whose senior officers, much
influenced by Darlan the politician rather than Darlan the
commander-in-chief, showed more disposition to regard their
fleets as bargaining chips than weapons of war. But Churchill
was forced to recognize the constraints on Roosevelt's freedom
of action. Churchill's decision in late June—and it was his
alone—to capture and destroy as much of the French Navy as
he could lay hands on reflected not only suspicion of Darlan
but also belief that bold and bloody strokes would convince
America that Britain meant to fight Hitler and all who collaborated with him.

On 4 June British and substantial French forces completed the evacuation from Dunkirk—Operation DYNAMO.
That day, in the House of Commons, Churchill was inspired
to say: "We shall defend our island, whatever the cost may be,
we shall fight on the beaches, we shall fight on the landing-
grounds, we shall fight in the fields and in the streets, we shall
fight in the hills; we shall never surrender, and even if . . . this

Island were subjugated . . . then our Empire beyond the seas, armed and guarded by the British Fleet, would carry on the struggle, until, in God's good time, the New World, with all its power and might, steps forth to the rescue and liberation of the Old."

But something more than the boldest defiance and the grandest rhetoric was needed to serve notice on friend and enemy alike that Britain would stay in the fight. On 10 June Roosevelt pledged "that the resources of the United States would be extended 'full speed ahead' to those struggling against Germany, and against Italy . . ." But the pledge was shorn of domestic political content and fell short of international impact. Action this day was needed. Darlan's pledges to the British government that the fleet which he had created would remain in French hands meant nothing to Churchill, who argued that French warships could only be physically secure from the German and Italian grasp if berthed in British, imperial, or United States ports. Churchill states his case unequivocally: "In spite of every kind of personal and private assurance given by Admiral Darlan to the First Lord of the Admirality and his naval colleagues [18 June] . . . an armistice was signed which was bound to put the French fleet effectively in the hands of Germany."

On 16 June Darlan had become minister of marine in Pétain's cabinet. Darlan claimed he could no longer give orders to the fleet. This was not true: Darlan remained commander-in-chief of the French Navy, but he was starting on the long road that led to brief power—and the assassin's bullet: from the first, he sought to be a man for all seasons. As Edouard Herriot remarked during the final days of the Third Republic: "This Admiral knows how to swim." Darlan also knew how to prevaricate, to maneuver. Churchill could never satisfactorily answer a question that Darlan implied rather than posed as they fenced amidst the ruins of France: Unless Hitler and Mussolini intended to extend their sway to North and West Africa, why should French warships be more secure from the victors of Compiègne if they were sailed to Gibraltar, Malta, or Freetown than if they remained at Oran, Casablanca, or Dakar?

This implied question has particular relevance to subsequent events; Churchill took the "worst case" interpretation of Darlan's rejoinders. If the French fleet was not sailed to British, imperial, or U.S. ports, it must be neutralized, or crippled. The units at Alexandria and in the French Antilles were relatively negligible. Moreover, the admirals commanding seemed more disposed to parley than fight, or flee. But the combined strength of the units at Toulon, Algiers, Oran, Casablanca, and Dakar presented a potential threat to the Royal Navy which was in no sense alleviated by the fact that many French warships were, by 25 June, also berthed in British ports. These ships were either old or small. They were seized with little bloodshed. Churchill concentrated his energies on the major units in the Mediterranean and at sea in the Atlantic.

Maritime strategy thus formed a central element in Churchill's pleas to Roosevelt after Compiègne. If an Anglo-American alliance was ever to emerge from the peril facing Britain, protection of the sea lanes must be the foundation. If Britain, having deterred or repelled invasion, moved to the offensive, maritime considerations would predominate. The Former Naval Person and the president would become Nelson and Mahan, defeating the enemy at sea, securing a base for offensive operations from which Hitler's European fortress could be stormed.

II

The bombardment of French warships at Mers el-Kébir and Oran by Vice Admiral Sir James Somerville's "Force H" on 3 July 1940 must be seen both as a tragedy and a necessity. Churchill ordered the bombardment not only to cripple French warships but also to serve notice on Roosevelt that he intended to fight; to fight at sea; to fight the King's enemies wherever they might be found. That the enemies were major units of the French Navy, found at Mers el-Kébir, emphasizes that Churchill's order to Somerville was only the more trenchant and imperative in consequence.

The operation order for CATAPULT reveals that Churchill intended to deal Vichy the most savage blow he could inflict: "The simultaneous seizure, control, or effective disablement or destruction of the accessible French fleet." This is certainly comprehensive, indicative both of Churchill's fears and anger. That Mers el-Kébir—and related operations during July and the following months—pushed Darlan toward collaboration with Hitler merely confirmed Churchill in his conviction that the former was not to be trusted anyway. Roosevelt kept his own counsel on all these issues; his ambassador at Vichy cultivated Darlan.

Mers el-Kébir was an act that all subsequent events only served to emphasize. Darlan insisted in Bordeaux before Pétain's government retreated to Vichy: "I did not create a fleet in order to offer it to the British." There is, indeed, ample evidence that Darlan created the fleet to serve his own political purposes; that Hitler understood this factor in the making of Vichy; but that, in a curious way, Darlan was consistent. On 3 June, before Churchill sought assurances, Darlan had threatened to sail the fleet to *British* ports "should armistice conditions include its surrender." Darlan's Anglophobia did not deflect him from his aim: to preserve his fleet, intact, not exactly in order to offer it to the highest bidder, but so that he could give France a bargaining asset if her forces were finally defeated in the field.

Darlan supported the armistice for his own purposes; we have to say, or surmise, that Churchill's particular detestation for Darlan—far exceeding fears about Pétain, or even Laval—reflected his conviction that although an armistice was inevitable, execration should still be heaped on the French government that signed it. Darlan thus became the major target for Churchill's abuse of Vichy; he was the only member of its government who could actively damage the British cause. Oddly, Churchill never seems to have realized that Darlan's notion of the French Navy as a political force differed in no way from General Maxime Weygand's obsession with the French Army in politics. Yet Churchill continued to nourish a certain affection for Weygand—and to entertain exaggerated hopes for his return to the Allied fold.

Did Churchill order the bombardment at Mers el-Kébir in order to destroy Darlan? We do not know for sure, but it seems likely that Darlan was as much a target as was the French fleet. If so, Churchill failed. Nor is this surprising, given the facts. Darlan was too slippery to be destroyed by Churchillian methods, *circa* 1940. Mutual detestation quickly burst into the open, but Darlan confined his reactions to rhetoric. On the day of Compiègne, Darlan warned Admiral René Godfroy at Alexandria that he would adopt a *"solution extrème, catastrophique pour tous"* if British naval forces sought to bar the French squadron's freedom of movement. Darlan ordered Godfroy to fight his way out.

Godfroy showed no disposition to comply with Darlan's orders, thanks to the cordial relationship that he established with Admiral Cunningham. This rebuff to Darlan seems only to have intensified his Anglophobia. On 1 July Darlan told the United States ambassador, William Bullitt, that "the Axis had won the war. The British had fled before the Germans and left France in the lurch, and now they would be defeated in five weeks. American intervention would come too late, if ever." Bullitt reported further: "Darlan noted that 'the French fleet had not been defeated and its spirit remained intact and he hoped and believed that the Officer Corps of the French Navy would play a great role in rebuilding France.' "

Yet Darlan, according to his lights, not only kept his word to the French Navy, but to Churchill as well. The latter attacked him for missing an opportunity to "become master of all French interests beyond German control ..." Darlan riposted by reminding Churchill that, at Briare on 12 June, he had pledged never to surrender the French fleet. It is also a fact, which Churchill ignores, that Darlan repeatedly sought compromise with him. Major units would be sailed to the United States. There was no response from Churchill—this was a French offer, not a British condition.

Worse was to follow. The French Naval Mission in London continued to function even after Compiègne; its staff, in touch with Darlan, were left in no doubt about CATAPULT. As this operation gathered momentum, Darlan certainly endeavored to reassure Churchill about the French fleet in terms of proposed amendments to the armistice, and the virtual immobilization of units berthed in North African ports. Amendments would give some assurance that ships in French ports would be immune from any sort of control by the German authorities. Immobilization would be effected under French control.

Churchill would have none of this: "Discussions as to the armistice conditions could not affect the real facts of the situation." The real facts, to Churchill, were the French fleet, as dominated by Darlan. Churchill intended to destroy both, or render the one useless, the other a liability to his fellow "Quislings"—and an embarrassment to any foreign power that contemplated dealings with him. Churchill's attitude to Darlan was consistent, and unbending. No answer was ever returned to Darlan's angry charge: "I admit to having been overcome by a great bitterness and a great resentment against England as the result of the painful events which touched me as a sailor; furthermore it seemed to me that you did not believe my word." Churchill did not believe Darlan's word; he did not believe the evidence of events—above all concerning North Africa, despite the three French territories remaining virtually immune from Axis *strategic* penetration in the years that followed the armistice.

Mers el-Kébir was thus a trial of strength between Churchill and Darlan. Its tragic genesis and even more tragic outcome—although damage to major units of the French fleet scarcely affected the overall naval balance of power, nearly 1,300 French sailors were killed—forced Churchill to intensify his war against Darlan, and Vichy, or admit to error of judgment. Somerville and his senior officers, all good friends of their recent ally, now an involuntary enemy, "hated the whole business," and protested strongly about it.

On 1 July Churchill ordered them to get a move on—the terms offered to Admiral Marcel-Bruno Gensoul amounted to no more than an ultimatum, to be accepted or rejected during a cruelly short period of six hours—but British public reaction showed how deeply ordinary people could understand the entire French tragedy. Total support for Churchill, together with a rapid, widespread welcome to de Gaulle and the few thousand who were with him, did not destroy other, equally generous, emotions.

III

Mers el-Kébir and its consequences only strengthened Churchill's resolve to secure practical assistance from Roosevelt. Churchill was quite aware that Roosevelt's diplomatic recognition of Vichy made such a resolve political rather than strategic: an American president was being indirectly challenged to accord Vichy only nominal recognition, putting his full weight and influence behind Britain and all who stood with her against the Axis and its satellites. On 5 July the Vichy government broke off diplomatic relations with Britain. The House of Commons solidly supported Churchill's decision about the French fleet. De Gaulle—"whose remarkable capacity for feeling pain" was noted by Churchill at the time—broadcast to France on 8 July in terms that showed where he stood in relation to Vichy, and Britain:

> I prefer to know that even the *Dunkerque*—our dear, magnificent, powerful *Dunkerque*—is stranded off Mers el-

Kébir, rather than to learn one day that she has been
manned by Germans and used to shell British ports, or
perhaps Algiers, Casablanca, or Dakar . . .

All serious-minded Englishmen must know that victory
could never be achieved if the sympathies of France were
enlisted under the banner of the enemy.

No Frenchman worthy of the name can for a moment
doubt that a British defeat would seal for ever his country's bondage.

Such sentiments were largely ignored in the isolationist
United States of 1940. Moreover, Operation MENACE, an
Anglo–Free French attempt on 23 September to capture Vichy-
held Dakar proved to be a fiasco. American reactions were
derisive. Insufficient attention was paid to the fact that de
Gaulle's success in rallying much of French colonial Africa to
his cause by the fall of 1940 had produced a strategic asset that
Churchill was not slow to exploit. Failure to seize Dakar—a
port of much importance in Roosevelt's strategic thinking—
lowered de Gaulle in widespread American estimation to the
level of an adventurer and, which was worse, an unsuccessful
one.

In 1940 Roosevelt did not measure Churchill by his support for de Gaulle. Roosevelt did not react to Churchill's defense
of de Gaulle after the failure of MENACE: "His Majesty's
government have no intention whatever of abandoning the cause
of General de Gaulle until it is merged, as merged it will be,
in the larger cause of France." Churchill's support for de Gaulle
was "an irrevocable step." This factor of support, coupled with
the complexities inherent in recognizing or fighting Vichy, had
no bearing on the protracted negotiations between Roosevelt
and Churchill whereby fifty elderly American destroyers were
exchanged for facilities in Canada and the Caribbean—the so-
called "bases for destroyers" deal. Roosevelt was inhibited by
isolationism, Congress, and the impending presidential elec-
tion. Nevertheless, Roosevelt could have waged a battle on
Churchill's behalf if he had not wished to keep all his options

open. De Gaulle, at the time, was virtually dismissed in Washington. Pétain—and Darlan—was another matter altogether. Relations with Vichy were among Roosevelt's options: that the bases-for-destroyers deal received diplomatic endorsement (on 3 September 1940) is only of importance in considering Roosevelt's and Churchill's emerging—and unequal— alliance. Impending conflict over Vichy was also another matter altogether.

In all essentials, Roosevelt's evolving maritime policy was based on his assessment of Vichy rather than Churchill. The policy was twin-track, but the line was more likely to be controlled by signals from Vichy than from London. Roosevelt knew Churchill would fight; that was not the point. Roosevelt did not know what Vichy would do; that was very much the point— for an America clinging to a neutrality like a cloak that could be wrenched aside by clumsy, precipitate acts. Vichy disposed of assets that were of as much concern to Roosevelt as they were to Churchill, and de Gaulle. The French fleet, if confined to the Mediterranean, posed no threat to the United States. Casablanca and Dakar in Vichy hands posed a potential threat; in German hands, a contingent, but specific threat.

Roosevelt thus saw North Africa as a political bridgehead for the prosecution of his own designs. Murphy paid his exploratory to Algiers in December 1940 precisely for that reason. Roosevelt's North African policies had not clearly evolved by the end of 1940; even if they had done so, it is doubtful whether Roosevelt would have confided them to Churchill. Lack of communication regarding this peculiarly sensitive area explains much of what a perceptive Polish agent of the British Secret Intelligence Service called "this great tangle of TORCH."

Roosevelt, in short, sought to evolve a foreign policy for a neutral United States committed neither to one party nor another. Roosevelt, in foreign policy terms, is remembered for two actions in the latter half of 1940: first, the bases-for-destroyers deal with Churchill; second, his reaction to the meeting between Hitler and Pétain at Montoire on 24 October. Taken together, these actions can suggest that Roosevelt had taken sides: Britain received fifty destroyers; Pétain was warned to watch his step.

The reality is different, but setting the record straight does Roosevelt no disservice. The record shows the president of the United States weighing the odds, calculating the national interest in a context in which his country's survival was not actually at stake. Roosevelt used the metaphor of the garden hose, handed to a fire-stricken neighbor over the fence, when "lend-lease" was debated at the turn of the year and throughout the early months of 1941. The metaphor was never particularly appropriate, but is wholly inapplicable to the bases-for-destroyers deal and the "warning" delivered after Montoire. In both cases, the national interest dominated; all else, in foreign policy terms, was subordinate. Nor could Roosevelt have done otherwise—unless he had committed himself to Churchill, and de Gaulle.

The bases-for-destroyers deal went through because "the climate of opinion in America had now come to favour the release of the destroyers, provided some compensating advantage was forthcoming . . . it was essential for the president to show that the United States was receiving valuable consideration for its gifts." Churchill, forced to give Roosevelt assurances before the deal was struck that the "British fleet"; would not be handed over the the Germans—an oddly wounding demand, a curious counterpoint to CATAPULT—admitted:

> There was, of course, no comparison between the intrinsic value of these antiquated and inefficient craft and the immense permanent security afforded to the United States by the enjoyment of the island bases.

The meetings at Montoire on 22 October between Hitler and Laval, and on the 24th between the former and Pétain, did produce some sort of reaction from Roosevelt, but it fell far short of what Churchill desired: not merely a presidential warning to Vichy but evidence that the United States administration would commit itself unequivocally on basic issues. Churchill was under pressure from his foreign secretary (Lord Halifax) and much of Whitehall to conciliate Vichy—and "drop that born loser de Gaulle." In effect, Churchill sought assurance from Roosevelt not only that a firm, prospectively Allied front must be displayed against Vichy, but also that support for de Gaulle was inseparable from the common cause. Churchill was careful not to be explicit on this point to Roosevelt. Between 21 October and 23 November, a month when Churchill signaled Roosevelt repeatedly, he concentrated solely on the issue of Vichy and maritime assets that the Axis might acquire, or seize. Nevertheless, we can discern Churchill's determination to back de Gaulle despite—or because of—opposition from his advisers.

Concurrently with Churchill's increasingly agitated signals to Roosevelt one finds strong, unequivocal expressions of support for de Gaulle. On 21 October Churchill broadcast to France in language that de Gaulle might well have used, not merely in terms of which he undoubtedly approved. Despite—or because of—Whitehall's collective desire to conciliate Vichy, Churchill's basic attitude was expressed thus: "We must not allow ourselves to become obsessed with the idea that we must never in any circumstances offer provocation to the Vichy Government." The observation was, in a sense, gratuitous: the "line of blood" would not be washed away by diplomatic soft soap, nor would it have been expunged even if Churchill had "dropped" de Gaulle. Churchill reminded Whitehall of basic issues during a period when he was increasingly anxious to commit Roosevelt to positive action.

If this was a ploy, it failed. On 20 October, Churchill signaled to Roosevelt:

> We hear rumours from various sources that the Vichy Government are preparing their ships and colonial troops

to aid the Germans against us. I do not myself believe these reports, but if the French fleet at Toulon were turned over to Germany it would be a very heavy blow. It would certainly be a wise precaution, Mr President, if you would speak in the strongest terms to the French Ambassador emphasising the disapprobation with which the United States would view such a betrayal of the cause of democracy and freedom. They will pay great heed in Vichy to such a warning.

On 24 October, Roosevelt, at several removes, stated to Pétain:

In the opinion of the United States Government the fact that the French Government alleges that it is under duress and consequently cannot act except to a very limited degree as a free agent is in no sense to be considered as justifying any course on the part of the French Government which would provide assistance to Germany and her allies in their war against the British Empire. The fact a government is a prisoner of war of another power does not justify such a prisoner serving in operations against its former ally. The Government of the United States received from the Pétain Government the most solemn assurances that the French fleet would not be surrendered. If the French Government now permits the Germans to use the French fleet in hostile operations against the British fleet, such action would constitute a flagrant and deliberate breach of faith with the United States Government.

Roosevelt continued: "Any agreement entered into between France and Germany which partook of the character abovementioned would most definitely wreck the traditional friendship between the French and American peoples, would permanently remove any chance that this Government would be disposed to give any assistance to the French people in their distress, and would create a wave of bitter indignation against France on the part of American public opinion. *If* France pursued a policy as that above outlined, the United States could make no effort when the appropriate time came to exercise its influence to insure to France the retention of her overseas possessions."

Roosevelt's message to Pétain was dispatched before the results, and implications, of the Montoire meetings could be reported to Washington, let alone assessed there. Roosevelt, in dispatching his message to Pétain—and receiving fervent assurances in return—did what he supposed Churchill wanted him to do. But whether or not Roosevelt discerned a deeper motive in Churchill's communiqués—or a more pressing need in them—he was determined not to commit himself to anything more positive than an expression of his contingent power to cease giving Vichy active, and not only covert, support.

Pétain was thus happy to reassure Roosevelt, given the prospect of active collaboration with the United States. At just the moment when Churchill sought assurance from Roosevelt—nay insurance from him—the latter was embarking on a policy of positive collaboration with Vichy, above all in terms of economic support, specifically in relation to North Africa. Churchill wanted Roosevelt to put Vichy on notice; Roosevelt had no intention of doing so, except in terms that *he* would dictate. Thus, by a further irony, Roosevelt's policy came eventually to unite Churchill and Whitehall in opposition to Vichy— in opposition to *him*. Churchill—with Whitehall—wanted to offer Vichy what later became known as "a policy of blessings or cursings": resistance to Hitler might mean lifting the blockade; effective removal of the French fleet from the Axis grasp might mean a standoff in relation to British—and Gaullist— attacks on Vichy-governed colonies. Roosevelt stepped in, offered his own terms to Pétain, challenged Churchill's view of France—and kept his options open.

2

1941
The Lean Year

I

A year that opened with Hitler as Europe's *Führer* but ended with him embroiled in war against the United States and Soviet Union eludes simple definition. A year that opened with Churchill standing alone but ended with Roosevelt and Stalin joining him as allies—of a kind—requires consideration about the conduct of grand strategy. A year that ended with Anglo-American strategy defined by Churchill's prescription for "closing the ring" around Germany suggests his emergence as the arbiter of major decisions. The facts contradict this supposition.

Despite momentous changes, 1941 can aptly be described as "the lean year" for Churchill—and de Gaulle. The phrase was coined in SOE's Baker Street headquarters to describe a succession of disasters, and failures, that afflicted secret agents and circuits amid the birth pangs of Résistance in France. But the phrase can be applied in a wider dimension as well. Little went well for Britain and de Gaulle's Free French during 1941. Much went so ill, indeed—not least in relations between Churchill and de Gaulle—that ARCADIA should be seen less as a triumph for the former than as a veiled hint by Roosevelt that the conduct of Anglo-American strategy was a matter for him to arbitrate. So far as Roosevelt subscribed to the strategy of "closing the ring" he did so on the premise that he would control the emerging alliance, above all in the political field. Nowhere was this conviction more strongly held than concerning the one area where Churchill believed a decisive strategic, and political, blow could, at the appropriate time, be struck: North Africa.

Roosevelt's conviction was, however, vitiated by three factors. Churchill was committed to de Gaulle, and for so long as he was Vichy remained Anglophobe, and actively so. Pétain was anxious to collaborate with both Hitler and the United States, but Darlan, alone in the Vichy government, seriously pondered the chances of exchanging one form of collaboration for another. Darlan's collegues continued to regard Roosevelt as a prospective ally of Churchill's, and were cool to American overtures. Weygand, who became Vichy "Delegate-General in North Africa" in October 1940, ignored overtures from Murphy which were, in truth, more notable for guesswork about the situation in the three territories than knowledge of its unique blend of opportunism and *attentisme*; British strategic resources were insufficient to provide the insurance policy that even a soldier less politically devious than Weygand might have demanded. Weygand's famous, if apocryphal, remark to Churchill was a pointed one: "If you come with twenty divisions I will embrace you; if you come with four I will attack you." The point applied equally well to anything that Murphy might say.

Churchill had stripped the strategic cupboard bare to mount offensives against Mussolini. Although at the end of 1940 the

Chiefs of Staff indicated that six divisions might be earmarked for North Africa, this was a purely notional figure, quite useless either as bluff or diplomatic ammunition. By the following March, General Sir Archibald Wavell's Middle East command, although swarming with troops, was short of front-line units. Maintenance of armored vehicles could never match the demands made on them. The Royal Air Force in the theater was mainly equipped with obsolescent aircraft. The Royal Navy at all times was fully stretched. Churchill certainly had no divisions to spare for offering Weygand a blessing, or a cursing.

Yet Churchill was determined to mount offensives against the Axis in the Middle East—and, prospectively, in French North Africa—at almost any cost. Churchill's commitment to offensive action in the region was one shared wholeheartedly with de Gaulle. By early 1941, Free French ground forces in the Middle East and the Horn of Africa numbered approximately 8,000, mostly colonial troops, of high quality but poorly equipped. Free France would mean little to friends, enemies— and critics—unless this derisory number could be substantially increased. Only one source was available, unless or until North Africa was seized or seduced from Vichy: Syria and Lebanon, where a Vichy force of approximately 30,000, well armed and equipped, posed not only a challenge to de Gaulle but also a threat to British strategy and Churchill's plans for implementing it.

De Gaulle's emissaries and agents made strong efforts to seduce this force from its loyalty to Vichy. Little success attended these efforts, but de Gaulle and Churchill shared a conviction that if Syria was invaded by Anglo–Free French forces two objectives would be attained: first, Hitler's power to challenge Britain in the region by means of Vichy collaboration would be thwarted; second, Free France would gain thousands of well-trained, well-armed soldiers and airmen. Attaining the second objective was foremost in de Gaulle's mind but, uncharacteristically, he deluded himself that rhetoric and intrigue were sufficient substitutes for reliable raw intelligence about the situation in Syria. De Gaulle wrote in his memoirs: "Towards the complicated east, I flew with simple ideas," but his journey from Brazzaville to Cairo in April 1941 foreshadowed a lean year of disappointment, and humiliation. Vichy Syria did not swing to de Gaulle: the omens were noted in Washington.

Less attention was paid in Washington to Darlan. There were signs, even as Darlan cultivated Hitler, that the former's bets were being hedged: Roosevelt had no intention of offering Darlan either a blessing or a cursing until he showed his hand. Moreover, Roosevelt, in 1941, took little interest in the Middle East as such. Active intervention by Vichy's Syrian garrison in support of the Axis was, in fact, unlikely. Use by the Luftwaffe of airfields in Syria and Lebanon was, however, a distinct possibility—and a serious threat, not only to Wavell's forces in Egypt and the desert, but to the British position in the Middle East as a whole. This position was by no means secure in Iraq and Iran, where Axis agents worked upon latent anti-British feelings not only among the rulers but also the oilfield workers. The stakes were high.

It is in this connection that Darlan's collaboration with Hitler during the first six months of 1941 assumed an importance to Churchill that did much to strengthen his animosity— and to sustain a relationship with de Gaulle when events concerning Syria and Lebanon produced violent disagreement. The Anglo-Gaullist invasion of Syria on 9 June (Operation EXPORTER) eventually thwarted Hitler in that area. But at the same time recriminations arose between Churchill and de Gaulle on the grounds—as the latter saw them—that French interests were sacrificed to British imperial ambitions. De Gaulle overstated his case, but he had a good one.

Both de Gaulle and Darlan failed to attain their immediate objectives in 1941. By the fall, de Gaulle and Churchill were reconciled in terms of the overriding issue of French liberation. However, disagreement about Syria and Lebanon— put virtually under British control once an armistice was signed on 14 July—left a residue of ill feeling which opponents of the

Free French Movement were not slow to exploit. Darlan hoped to collaborate with Hitler not only as one whose New Order seemed impregnable, but also so that he could consolidate his power within Vichy. As vice-president of the Council of Ministers, foreign minister—and much else—Darlan appeared to others apart from Pétain as the latter's "Dauphin." But Darlan feared to commit himself wholly to any cause that offered dangers, not only prizes. Hitler offered Darlan command of *la grande flotte Européenne*. Pétain has recorded that Hitler saw Darlan as his man—but only up to a point: Darlan was prospectively important *"jusqu'à l'embrasser, lui et ses cuirassés."* The French fleet, in short, was Darlan's to offer—or withhold.

On 11 May Darlan met Hitler, cordially. Their first meeting, on Christmas Day 1940, had exposed Darlan to Hitler enraged. The second occasion witnessed an, apparent, meeting of minds. Hitler's card was a pledge to sustain Vichy as an entity, at home and overseas. Darlan, perfectly indifferent to Vichy in Pétainist terms—"work, family, fatherland," and all the bogus ideology of the right reflected in this phrase—saw more clearly than his colleagues that the regime would be reduced to absurdity if Hitler sent his panzers into the Unoccupied Zone. On 11 May, Hitler hinted that Vichy would remain in being, nay, increase in recognition. "Greater French concessions would be rewarded with greater German concessions." Hitler wanted Darlan to make war on Britain, but even at this moment, poised for the attack on Crete as prelude to a concerted offensive against Britain in the Middle East, hesitated to force his collaborator's hand.

Darlan read Hitler's hand with professional skill. Reporting to the Vichy Council of Ministers on 14 May, Darlan argued: "If France supported Britain or even attempted to play her off against Germany she would suffer for it during the war and in the final peace; if, on the other hand, France collaborated with Germany by producing for her and giving her *'certaines facil-*

ités,' without however, *'nous ranger à ses côtés,'* then she would suffer minimal territorial losses and play *'un rôle honorable, sinon important, dans l'Europe future.'* " Darlan showed *his* hand at this point, to the extent that he ever did so. Decoded—*sinon* is a word of varied interpretation—Darlan was telling his colleagues, his subordinates, that Vichy could survive, and flourish, in Hitler's New Order, not otherwise.

Syria thus provided an ideal means for Darlan to collaborate with Hitler, to make war on Britain by proxy. On 27–28 May the "Paris Protocols" between Germany and Vichy France were signed. This substantial reaffirmation of the Compiègne Armistice gave Hitler a toehold in North Africa, should he need to reinforce Rommel from Tunis, but is important mainly for the *"facilités"* that he secured in Syria. This provided for the stationing of Luftwaffe units in Syria, not merely for their passage en route to Iraq. Syria was to become a Nazi bridgehead, from which both overt and covert operations would be conducted against British interests.

In return, the protocols, on paper, reduced occupation costs; provided for the return home of 80,000 prisoners of war; "guaranteed the French Empire's independence"—and blurred somewhat the distinction between the two zones in Metropolitan France. French citizens, on paper, would be able to travel with relative ease between the two zones. Darlan argued to his fellow citizens on 31 May that Hitler's Germany was a better friend to France than Britain could ever be. More to the point, Weygand, backed by his subordinates in North and West Africa, persuaded Darlan to fudge the issue of German facilities in these territories. Nothing loath, Darlan argued to the German emissaries at the protocol meetings that little could be done in this direction until "the . . . strengthening of French defensive means" had been completed.

Roosevelt had protested, mildly, to Pétain once the meeting between Hitler and Darlan on 11 May had been assessed in Washington, but drew nothing better from his respondent than a mendacious remark to the effect that "he does not intend

to go beyond the requirements of the Armistice Agreement."
Roosevelt appeared satisfied with this reply, and with Leahy's
odd message at the time that "our excellent contacts have
absolutely frozen up on us." In truth, Roosevelt and Leahy were
relatively indifferent to the implications of Darlan's Syrian poker
game, provided no injury was caused to American interests or,
which came to much the same thing, prospective collaboration
with Vichy in North Africa was in no way frustrated. Murphy
was sent *en poste* to North Africa in April 1941, after his initial
visit of December 1940, in the expectation that immediate results
would be achieved. His instructions, in fact, were to lay plans
for the future, whatever Weygand might say, or decline to do.

During the Anglo-Gaullist campaign in Syria, it was Darlan rather than Hitler who pushed collaboration just about as
far as it would go. Although a Nazi-inspired coup in Iraq had,
briefly, posed a serious threat to British interests, the "Golden
Square" of idealogues had been routed by early June. German
support had been inadquate, and tardy. No decisive Luftwaffe
intervention took place, despite Darlan having given permission for aircraft to refuel in Syria on 5 May, a week before his
critical second meeting with Hitler. Darlan was in the position
of one whose ingenuity in terms of self-preservation and ambition was always liable to make enemies rather than allies.
Weygand bitterly opposed Hitler's prospective moves into his
fief; he wanted to preserve it for his own use. Darlan was also
opposed by those in Vichy and the armed forces who saw collaboration with Hitler as a virtual guarantee that Syria and
Lebanon would be swallowed up—by Britain.

Darlan nevertheless succeeded in keeping himself afloat
throughout 1941 by propitiating Weygand—until he dismissed
him in November—and checking collaboration with Hitler at
just the point where an irrevocable step might have been taken:
the active commitment of the French fleet to convoy North
African reinforcements to Syria. The day of BARBAROSSA
saw Darlan contemplating this Rubicon. But once the invasion
of Russia had been launched, Darlan knew that, however much

Britain's destruction remained a phobia with Hitler, the dimension of war had utterly changed. Syria, so to speak, became a rear area. Darlan's direct collaboration with Hitler had been tried, and found wanting. Yet, seeking to retrieve rather than retain his ascendancy in Vichy, Darlan sought collaboration with Hitler's subordinates. Darlan made no absolute commitment regarding the French fleet; he proposed discussions, and awaited German reactions.

German reactions were negative, or were so in Darlan's terms. A partial welcome was given to Darlan's proposal for discussions, but in words intended to convince him "that Axis resources were stretched to the limit." Darlan was given a foretaste of German defeat, and thereafter began to regard Leahy as a man to be cultivated. Hitler remained interested in North and West Africa, but Darlan, alerted to sentiment there, refused to play that card. By the end of June, with EXPORTER getting into its stride, both Hitler's and Darlan's subordinates had agreed to write Syria off the collaboration list, whatever the cost to Vichy pride.

Darlan's Syria policy had reached a dangerous stage. French destroyers based at Beirut attacked British warships. A French destroyer was sunk on 16 June by Royal Navy aircraft operating from Cyprus; a French submarine was sunk on the 25th. Other clashes threatened to intensify despite the fact that, after the Crete campaign, the Mediterranean fleet was "at so low an ebb" that a French naval offensive might well have given the Axis maritime ascendancy, at last, in the one dimension of Middle East war where Britain remained dominant. On 14 July 1941, ". . . Vichy gave the Germans formal notice that France would be unable to carry out the provisions of the Paris Protocols until various preconditions—i.e., German political concessions—had been met." Hitler was, apparently, furious at Darlan's show of defiance. But with BARBAROSSA, in his generals' collective view, already foreshadowing 1812, even a demonic Hitler was unable to impose his will on one who knew how to keep afloat however turbulent the water.

Darlan had survived, to collaborte another day, a fact duly noted
in Berlin—and Washington.

II

The meeting in London on 12 September 1941 (the first for
many months) was a milestone in the history of Churchill and
de Gaulle in war. Nevertheless they failed to discuss, let alone
resolve, the issue that had governed much of de Gaulle's
behavior for the past twelve months: Where, precisely, did
Churchill and the British Government stand in relation to Vichy,
to Darlan above all? In consequence, Churchill and de Gaulle
also ignored the issue whose resolution should have followed
logically from any consideration of Darlan, and Vichy: Résistance. As a result of this failure, no attention was given to the
prospective role of North Africa as a base for supporting an
anti-Vichy Résistance in the Unoccupied Zone. Not until the
spring of 1942 did the British Chiefs of Staff, hardly Gaullist
in sympathy, begin to think along these lines. By then Roosevelt and Murphy were busy with conspiracy.

Churchill's animosity toward Darlan never diminished.
Talking to MPs in the House of Commons Smoking Room on
1 April, Churchill had declared of Darlan, "I should like to
break that man. Expressing gratitude to Germany, which has
humbled his country into dust."

Darlan's ability to swim with the tides of fortune and misfortune alike was, as we shall see, acted upon, not merely noted
in Washington. But the ability to swim was noted neither by
Churchill nor de Gaulle. Churchillian outbursts were no sub-
stitute for lack of clear British objectives concerning the liberation of France not only from Hitler but also from Vichy. In
1941 the latter was virtually synonymous with Darlan's actions,
and calculations. Churchill and de Gaulle not only came to the

edge of a calamitous breach in 1941 because of disagreement about Syria; they also, despite the belated September reconciliation, failed to consider either cause, implications, or concurrent events. De Gaulle, moreover, remained convinced that Churchill was prepared to deal with Pétain if the opportunity arose. The meeting had been preceded by renewed outbursts from de Gaulle, culminating in an interview with the Chicago *Daily News* in late August "where he had given free rein to his anglophobia." On 1 September Churchill told the cabinet that de Gaulle's actions were "disturbing," and that, for the time being, Whitehall should adopt "a cautious and dilatory attitude" to the Free French.

At that time Whitehall had needed no prompting on this score. In fact, however, the tide of official British opposition to de Gaulle was beginning to turn. Churchill's selection of "disturbing" was deliberately ambiguous; despite rebuffing de Gaulle over Free French claims to Syria in the House of Commons, Churchill saw that de Gaulle was suffering from unavoidable stress, not mere humiliation. On 12 September, in a meeting that extended throughout the day, de Gaulle apologized for his difficult temperament and made handsome, unusual amends for almost unpardonable verbal violence. Churchill, the most magnanimous of great men, responded in kind. The bond was reestablished and strengthened.

De Gaulle, nevertheless, was determined to unburden himself about Syria. He spoke from the heart rather than the head: "Recent events there had profoundly disturbed him and cast doubt in his mind as to the attitude of many British authorities toward him and the Free French movement. These events, added to the great difficulties of his personal position, to his isolation, and no doubt to the factor of his personal temperament, had led him to utterances that must clearly have been disagreeable. He wished to apologize for these utterances." Churchill's response was handsome, if a touch disingenuous: "He had been at great pains before General de Gaulle's arrival in Egypt to make it clear to all concerned that the General was the man he trusted and the man with whom he proposed to work. Everything had been done to smooth the path before General de Gaulle." The bond was reestablished—and strengthened—because Churchill and de Gaulle were together fighting in a universal war. But another year and more was to pass before Darlan brought them shoulder to shoulder again.

Vichy as such was seen by Churchill and de Gaulle from widely different aspects throughout most of 1941. High ideals are best shared in common adversity; separation reveals unavoidably different perspectives of the same beliefs, accentuates what is not shared, in belief or action. Churchill was poorly provided with political intelligence on Vichy in France, but the ENIGMA gave him a good picture of Darlan's activities in Syria and in relation to Iraq. Churchill knew in advance of Luftwaffe movements into Syria; he also knew about Darlan's contemplated commitment of the French fleet. Fearing these movements as he did, Churchill saw Darlan as a menace in strategic terms. In stark contrast, de Gaulle saw Churchill's response to Darlan's actions in predominately political terms. The revolt in Iraq had been crushed a clear week before EXPORTER was mounted. De Gaulle could well have asked: Was this operation really was necessary—as a means of denying Fighting France a rightful place at Britain's side?

Failure to discuss, let alone agree about, these issues precluded consideration of Darlan's role in Vichy. Thus Darlan was ignored. This double lapse ensured that North Africa was likewise ignored. A dangerous ignorance about Roosevelt, and Vichy, was betrayed. Roosevelt's policy toward Vichy was based, ostensibly, on economic aid to North Africa. The British government collectively opposed this policy, indeed tried to thwart it in various ways. But Churchill and de Gaulle, preoccupied with reconciliation, ignored the implications of Roosevelt's acts. A year before, these two men had not only been joined in a common cause, but had also agreed on the necessity to include

Vichy among the king's enemies and those of France. Now they could do no more than effect a reconciliation.

Occurring when it did and triumphing over personal opposition to de Gaulle among disaffected individuals, this reconciliation remains significant—unique, perhaps—in the relationship between Churchill and de Gaulle. This opposition, which increased in venom as it went underground, became more vicious as Whitehall, gradually, obeyed Churchill's injunction after the 12 September meeting: De Gaulle is to be supported by all means in our power. "The order for departmental caution was rescinded." But the injunction reflected reconciliation, not concerted policies. The injunction was hardly construed literally. Not until the spring of 1942 did the Chiefs of Staff bring themselves to consider de Gaulle in any but a hostile light. By the end of 1941, however, much prompted by Anthony Eden, the Foreign Office had swung to the other extreme:

> De Gaulle and the Free French are saving the soul of France. It was a magnificent act of faith to resolve, single-handed, upon the creation of a Free French movement. Everything goes to show that Gaullist sentiment is particularly strong in occupied France, and indeed that the great majority of the population are supporters of the cause. Even in unoccupied France, although here support may be less robust, the movement is visibly gaining ground. The Cross of Lorraine, adopted by General de Gaulle, is increasingly being worn as an emblem of national revival.

Alas, all this was hyperbole, bearing little relation to the realities of the situation in either zone—or in London. In 1941 SOE and the Free French were very far from being in agreement about the nature of Résistance, the most effective means of supporting it, or the ultimate objective to be attained. There is also, alas, a further indication of the lack of genuine cooperation between Churchill and de Gaulle in the last quarter of

1941. This is their failure—and that of Whitehall collec-tively—to appreciate, and act on, the report that Jean Moulin handed to de Gaulle and "the British authorities" shortly after he arrived in London from France—via Lisbon—in late October.

Moulin, who was to die a martyr's death in June 1943—by then as much an emissary of SOE as de Gaulle—had been, at forty-one, the youngest prefect in France. Dismissed by Vichy in November 1940, he was immediately assessed by the Ger-man command in Chartres as a man to watch, persecute, tor-ture. Moulin escaped to Avignon, where he began his long, heroic career as a résistant. But Moulin first—and last—observed. What he observed and reported came, in effect, to this: Although "the only question at stake is the fight against the Germans," the seed bed for Résistance was hatred of Vichy. Hence Résistance movements must be built up primarily in the Unoccupied Zone, with the emphasis on political action, not sabotage or other acts which, while providing a temporary fil-lip, brought reprisal sufficiently brutal to deter further ges-tures. In sum, Résistance movements, however active in perfecting their role as an adjunct to any campaign for the lib-eration of France must, as their primary task, prepare for the immediate aftermath: chaos would reign—and civil war break out—if such movements were unable to restore the fabric and substance of organized society.

This argument was much more than "a prefect's point"; the only possible inference to be drawn was that Résistance in France required a leader who could weld separate—and potentially conflicting—groups into a movement that, even if not homogeneous, possessed a highest common factor of objective, intention, and method. The reader will at once appreciate the importance of Moulin's report for de Gaulle; he will have no difficulty in appreciating that Whitehall, collec-tively, was not particularly enamored of it. The French National Committee had been formed in London on 24 September, vir-tually at Churchill's insistence, as a device whereby de Gaulle would be something more than first amongst equals with his

Free French colleagues but something much less than their master in all things.

This device exploded in Churchill's face. Some particularly stupid underground intrigues against de Gaulle served only to strengthen his position. Moulin's report was scrupulous throughout in linking "the British cause" to that of de Gaulle. Nevertheless the reader was left in no doubt that its author was providing the latter with the means of becoming much more than leader of the Free French, "recognised" in that role by His Majesty's Government—but no more. Moulin's report pointed to the liberation of France, powerfully aided by a Résistance movement which, in deriving its inspiration from de Gaulle, looked to him to lead the nation in its postwar return to civilized values and a free society.

Churchill and de Gaulle met again on 27 October, when some discussion did take place on Moulin's report. De Gaulle made no demands at this meeting; he merely "raised directly with Churchill the question of establishing in France an organization to 'organise the French people for a nationwide uprising at the appointed time, whose activity should be co-ordinated with future military plans and considered in relation to similar action in other European countries.' " This, for de Gaulle, was pretty anodyne. But the comment, designed as a trailer for future political action, missed the essential operational points: How were Moulin's recommendations to be given the backing of properly trained agents? Where should those agents be based? What relationship should Résistance develop with conventional military forces when the campaign for Western Europe's liberation was mounted?

The lean year ended with Churchill and de Gaulle reconciled, but no more, despite Moulin's advent and the support for his return to France provided by SOE. Momentous events were in the offing, but enduring calamities and the pains of frustrated expectation had made for divided counsel. Moreover, much remained obscure in Vichy. Weygand's dismissal by Darlan on 18 November finally convinced Churchill that even covert relations with Vichy, except at the intelligence level, were futile. De Gaulle was regarded as but a gallant comrade; his possession of strategic assets had produced conflict, not harmony. Nor had de Gaulle become, in Churchill's eyes, the leader of all Free French citizens, however much he should legitimately be regarded as the symbol of resistance to Compiègne. In consequence, the relationship between Churchill and de Gaulle was not revived at a level sufficiently cordial, alert, and vigorous to comprehend, let alone counter, the evolution of Roosevelt's Vichy gamble.

III

Roosevelt had reacted calmly to the Montoire meetings, and although six months later the United States Navy was actively engaged in the North Atlantic, Roosevelt's attention had become concentrated on U-boats operating from French ports in Brittany, not those that might do so from Casablanca, or Dakar. Roosevelt remained convinced that the Monroe Doctrine must be extended to the North and West African shore, but throughout 1941 expressed no concern that the necessity to do so would be hastened by German moves in that direction. The war had moved east, where Hitler would be defeated. This was Darlan's conclusion also. But Roosevelt was able to provide material support to Russia well before Pearl Harbor forced America into war. One commitment having been made, Roosevelt reverted to his policy of conducting war by proxy—the cultivation of Vichy, a satellite, whose "caitiff government" could be bought. The phrase is Churchill's; but Churchill did not believe that Pétain, Laval—or Darlan—could be bought.

Churchill's instinctive opposition to Vichy and all its works served only to strengthen Roosevelt's conviction that collaboration with Pétain and his colleagues made sense for the United States. Moreover, Churchill's loyalty to de Gaulle acted as a goad on Roosevelt. Although Roosevelt did not meet de Gaulle face-to-face until the Casablanca conference in January 1943, instinctive antipathy to him—as one who could destroy his policy of collaboration with Vichy—increased throughout 1941, reaching a stage of some protest to Churchill over the St. Pierre et Miquelon affair during Christmas week. By one of those ironies that liberally accompanied de Gaulle's career, these Vichy-governed islands off the coast of Newfoundland were seized for Free France by his one-time opponent within the Free French movement, Admiral Emile Muselier. The minute colony was important: its radio station pumped out Vichy propaganda; the German Naval Command was known to be interested in the islands as a U-boat base.

Despite these factors, Roosevelt, pestered by his secretary of state, Cordell Hull, reacted with strong condemnation. Churchill, as always on such occasions, stoutly backed de Gaulle—the affair was, in any case, much to his taste. Churchill never failed de Gaulle when the issue was vital to the preservation of British freedom and preliminary to French liberation. The Battle of the Atlantic, bitterly fought by Britain throughout 1941, was certainly such an issue, but although it was one vital also to the security of the United States, the St. Pierre et Miquelon affair served only to widen the breach between London and Washington concerning Vichy, and de Gaulle.

In October Roosevelt appointed an old crony, William Donovan, to establish an intelligence service. Donovan was euphemistically designated Coordinator of Information; his real task, however, was to establish an intelligence service whose members would operate in North Africa as elements in Roosevelt's Vichy policy. But the twelve consuls whom Roosevelt dispatched to North Africa early in 1941 were in no sense trained intelligence officers. Moreover, Murphy was incapable of making accurate assessments in terms of the difference between reliable and spurious intelligence. Such intelligence about the situation in North Africa as came the way of British authorities was not transmitted to Washington. The intelligence came to this: ". . . when the eventual defeat of Germany had become more apparent, the French [North] African Army, if assisted from overseas, might be able to contribute much to the cause of the democracies. [But] France would not return to the war before 'the intelligent moment.' "

Attentisme was thus defined in North African terms. Murphy, however—"Anglophobe and Vichyphil"—came to convince himself as he set out to execute Roosevelt's personal instructions that establishing the intelligent moment depended on the power of American blandishment. Thus, throughout 1941, British and United States policies concerning North Africa moved further apart. The British position, while in no sense Gaullist, was tacitly opposed to maintaining the Vichy administration in authority. Any successor must reflect the fortunes of war, wherein North Africa had been seized by force of arms. The United States position took the maintenance, indeed the strengthening, of the Vichy administration as a basis for policy and action. The Americans also assumed the existence of a conspiracy in North Africa whose members would acquire a new loyalty—to all things American.

Roosevelt had directed Murphy to report personally, bypassing the State Department concerning "anything of special interest." This directive was no more precise than the Churchillian 1940 exhortation to SOE: "And now set Europe ablaze." But whereas SOE had been tasked to stir things up, Murphy was enjoined to calm people down, and to press the flesh. Murphy should have realized that bushels of wheat and barrels of oil might keep North Africa going economically, but would never induce Weygand or anybody else to foment conspiracy on America's behalf. Washington, collectively, was always much less devious than Roosevelt, vastly less sanguine than Murphy. By the end of the year the State Department could well have echoed Leahy concerning Vichy in France. The observation certainly applies to North Africa: "It is impossible to guess what will happen in France tomorrow or the next day, and almost as difficult for me to point to any useful accomplishment that we have made since my arrival." Darlan, however, was another matter altogether. Leahy, indeed, regarded his cultivation of Darlan as rather more than a useful accomplishment.

Unlike Leahy, Murphy did at least speak French. But he emulated Leahy throughout 1941 in cultivating only those who seemed likely to favor Roosevelt's version of a liberated France.

> The President did not ask the Admiral [Leahy] to seek among the grass roots of France to determine whether the Pétain Government represented the elements with which the United States ought to maintain contact. He was not asked to cultivate Jews, Socialists, or Communists; he was told to maintain close relations with Marshal Pétain, to associate with high officers in the French Navy . . . His task was simplified by the fact that many Frenchmen could see, without too much American persuasion, that minimum cooperation and preservation of the fleet was to France's interest. The result was that instead of Leahy's persuading the French, it was the French who persuaded Leahy that some resistance to the Germans existed within the framework of the Vichy government . . . there was no need for an exterior, "illegal" resistance such as de Gaulle had established in London.

Leahy was right to imply that he preferred to guess rather than seek. Leahy's 1941 ended with Darlan providing further reassurances about the French fleet. Darlan's words had to be taken at face value by Roosevelt because he had no way to verify them.

Murphy's position was far more invidious than Leahy's. Murphy was spared Darlan's taunt to Leahy—emulating Weygand, and several times repeated in 1941: "Come to Marseilles with 500,000 men, 6,000 planes and 3,000 tanks, and then we shall welcome you." Even Murphy might have seen the taunt for what it was worth: make sure you get it right before I commit myself. But Murphy had much of Doctor Pangloss in his composition, and as we survey his hustle and bustle across North

Africa during 1941 the wonder is that he never appeared to doubt the validity of his apparent discoveries.

We meet in Murphy's report those who play a prominent, if dubious, role in the latter half of 1942—Henri d'Astier, Jacques Lemaigre-Dubreuil, Jean Rigault, assorted soldiers, many officials, a solitary, secure British agent, André Achiary. In 1941 Murphy could do no more than promise, provide—and sometimes withhold the wheat and the oil; those whom he met were of the right, the far right in most cases, *Cagoulard* in at least one instance. Murphy cast his net more widely than Leahy, and the pseudo-consuls occasionally reported items of passing interest. But Murphy moved and had his being more easily among those whom, as de Gaulle was scornfully to remark, "he met at dinner."

On the eve of ARCADIA, therefore, Roosevelt had little to show for his efforts at collaboration with Vichy. Although Leahy's cultivation of Darlan remained the kernel of Roosevelt's policy, "There is no evidence that American policy, when put to the test, was able to exert any significant influence on Vichy." The reason for failure in 1941 does not lie in the fact that Leahy and Murphy were credulous. Nor is the answer found in the fact that although Churchill did what he was told in "the small ways," he resisted Roosevelt whenever the latter tried to coerce or blackmail crudely. Churchill not only backed de Gaulle over St. Pierre et Miquelon; he also resisted all attempts to end the Royal Navy's blockade of Vichy ports.

In July and thereafter, relations between London and Washington were strained less concerning Syria—to which Roosevelt remained mostly indifferent—than over the blockade, and American trade with Vichy North Africa. But when Sumner Welles (the assistant secretary of state) also threatened that lend-lease aid might be affected if the blockade was not lifted or American trade curtailed, Churchill and Whitehall collectively resisted. The blockade remained, and the trade in question, while enabling North Africa to survive economically, was chiefly beneficial to *entrepreneurs* of the Lemaigre-Dubreuil variety. Roosevelt could well have echoed Leahy's words. But Darlan was, prospectively, another matter altogether.

Roosevelt was playing a long suit. His Vichy gamble did not depend on immediate success. The gamble might well depend on Darlan for success, but this was a factor that Churchill—and de Gaulle—failed to grasp. They did so because they did not realize the long-term, indeed "post-war," nature of Roosevelt's Vichy policy. Unlike de Gaulle, who set out to create a movement, Roosevelt was determined to capture individuals in a system he saw as without substance, a France he believed was finished. Success was important to de Gaulle in terms of immediate, and sustained, achievement; Roosevelt could afford to wait. Thus Churchill and Roosevelt conducted a strategic review during ARCADIA with basic disagreements either unrevealed or ignored. Churchill dealt his strategic cards masterfully to a president and advisers in no mood for outright opposition. Yet Churchill, who had survived a far more testing year than 1940, was loath to push his advantage home.

Churchill had also grasped that, whatever might appear on the record, Roosevelt's energies for months to come would inevitably be concentrated on the Pacific. Churchill claimed that, before Pearl Harbor, he had had to woo Roosevelt but that after the event he consummated a relationship and adopted a tough approach: "The President is now in the harem!" This strained, infelicitous metaphor betrays in reality a continued anxiety on Churchill's part that Roosevelt would eventually crush all schemes but his own for Vichy, and North Africa. Yet although the anxiety is apparent, the true nature of Roosevelt's Vichy policy was, in 1941, beyond Churchill's ken.

Churchill noted in preparation for ARCADIA:

We ought, therefore, to try hard to win over French North Africa and now is the moment to use every inducement and form of pressure at our disposal upon the Government of Vichy and the French authorities in North Africa. The German set-back in Russia, the British successes in Libya, the moral and military collapse of Italy; above all, the Declarations of War exchanged between Germany and the United States, must strongly affect the mind of France and the French Empire. Now is the time to offer to Vichy either a blessing or a cursing. A blessing will consist in a promise by the United States and Great Britain to re-establish France as a Great Power with her territories undiminished (except for the changes in Syria and certain adjustments which may be necessary on the frontier of Spanish Morocco). It should carry with it an offer of active aid by British and United States Expeditionary Forces, both from the Atlantic seaboard of Morocco and at convenient landing points in Algeria and Tunisia as well as from General Auchinleck's forces advancing from the East. [Sir Claude Auchinleck was commanding British forces in the Middle East.] Ample supplies for the French and the loyal Moors should be made available. Vichy should be asked to send their fleet from Toulon to Oran and Bizerta and to bring France into the war again as a principal.

Churchill was determined not to abandon all the implications of his strategy in pursuit of a policy designed to influence Roosevelt. Churchill continued: "This would mean that the Germans would take over the whole of France and rule it as occupied territory." This was a contingency that Roosevelt always refused to consider, because it would extinguish his Vichy policy at a blow. Churchill, therefore, amended his warning: "There is, of course, always the chance that the Germans, tied up in Russia, may not care to take over Unoccupied France even though French North Africa is at war with them." In reality, Churchill knew from the ENIGMA that a German occupation of "Vichy France" in the event of an Anglo-American force descending on North Africa was more likely than not. Churchill also believed that such a descent, uninvited, would be made whether French forces resisted or not. In order to influence Roosevelt toward a consideration of strategic issues and wean him from political gambles, Churchill concluded this and wean him from political gambles, Churchill concluded this part of his argument with a most uncharacteristic resort to begging the question:

> Our relationship with General de Gaulle will require to be reviewed. Hitherto the United States have entered into no undertakings similar to those comprised in my correspondence with him. [The "undertakings" were, in fact, with the British government and, to that extent, "correspondence" must be seen as wholly disingenuous.] Through no particular fault of his own he has not been of any important help to us. Indeed, his Movement has created new antagonisms in French minds. Any action which the United States may now feel able to take in regard to him should have the effect *inter alia* of re-defining our obligations to him and France so as to make those obligations more closely dependent upon the effective effort by him and the French nation to rehabilitate themselves. If Vichy were to act as we desire about French North Africa, the United States and Great Britain must labour to bring about a reconciliation between the Free French (de Gaullists) and those other Frenchmen who will have taken up arms once more against Germany. If, on the other hand, Vichy assists in collaboration with Germany and we have to fight our way into French North and West Africa, then the de Gaullist Movement will be of value and must be aided and used to the full.

Further than that Churchill would not go. He had been laboring on his strategic review for months; despite appalling news from the Far East and the Pacific, the invasion of North Africa remained at the center of Churchill's strategy for the prosecution of war against the Axis. Churchill would do much in attempting to influence Roosevelt to accept a comparable preoccupation. But Churchill would not fudge the issues beyond a certain point—and he had no intention of abandoning de Gaulle. On 1 January 1942, two weeks after Churchill's North Africa paper had achieved its final revision, Jean Moulin returned to France.

3

1942
Une Place d'armes

Roosevelt accepted ARCADIA's prescription for Allied offensive operations in 1942. But the president's acceptance reflected both his instinctive perception that Stalin's Russia was Hitler's principal adversary, and his determination to fashion an Anglo-American political strategy to suit his own purposes. Therein lay a lurking crisis for Churchill: Roosevelt would come to see Stalin as coeval; the investment of North Africa would be part of an American-dominated political process, preliminary to American domination of a "liberated" Western Europe. But the prescription, although nominally accepted by Admiral Ernest J. King and General Henry Arnold (the U.S. Navy and U.S. Army Air Force members of the Joint Chiefs of Staff), was sternly contested by General George C. Marshall, the army chief of staff, in discussions within the organization that resulted from ARCADIA: the Combined Chiefs of Staff. At this level of Anglo-American command and control, much of 1942 was dominated by Marshall's campaign to make a reality of "Germany first."

Marshall believed in the feasibility of a direct, cross-Channel assault on occupied Western Europe, and the subsequent invasion of Germany. Marshall opposed the invastion of North Africa as a wasteful diversion from "Germany first," and said so with all the considerable intellectual resources at his command. Marshall's staff included a certain Brigadier General Dwight D. Eisenhower—in 1941 merely a lieutenant colonel—who, for whatever reason, shared his doubts about North Africa. Marshall's opposition to GYMNAST and SUPER GYMNAST—British code names for a North African operation, later to be TORCH—was, however, essentially futile. Once Roosevelt had made a decision—even, as in this case, disguised as compliance with Churchill's arguments—none could shift him. By later summer, Marshall was forced to accept the presidential decision, thereafter unenthusiastically to seek the means whereby TORCH could become a feasible operation of war.

In April Pierre Laval returned to power, ousting Darlan from all office except "Commander-in-Chief of the French Armed Forces." Darlan remained Pétain's "Dauphin," but more so in his own estimation than that of rivals and supporters. Laval's return to power—at Hitler's bidding, to do as he willed—effectively disposed of Pétain. A few frail decencies had survived in Vichy during Laval's absence. His return was marked by complete adhesion to Hitler as a force for evil. The return was signaled by active anti-Semitism in terms of planned liquidation, and by the imposition of forced labor on French Gentile youth. The *Service d'Ordre Legionnaire* (SOL), formed in January to emulate the SS, was immediately strengthened, particularly in North Africa. In January Roosevelt had told Pétain that "the

United States was about the best friend which France had."
The words, puzzling in January, were hollow by April.

On 27 April, Leahy reported to Washington: "Laval is ready
to defend France and the French Empire against all comers
and he specifically stated that if the British or the Americans
should attempt to make a landing either on the soil of Metropolitan France or on French territory in North Africa, he would
offer resistance to the best of his ability." Leahy was on his
way home—for personal reasons rather than as an expression
of Roosevelt's undoubted concern over Laval's new role; this
valedictory has an ironic ring. Indications of Laval's return had
caused the State Department to issue a wish-fulfilling statement hinting that "trustful relations" with Vichy might be pre-
served.

Laval returned; Leahy left Vichy; diplomatic relations were
maintained. To be "Dauphin" in such circumstances was to
invite ridicule, or elimination. Darlan's day in Pétain's Vichy
was done. By late 1941, Darlan was convinced that Germany
would not achieve Hitler's ambition; by early 1942, Darlan saw
further evidence of America's latent power—and of Roosevelt's determination to maintain Vichy in being, by one means
or another. Darlan began to plan for another day, in another
country, with new masters, fresh opportunities. If Roosevelt was
to acquire a new French friend, Darlan would be the man to
offer himself. Murphy was instructed accordingly. Marshall had
a good strategic case for "Germany first"; Roosevelt, in his own
estimation, had a political case for "North Africa first"—provided Darlan became his satellite.

II

Relations among Churchill, Roosevelt, and de Gaulle may be
dealt with briefly. The one critical factor until just before the
Allied landings in North Africa is Churchill's determination to
keep de Gaulle in check, much as Roosevelt, operating through

Murphy, kept North African Vichy in play. From midsummer 1942 until Roosevelt's collaboration with Darlan finally compelled retaliation, Churchill took the line of least resistance, and sought to condemn those who followed their own convictions. Briefly, in June, and after rebuffing Eden's defense of de Gaulle, Churchill even found time to say a good word for Vichy.

Throughout these long months of 1942, therefore, de Gaulle endured the further pain of a relationship with Churchill that was only assuaged by occasional warmth and understanding. Yet de Gaulle feared no final break: even in September, when the relationship reached the point of greatest strain—Churchill suggesting to Roosevelt on the 15th that de Gaulle be "kept out of the TORCH picture"—the subject of the proposed exclusion could afford to declare *"Je tiendrai les conséquences."* Apart from the intelligence about TORCH that de Gaulle acquired in London (from the Foreign Office, not SOE), his representatives in Washington, although politically ineffective, did not lack for sympathizers in the middle reaches of Roosevelt's civilian and military hierarchy

De Gaulle knew French North Africa would be invaded (but not when), and that Roosevelt, not Churchill, would dominate events. De Gaulle would have been silently contemptuous of the tone, words, and purpose of Churchill's 15 September wire to Roosevelt—"In the whole of TORCH, military and political, I consider myself your lieutenant asking only to put my viewpoint plainly before you . . . This is an American enterprise in which we are your helpmates . . ." But de Gaulle saw quite clearly that Roosevelt was the arbiter of Allied fortunes in matériel terms. De Gaulle publicly acknowledged this fact; meanwhile his intelligence services conveyed to him the equally material fact that, in certain British quarters, TORCH bore a direct relationship to the Résistance which Jean Moulin had been charged to create.

Roosevelt could only destroy the relationship between Churchill and de Gaulle—and thus affect the future of France—

if he insisted on an absolute breach. Roosevelt, although consistently hostile to de Gaulle, never did insist. In a curious way—or by yet another paradox—Roosevelt's prospective, covert alliance with Darlan worked in de Gaulle's favor: for the United States—"the arsenal of democracy"—to have wholly repudiated de Gaulle and his fighting Frenchmen would have revealed Roosevelt as positively—and publicly—committed to Vichy. Roosevelt could never show his hand so boldly. Churchill perceived these factors well enough when, on the eve of TORCH, he enjoyed a rare chance to put his viewpoint plainly. Churchill dissuaded Roosevelt from addressing Pétain publicly as "My dear old friend."

The archive for 1942 can be read as sustained attempts by Churchill, almost desperately anxious to conciliate Roosevelt, to cut de Gaulle down to the size of a mere French adventurer. The objective interpretation shows that Churchill allowed almost exactly the opposite situation to develop. Despite gallant endeavor, the Free French contribution to war remained unavoidably limited—in material terms. The contribution remained wholly dependent on British financial and material support. It lay within Churchill's power rather than Roosevelt's to repudiate de Gaulle at a time when American resources were becoming the arbiter of British fortunes.

Failing repudiation, de Gaulle's position could only strengthen, provided a British-supported French Résistance acknowledged de Gaulle as something more than a symbolic leader. Churchill knew, and unwillingly tolerated, this fact. Throughout 1942, Churchill and de Gaulle marked time. IRONCLAD is one example of this process; Churchill let it be known that the invasion of Madagascar was intended to install "the de Gaullists." Churchill's congratulations to de Gaulle after the heroic defense of Bir Hacheim in the Western Desert by General Pierre Koenig's First Free French Brigade Group furnishes a more telling instance of the relationship under strain, but enduring.

Koenig and his "stout-hearted troops" were supported

strongly at all times by a hard-pressed Royal Air Force. French and British men at arms were once more fighting for a common cause. Churchill and de Gaulle met on 10 June at Ten Downing Street—scene of so much. Churchill, momentarily free of Roosevelt, spoke from the heart: "It is one of the finest feats of arms in this war." This was not only generous, but strictly accurate. Bir Hacheim, fought between 27 May and 11 June—and thus still waged as Churchill spoke—thwarted Rommel on his right flank, and had much to do with preparations that the British Eighth Army thereafter made to deny Hitler Egypt, and the Suez Canal.

Bir Hacheim was much more than a gallant, costly, effective feat of arms. The Free French had, indeed, become the Fighting French, no longer a gesture of defiance, but prospectively the France for whom Churchill had fought in vain during his first meetings with de Gaulle. De Gaulle was right to exclaim after hearing Churchill's generous praise: "Men of reason have endured. Men of passion have lived!" Churchill, always candid when moved, confided Roosevelt's Vichy policy to de Gaulle. Churchill neither defended nor attacked the policy, but certainly dropped his "lieutenant's" role in declaring, "I am the friend of France! I have always wanted, and I want, a great France with a great army. It is necessary for the peace, order and security of Europe. I have never had any other policy!" Whether Churchill, inspired by Bir Hacheim, conscious that at Alexandria and Fort de France French warships lay moored and idle, sensing that Laval's Vichy would vie with Hitler's Germany in cruelty and repression, spoke from the heart or the head matters not. De Gaulle responded, but inimitably—and revealingly:

> That's true. You even had the merit, after Vichy's armistice, of continuing to play the card of France. That card is called de Gaulle: don't lose it now! It would be all the more absurd since you have reached the moment when your policy is succeeding and when Free France has become the soul and frame of French resistance. On these

bases I too am faithful to you. But I have very few resources with which to bear the responsibility for the interests of France. This involves great difficulties for me. I ask you to help me to overcome them. I agree that, on the whole, you are not ill-disposed towards us. But there are grave exceptions. Also American policy towards us is atrocious; it aims at our destruction. Do you know that, for Memorial Day, the American Government invited the Vichy military attachés and did not invite our officers? For the Americans, the Frenchmen of Bir Hacheim are not belligerents.

De Gaulle's outburst contained two elements that might have been calculated to infuriate Churchill: first, de Gaulle equated himself with France; second, he attacked Roosevelt. In 1940 Churchill had seen de Gaulle as embodying the true spirit of France. Two years later he was still convinced, despite ambiguous observations to Roosevelt, that de Gaulle was capable of great things. But neither in 1940, nor two years later, did Churchill accept de Gaulle's *political* identification of himself with France as such. This distinction owed nothing to Roosevelt's hostility. Nor was Churchill influenced by individual opposition to de Gaulle's pretensions. Churchill shared de Gaulle's views; however, he saw no reason to support the Frenchman's personal political ambitions, least of all when he denied having them.

Churchill's reaction to the Moulin report reveals more clearly than other evidence his refusal to back de Gaulle in 1942 as a future political leader of France. Acceptance of de Gaulle as the symbol of Résistance was one thing; acceptance of de Gaulle as a future president of France another. Churchill was well aware that the distinction would become more apparent than real, but his own attitudes, coupled with subservience to Roosevelt, made him reluctant to acknowledge the fact. By the end of 1942, Churchill's attitude had begun to change, fundamentally. But in mid-1942 he drew a clear distinction—in his own mind—between de Gaulle the fighting Frenchman and de Gaulle the ambitious politician.

The distinction did not even exist in Roosevelt's mind. In the view of one of de Gaulle's few confidants, Maurice Dejean, Roosevelt was committed to "a sort of capitalist democracy in France after the war by supporting Pétainist elements in Vichy and encouraging the establishment of a successor government to Vichy which would be heavily dependent on the United States." These pregnant words aside, the appointment on 9 July of Admiral Harold Stark as Roosevelt's personal representative to de Gaulle's headquarters in London was an important step. It marked a significant stage in the almost unwitting evolution of an American policy toward Fighting France and its leader which, while denying the value of one or the legitimacy of the other, reluctantly acknowledged the existence of both.

In July 1942, Stark was commander of U.S. naval forces in the "European Theater of Operations," an appointment devoid of much real strategic importance, but carrying rank and prestige. The dual appointment could be construed as Roosevelt's gesture toward a de Gaulle he could not wholly repudiate, but whose pretensions he would continue to oppose. In fact, Stark and his Francophile subordinates took their mission to de Gaulle rather more seriously than Washington intended. Whitehall, by July 1942, had Gaullist characteristics here and there that were hard to define but, by anyone of imagination, impossible to ignore. Stark did not ignore signs of the times. His appointment came to serve de Gaulle's ambitions well.

The change in terminology from "Free French" to "Fighting France" followed Stark's arrival in London, and not entirely by coincidence. The rewording could also be construed as an American attempt, with British acquiescence, to relegate the movement that de Gaulle had created from the expression of an undefeated France to a collection of Frenchmen who had enlisted under the Allied banner. Throughout June and July able diplomats in London—and Washington—spent much time on these matters.

In the event—and by a final paradox—*"La France Combattante,"* while no longer equating de Gaulle with leadership
of the movement, provided him with precisely what he sought.
". . . the new definition [of 14 July] made it clear that the persons and territories constituting *'La France Combattante"*
formed a unity for the purpose of continuing the war . . . it
recognized General de Gaulle's movement for the first time as
a symbol of French resistance in general, whether in France
or elsewhere . . . the [French] National Committee was recognized as representing the unity of *'La France Combattante.'*" De Gaulle's contribution to this ostensibly
terminological debate was adroitly muted. His instinctive
political skill was never better expressed than during the time
when Roosevelt and Churchill were embarking on "this great
tangle of TORCH."

Considered from these aspects, the meeting between
Churchill and de Gaulle on 10 June could have provided
Churchill with a unique opportunity to offer de Gaulle either
a blessing or a cursing. Churchill, committed to de Gaulle the
man, the patriot, did neither. After de Gaulle had spoken,
Churchill merely said: "The Americans do not wish to give up
their policy with Vichy." Churchill went further in exposi-
tion—although he made no attempt to explain why Roosevelt
was prepared to grant a form of recognition to the French
National Committee while playing the Vichy card for what it
was worth. All that concerns us here, however, is loss of another
opportunity to tackle the crucial question: Given such an
American commitment to Vichy, how would it be possible for
any effective Résistance movement to develop in France, above
all in the Unoccupied Zone?

De Gaulle was reluctant to acknowledge the British contribution to French Résistance. His reluctance sprang from
pride—in his own judgment and in France. Jacques Soustelle
and others on the French National Committee openly
acknowledged the British contribution. This attitude earned
no plaudits from de Gaulle. But what really hurt de Gaulle's
pride was the simple, unpalatable fact that effective Résistance

depended on British support in practical terms: agents; naval vessels, and aircraft; arms; munitions; sanctuary in the United Kingdom and elsewhere; *cash.* Both Churchill and de Gaulle failed to tackle, let alone settle, the issue of where British support became political—the future of France—rather than strategic: what support could Résistance give to *British* military objectives? Failure can only be explained by the fact that tackling, let alone attempting to answer, the question raised an even more fundamental issue: Was de Gaulle the only Frenchman capable of uniting Résistance groups? De Gaulle—and Jean Moulin—believed there was only one Frenchman who could make a realistic Résistance. Unity required more than symbols. De Gaulle decided to extend "L'Appel" of 18 June 1940 to potential résistants.

On 23 June de Gaulle published a manifesto intended to match that broadcast from Brazzaville nearly two years earlier. Although the second manifesto was rhetorical rather than specific, it was de Gaulle's first direct attempt to ally himself with the forces of Résistance. Reading between the lines, one detects the skill with which de Gaulle matches Moulin's case for internal stability being a product of Résistance with a demand that "the nation must once again exercise absolute sovereignty over its destiny. Any usurpation, whether inside or beyond our frontiers, must be destroyed and swept away." De Gaulle had embarked on the second stage of "L'Appel," and it was one that neither Churchill nor Roosevelt could arrest or divert. By September, Churchill and de Gaulle are again locked in sterile verbal conflict. But arguments are irrelevant to the momentum of events. TORCH is in motion, with de Gaulle excluded from its deliberations. Résistance is stirring; de Gaulle will be something more potent than a symbol, and that shortly.

III

Allied Forces Headquarters was established at Norfolk House, St. James's Square on 6 August. Eisenhower, "Commanding

General in the European Theatre of Operation"—an appointment that Marshall had intended as preliminary to tackling "Germany first"—became "Commander in Chief Allied Expeditionary Force"; he immediately found himself embroiled in a situation of political contradiction and strategic ambiguity for which neither his experience nor his talents had prepared him. At no time between 4 August and 8 November did AFHQ represent anything more than a collection of individuals; at no time during those three anxious months was Eisenhower personally or AFHQ collectively able to decide unambiguously whether TORCH was an operation of war or an exercise in political calculation.

More to the point—as belatedly perceived—no adequate appreciation was ever attempted, let alone achieved, of what kind of political situation might exist, or evolve, after the Allied landings. Nothing illustrates these truths better than the decision to send Eisenhower's deputy, Major General Mark Clark, to a secret rendezvous with Murphy less than three weeks before D-Day. Clark's mission, shorn of its subsequently contrived melodrama, had one simple aim: to discover just what the hell was going on.

In briefly considering these three months, it is essential to establish in the reader's mind the fact that strategic planning for TORCH took place in London, not Washington. The Combined Chiefs of Staff was established in Washington, but London was, or was supposed to be, the center for planning and executing strategy in "the European Theatre of Operations." French North Africa, within the ARCADIA prescription, was part of that theater for operational purposes. Despite that fact, a central paradox dominates the period: Neither Eisenhower, nor anybody else, was able to pull together the many conflicting elements of strategy and politics that dominated London concerning French North Africa, and France, by the third year of the war. TORCH remained "this great tangle" because neither organization nor personal volition existed to ensure clear communication so that contradictions could be resolved. Mark

Clark's challenge reflects simple, human bewilderment at the higher levels of Allied decision-making. The challenge should have been made at all levels, but lack of time, understanding, and experience ensured that it was not even contemplated.

What were these contradictions, and how did they affect Eisenhower and AFHQ, hence ultimately TORCH itself? There were three contradictory elements: British strategy for returning to the Continent of Europe; operational planning for TORCH as such—largely dominated by lack of time, intelligence, and resources; and the political nature of the operation in question. The British outlook on these matters is considered first, because it reflected aspirations that developed into policies well before the United States was forced into war. The Chiefs of Staff thought in strategic terms, but the process drove them to quasi-political conclusions.

The British Chiefs of Staff wished to establish a base in North Africa for offensive operations against the Axis so that "closing the ring" could become an option, not remain merely an aspiration. Such narrowly strategic considerations are beyond the scope of this book. But the Chiefs also wished to establish such a base so that clandestine operations in support of the French Résistance in the Unoccupied Zone could be mounted. The Chiefs, in April and May 1942—when directives to SOE were issued—had little or no interest in the ideological dimension of Résistance. Still less did the Chiefs support de Gaulle in his ambition of leading such a Résistance to a liberation from which he would emerge as the political leader of a newly independent France.

So far as the Chiefs thought about such a consummation, they disliked and opposed it. The Chiefs' interest in French Résistance was quite simple: as an "adjunct," in terms of sabotage and the like, to conventional military operations on the mainland of Western Europe when—and if—these should take place. The Unoccupied Zone was considered to be the most feasible area for Résistance in these terms—provided the relative proximity of French North Africa was guaranteed by the establishment there of a secure base, indeed a sanctuary. Such a base, by definition, could only become and remain secure in the context of an anti-Vichy administration.

The directives issued on 27 April and 11 May 1942 reveal with sufficient clarity the Chiefs' thoughts about French North Africa after ARCADIA had put the area in the forefront of Allied strategic planning. The directives stressed the need to avoid "premature uprisings" in France—but put equal emphasis on organizing and executing "subversive activities" in North Africa. In particular, the directives established new principles: In North Africa, SOE would be responsible for operations, the Secret Intelligence Service (SIS) for intelligence. SOE would acquire a regional headquarters in Gibraltar, which would enable a communications network independent of SIS to be established. Aircraft from the Royal Air Force Special Duties flight (tasked to support SOE) would engage in leaflet drops over North Africa and in other "subversive activities."

The directives made no specific reference to SOE-supported resistance in the Unoccupied Zone nor—rather obviously—to the political objectives that should be attained in North Africa. But SOE was tasked to establish itself, eventually, in North Africa as preliminary to operations outside it. SOE found in North Africa by November 1942 a situation that bore little or no relation to what the Chiefs of Staff had laid down six months before. That is not the point: the Chiefs knew by early 1942 that SOE, while divided into sections serving Gaullist and non-Gaullist interests, was united in being "anti-Vichy . . . it was its only political creed." The common denominator between the Chiefs and Baker Street was simply this: No Gaullist movement existed in North Africa, nor should British authorities, civil or military, overt or covert, do anything to encourage one. But the establishment of a base in North Africa, including clandestine and subversive elements, predicated an anti-Vichy administration after invasion (either by invitation or force), whether or not control of civil affairs was vested in some form of "Allied Military Government" or left to suitably cooperative French officials.

Thus we have the British aim—as the soldiers would put it—producing the first contradiction between Roosevelt's and Churchill's objectives concerning North Africa and France. But the contradiction only became apparent after invasion, because the preceding six months were dominated by operational factors, primarily lack of human and material resources. Immediately after Eisenhower's appointment, and indeed throughout August (when D-Day was still intended to be 15 October), he issued a stream of warnings to Marshall that reflected his fear that TORCH was not an operation of war but a political gamble. Eisenhower had sensed this factor well before his appointment but, in endeavoring to make sense of an operation that could only succeed if force was available should conspiracy fail, he made his apprehensions plain. Eisenhower did not believe that strategic objectives could be gained by political means, and said so to Marshall, who agreed with him: "A failure in SLEDGEHAMMER [the abandoned cross-Channel operation] for which the [American] public has been adequately prepared, could have been accepted, but failure in TORCH would only bring ridicule and loss of confidence."

Marhsall's and Eisenhower's fears were focused on the perils of landing well inside the Mediterranean, inviting an Axis riposte that could not be met. Both chief of staff and his subordinate wanted to exclude landings at Algiers—whereas Churchill was insistent that these must take place. Both Marshall and Eisenhower flatly refused to contemplate Tunis as a point of assault, let alone Tripoli, as the British Chiefs of Staff wished. Uneasy compromise on Algiers (assault on Casablanca was not disputed; Oran caused no dispute) nevertheless revealed the problem of dispersing forces that were initially limited in numbers and doubtful in quality. In particular,

The planned pattern of the assault [on Algiers] cut down to the narrowest of margins the possibility of occupying Tunisia within a brief period of Allied superiority over the Axis forces likely to be sent there. If the initial attempt should fail, the operations would be protracted in proportion to the strength which the Axis powers chose to commit.

On paper—in St. James's Square—Tunis was to be captured on D + 90, a time scale that reflected Roosevelt's priority aim of securing a political base throughout North Africa rather than the possibility that resistance would be encountered from both French and Axis forces. In the event, Tunis was not occupied by Allied forces until 15 May 1943—D + 172, or nearly six months after the initial landings. "The military promenade to Tunis which the Allies had anticipated became a soldiers' battle reminiscent of World War One." During those unexpected months of battle, and because assumptions were confounded, the political situation in North Africa underwent metamorphosis.

The Combined Chiefs of Staff, immersed in the higher direction of the war, gave little detailed attention to TORCH. On 6 October—by which date D-day had been moved to 8 November—the Chiefs issued a directive remarkable alike for imprecision of language and an Olympian tone. The Combined Chiefs can be excused for much, given the unresolved tensions that defined their deliberations, and the fact that TORCH was but one among many grave issues. But the Combined Chiefs must be accused nonetheless of allowing Roosevelt's policy assumption to pass without criticism or amendment. This assumption was that the intended blessing of an ostensibly American presence in North Africa would, of itself, deny the need for credible forces.

The Combined Chiefs' directive reads: "The objective [of TORCH] must be complete annihilation of Axis forces . . . in order to ensure communications through the Mediterranean, and to facilitate operations throughout the theatre and the European continent." This broadly expressed directive was preceded and followed by two paragraphs of considerable ambiguity: ". . . favourable conditions [should be created] for extensive offensive operations to the East through Libya against the rear of Axis forces in the Western Desert." Further: "No offensive action is to be taken against Vichy French forces unless these forces take definite hostile action against us." Invasion is, in itself, an offensive action: the words quoted beg this rather fundamental question.

By 6 October, two months after his appointment, Eisenhower could no longer beg fundamental questions. Eisenhower's staff reckoned that TORCH had "only a fifty per cent chance of success." Eisenhower could no more afford failure in TORCH than Marshall. On the same day that the Combined Chiefs established TORCH's objective in *strategic* terms, Eisenhower acquired a political adviser, a British official, moreover—and an outspoken critic of Vichy as well. Mr W.H.B. Mack, counsellor in the Foreign Office, was appointed "Head of the Political Section of the Commander-in-Chief Allied Expeditionary Force." Thus we come to the second main contradiction, the most twisted thread in the great tangle of TORCH. Vichy ground forces in North Africa numbered approximately 100,000, variable in quality and armament; yet they were not only familiar with political conditions and terrain, but also overwhelmingly superior in numbers compared to the Allied assault parties that would be directed onto the beaches and other landing points at H-Hour on D-Day. Could this disparity be reduced, if not wholly removed, by the exercise of some kind of political legerdemain?

This was, of course, the purpose for which Roosevelt had sent Murphy to North Africa. Before we consider why and how Murphy failed to carry out Roosevelt's purpose, it is essential to grasp that, by October, Eisenhower had been forced through circumstance to dilute his skepticism about attaining strategic objectives by political means. Eisenhower was driven to contemplate the factor of conspiracy, not that he might embark on it himself, but in order to ensure that his exiguous forces were neither defeated on the beaches nor humiliated in a pitched battle. In making this decision, Eisenhower not only put himself in Murphy's hands, but did so in a context where neither the commander nor the conspirator had acquired reliable political intelligence about the situation in the area that, between them, they had been directed to subvert and occupy. Such intelligence as came Murphy's way he sent to Washington, and it remained there. SIS operations in North Africa were in the hands of RYGOR, a Polish circuit. Unfortunately—to say the least—the intelligence thus acquired was not distributed to AFHQ.

"Most of what the Americans knew or thought they knew about the situation in North Africa came from Mr Robert Murphy." But at least the "Americans"—in Washington—thought they knew: Eisenhower and AFHQ knew that they did not know, and were thus driven to two expedients which, in being themselves contradictory, added further to "a dizzying confusion." The first expedient was to rely increasingly on Murphy, not as an intelligence source but as a conspirator; the second expedient was to establish political assumptions, some of which may have reflected Mack's anti-Vichy outlook, but also indicated that Eisenhower remained not only basically skeptical about conspiracy but was instinctively hostile to doing business with Vichy. Eisenhower's staff, therefore, concocted a formula just before Mack's appointment that appeared to settle these conundrums. In reality, the formula did not even paper over the cracks.

"The relationships that will apply among Donovan, Mack, and Murphy are as follows: Donovan is to provide my headquarters with one or more specialists who are to be incorporated into the Staff Section headed by Mack. The activities that Donovan's organization will be expected to execute, will be communicated to him by my headquarters after study by Mack's Section. Donovan is to do nothing that has not been previously cleared by my headquarters. Murphy is to head the Civil Affairs Section on my staff *after the beginning of the operation.* During the period before the beginning of the operation, Murphy is the sole agent in the affected area through whom political maneuvering will take place. In this position, he will suggest activities that Donovan's organization will be expected to execute, but these suggestions will normally reach this headquarters and be communicated from here to Donovan."

On 6 October, a little flesh was put upon these bones. Mack's appointment was enshrined in a directive: "It will be your duty to ensure the integration of the plans of the Special Operations Executive, the Secret Intelligence Service, and the Political Warfare Executive." Mack was directed to liaise on these matters with General Eisenhower and "Colonel Donovan's Organization." PWE was a propaganda organization, administratively under Foreign Office control (and much influenced by its prevailing outlook towards Fighting France and de Gaulle), responsible for acquiring intelligence overtly (and on the distribution for the less sensitively acquired covert material), then reporting on events as they developed. At this point in the steadily accelerating momentum of Eisenhower's apprehensions we may merely note that by Mack's appointment he had introduced a Gaullist Trojan Horse to AFHQ.

Eisenhower had asked for political guidance on 21 August, and it is some measure of his operational preoccupations that he was prepared to wait six weeks before he was given it—and then only in the sense that Mack was appointed. But the interest, and importance, of this appointment lies not so much in the fact that Mack was a British official; or in the inclusion of SOE, SIS, and OSS under his wing for operational purposes (the provision of political intelligence from two of these three sources remaining a matter of individual contact); or in Eisenhower's determination to provide himself with intelligence independently of Murphy. However much the latter remained responsible for "political maneuvering"—which, states Eisenhower, "is controlled by the President"—Eisenhower was clearly concerned that neither he nor AFHQ knew what the conspiracies and factions, hatched and fashioned by Roosevelt's personal representative in North Africa, were actually expected to achieve.

Yet there is, of course, a far more important element in

Mack's appointment and his terms of reference than Eisenhower's concern for guidance as such. Eisenhower was to be advised by an official whose main source of operational intelligence, in terms of what had to be done just before, on the eve of, and in the period immediately following D-Day, would be "organizations" whose members were, on balance, anti-Vichy in outlook. Stewart Menzies, Director General of SIS, does not come into this category, but collectively, SOE was anti-Vichy both from prospective Gaullist sentiment and hard-won experience. By the same token, OSS in North Africa had come to make three main assessments: No "great leaders" could be relied on; middle-rank elements in the civil administration and armed forces might prove useful; "patriot groups" must be considered as the one reliable source of committed conspirators whose members would be willing and able to act decisively on the night of the Allied landings. Mack had a mind, and could use it to ask the awkward question, but in October was in no position to give Eisenhower positive advice or specific recommendations. Mack was denied effective status—and he lacked reliable raw intelligence about the North African political situation.

We should not be wholly surprised, therefore, to discover that, on 10 October, with D-Day less than a month distant, Eisenhower posed this question for the combined cogitation of his staff: "Is it the object of policy (1) to have an independent French government established in North Africa in the place of the Vichy government and (2) to disrupt the Vichy government?" Murphy had been given his political directive personally by Roosevelt on 22 September, of which, in the context of Eisenhower's doubts, there is one key paragraph: "No change in the existing French Civil Administration is contemplated by the United States. Your task will be to preserve French sovereignty in Algeria, and the French Administration of Morocco and Tunisia." Contradiction, hidden like rocks beneath the surface, was all but complete between Eisenhower's military objectives and Murphy's political brief.

"Civil Administration" did *not* mean mere bureaucrats. The phrase, in the broader context of "political maneuvering," meant preserving what had become, after June 1940, an essentially political structure—Vichy, albeit in North Africa. As we move toward Mark Clark's meeting at Cherchell we find, therefore, a situation where Roosevelt and Murphy were maneuvering toward the maintenance of that political structure, while Eisenhower and his advisers were embarking, if almost unwittingly, on a process designed to replace it. Eisenhower was driven by circumstance to accept Darlan's diktat after D-Day. It is clear from the evidence that he was not prepared to ensure the preservation of Vichy in North Africa as he sat in London struggling to establish a political framework for the support of a hazardous military operation. In these contradictions and conflicts will be found at least some of the reasons for the bold hand that Darlan played and the ease with which he brought off a grand slam.

IV

Two events had occurred in June that gave definition to what otherwise remained a collection of suppositions about Anglo-American clandestine operations. Donovan and Sir Charles Hambro (SOE's "Executive Director") reached agreement on division of responsibilities; a member of Hambro's staff wrote a memorandum on returning to the Foreign Office which reveals what committed Gaullists in SOE believed was the right prescription for war in the shadows. The crux of the Donovan-Hambro Agreement was that North Africa became primarily an OSS responsibility, but SOE acquired specific roles there that, in certain cases, made it the senior partner in combined covert operations. Hambro and his colleagues perceived that various American sources had acquired useful raw intelligence about the political situation in North Africa. Donovan and his SOE opposite numbers also knew that something concrete had to be done if this intelligence was ever to form the basis of operations.

The agreement thus reflected Whitehall's enforced acceptance of the apparently major American role in TORCH, but intelligently accepted a fact that no amount of fudging or blandishment could change: OSS was brand new, established by presidential directive on 13 June. OSS, therefore, to put the matter in terms, knew little about covert operations, particularly of the rougher sort, specifically where people met violent ends, in hot, or cold, blood. SOE knew a certain amount about these things, sufficient for one OWI report to note with disdain in January 1942: "The British are commonly accused of being cynical about handling their agents and ruthless in exploiting them to get the job done." We should remember what one distinguished member of SOE was told when recruited: "You shouldn't object to fraud—and you musn't object to murder."

Despite the Office of War Information (OWI) philippic, Donovan was quite prepared for Baker Street to write the operational directives for OSS in North Africa. War in the shadows demands a certain style, and acquires a political dimension from sheer force of circumstance. The June memorandum advocated that support for Résistance take a specifically anti-Vichy cast; that assassination *in extremis* should not be ruled out; and that the Vichy administration, specifically in North and West Africa, should be seen, and treated, as a threat to British interests.

The memorandum concluded its case for subversive action by stating: "One of the really great virtues of this new instrument of war [SOE] is that you can use it without committing HMG [the British government]. Even if there is a suspicion that HMG may be behind any subversive movement there is usually no proof to that effect; even if there is proof that British authorities are responsible the necessary gestures of repudiation can be made."

Thus, while Marshall and his peers continued to debate grand strategy, Donovan's OSS and Hambro's SOE moved toward a plan of campaign in—and, prospectively, from—North Africa which, in its combination of intelligence about the situation there and appreciation of operational requirements came to differ fundamentally from much that was pondered by Eisenhower, and AFHQ. That the OSS and SOE plan of campaign for operations in North Africa was, in the first instance, intended to support TORCH must not distract attention from these fundamental differences. For what had Donovan's "knight errants" discovered? Unlike Murphy, the "Consuls" and the forerunners of OSS had done more than dine with the right people.

The rather crucial discovery had been made that Murphy's conspiracy was a figment of his imagination; that no "great leaders" existed; but that from embryonic "patriot groups" there might be found young men and women who would serve the Allied cause—in serving the cause of France. These were the young men and women—"mostly Jewish and left-wing"—who had left France to join those of like mind in North Africa, fortified by the belief that Vichy was as vulnerable there as it was vicious in the motherland. As de Gaulle remarked at an early stage in his career in exile: *"Je n'ai pour moi que les Juifs et les métèques."*

Even in August 1940, the U.S. Consulate in Rabat noted that General Auguste Noguès was "nervous of government authority." This somewhat oblique reference to Noguès's congenital *attentisme* gains force from "a remarkably perceptive analysis" which was received in the Foreign Office in late July 1941. The analysis pointed to the possibility that the authorities in North Africa "semi-independently of Vichy, may gradually achieve a position in which they will be able to pretend that their policy has brought them to a point where they are morally aligned to the United States in hostility to Germany, and that, looking back on events since the Armistice, their policy has been justified by its material results." After some further shrewd reflections on the "maneuvers" of Weygand, Pierre Boisson, and others, the report concluded: "From the point of view of our own dealings with France after the war it would, I think, be unfortunate if the Vichy politicians [in North Africa] were able at the last minute to scramble down on the right side of the fence, and were to succeed in justifying to French metropolitan opinion the shifts and intrigues and treacheries that have characterized their conduct of affairs."

On 31 January 1942, Donovan summarized his North African agents' reports to date as follows:

> As far as the military leaders in French North Africa are concerned, we do not believe great hopes should be based on them. In particular, [General Alphonse Juin] was sent to Morocco after Weygand was recalled, and it appears probable that his nomination, made by Darlan, was agreeable to the Germans. Juin was freed [from a German prisoner-of-war camp] after promising never to take up arms against Germany or undertake anything against her which other French officers refused to do.

The report then continues in strictly objective terms. Admiral Raymond Fenard, Admiral Jean Esteva, Yves Châtel, General Louis Koeltz and General Robert-Jean Odic were, with some qualifications, regarded as "cool-headed"—and possessing virtues—but mainly characterized by *attentisme* and *sauve qui peut:* "In the present public misfortune, they cling to the prestige and integrity of Marshal Pétain . . . One must not hope that they will rebel against their chiefs . . ."

We then find bigger game: "General Noguès, to whom a part of these preceding observations could be applied, is nevertheless a slightly more complicated case." The detailed analysis that follows comes to this: From family connection and prestige—son-in-law of Théophile Delcassé, Resident-General of Morocco since 1936—Noguès might be thought a soldier stirred by German conquest to set up the standard in North Africa. But not so: "He did not hesitate to tell us that he had been misinformed at the time of his appeal [in 1940] for resistance . . . the decision not to attempt a hopeless struggle in

Africa was wise." Donovan's words were echoed by Consul J. Rives Childs in Casablanca and his colleagues elsewhere in North Africa. As we shall see, Murphy saw matters in a different light.

Donovan's report concludes with an interesting picture of the French Navy, whose morale was considered far superior to that of the Army and Air Force—but mainly because pay had been doubled and conditions of service improved. "Most French sailors would obey orders even in the case of an Allied offensive, and if they knew it in advance " Equally valid, however, was the comment that the fleet spent little time at sea. Men would fight their ships but if both were trapped in harbor, resistance could be crushed.

The reports to Donovan carry conviction because subsequent events proved them to be accurate. Nevertheless, in the Washington of early 1942, Roosevelt personally, his entourage collectively, sought assurance that Vichy, intact in North Africa, could be detached entirely from the Axis grip. This assurance was not forthcoming—from OSS. However, Colonel William Eddy's agents began to report potential for active cooperation with the United States. Certain names begin to appear on the OSS file: Henri d'Astier de Lavigerie [sic]; "Rigaud and de St. Hardouin"; José Aboulker and Bernard Karsenty; "Doctor Raphael Aboulker, Doctor André Morali and Pierre Alexandre," Colonel [Emil] Jousse, General [Charles] Mast; Commissaire [André] Achiary, Commissaires Bringard, Esqueyre; "Commissaire Muscatelli, MM. Jacques Brunel and Raymond Lavaysse."

The names were to become familiar enough by 8 November 1942. But, in these early months of Murphy's conspiracy with seemingly more potent figures—d'Astier, indeed, among them—Washington was indifferent to reports of prospective revolt against Vichy, hostile to suggestions of Gaullist tendencies. René Capitant, editor of *Combat* in its North African version, was not a name to arouse interest in Washington when Bataan and Corregidor made the headlines; "[Louis] Joxe,

influential Gaullist propagandist," would not have been welcome in the State Department; that Raphael Aboulker was
President du parti Radical Socialiste, and his son was, by early
1942 *"Chef de l'organisation des Groupes"* (a prospective honor,
not a reality) only led those opposed to Donovan and all his
works to argue strongly that no deals could be made with men
of the left who were planning what OSS, most oddly, called
"the Putsch."

SOE, directed by the British Chiefs of Staff to operate from
North Africa was, by July, cooperating with an OSS whose
intelligence on the situation there suggested that support for
any Allied invasion would not be found in high places. The
intelligence also indicated that resistance to the invasion was
likely, ineffectual perhaps on land but, overall, serious enough
to prevent rapid establishment of a bridgehead, and the assertion of strategic and political advantage. SIS, directed by the
Chiefs to acquire intelligence, depended on four sources: its
own agents; RYGOR, the Polish Circuit; a very limited Fighting French operation; and Vichy intelligence officers who had
either continued to operate in liaison with their British opposite numbers or had decided to abandon Vichy, covertly.

Reports from these sources tended to support the OSS
conclusions. But, as must be stressed again, intelligence on
these matters did not reach AFHQ—or SOE. We may also note:
"During the planning of the Anglo-American descent on French
North Africa, as on the decision to undertake it, the influence
of intelligence was subordinate to that of logistic, strategic, and
political considerations." And further: "U.S. official accounts
made it clear that the U.S. position paid little regard to intelligence assessments."

What then led Colonel D.R. Guinness, of SOE's Planning
Staff, to write two directives for Colonel William Eddy (as OSS
station chief in North Africa) on 10 September and 12 October
1942 which established, in pretty unambiguous language, the

basis for sabotage by "patriot groups" who were known to be
wholly immune from the *attentisme* and self-interest that dominated the motives of those whom Murphy cultivated? The
answer is this: The entire concept of Résistance in occupied
territories, as supported by SOE, lay in opposition to and action
against existing *authority*, whether legitimate, enforced, or
usurped. Moulin's argument that French Résistance must form
the basis of an authority that would command national assent—
de Gaulle's call for "unity" being its rhetorical expression—
gave intellectual strength to what was, essentially, a revolutionary appeal, if one devoid of obvious political content.

SOE, driven to comparable conclusions by force of circumstance, was disliked in Whitehall as a result, but did come
to see the issues at stake, whether in France—or North Africa—
rather more clearly than those whose minds ran in the grooves
of orthodoxy, and habit. To that extent, but only to that extent,
Guinness's directives, in September and October, reflect a certain congruity of ideas with Gaullism. This was the case however much SOE had been directed by the British Chiefs of
Staff—not, be it noted, by AFHQ—only to operate in support
of conventional military operations, whether in North Africa
or elsewhere.

Nevertheless, nobody should assume that either the Guinness directives or the thoughts that he subsequently put on paper
reflect any desire or intention as such to openly support the
Gaullist cause. Even by late November 1942 and in Algiers,
such avowal would have been denied by SOE's unwritten creed
that "its only politics were to be resolutely anti-Vichy at all
times"—and by what certainly appeared to be a marked lack
of support for de Gaulle personally in North Africa.

A clandestine press was the first requirement: René Capitant's *Combat* was not only being widely distributed throughout North Africa by mid-1942, but was also avowedly Gaullist
in tone, and content. But a RYGOR report is timely in this
context: "Gaullist elements exist in Morocco, but they are
unorganised, with no overall control . . . they make little head-

way with their propaganda because of the strength of the Légion [des Anciens Combattants] and the SOL." However, according to Soustelle, there were Gaullist links in Morocco with the U.S.consulates at Rabat and Casablanca.

Tangier, the Spanish territory within French Morocco was, indeed, an intelligence-gathering free-for-all, where SOE, SIS, and the Fighting French were well established. Tangier's proximity to Gibraltar, where de Gaulle's representative (Captain Vaudreuil) maintained links with SOE and SIS, enabled some assessment to be made in Baker Street of what might be achieved in North Africa, eventually. In mid-1942 with Donovan and Hambro seeking accord or combined clandestine operations, Baker Street was more concerned with its own affairs then the pressing needs of Eisenhower, and AFHQ.

Eddy, the "tall, corpulent American, with a round, happy face," had been stationed in Tangier since December 1941 with the rather implausible appointment of assistant naval attaché. Eddy was an Arabist—of less use in North Africa than commonly supposed; a Marine of inconsistent but decided views. He was eventually to differ from Murphy about many things, not least in being, in those days, Anglophile. He was also well aware that although he might acquire reliable intelligence, eventually, on the North African political and military scene, he, his colleagues, and the agents whom they recruited would remain dependent on SOE for much else.

Eddy's directives, as drafted by Guinness, resulted from his visits to London between 9 August and 5 September—by which time Murphy laid his own plans for preserving, not sabotaging, Vichy. Eddy's prolonged absence from North Africa was, therefore, unfortunate, to put it mildly. It did, however, reflect the need to produce a plan of operations that would enable TORCH's assault parties to establish bridgeheads at Casablanca, Oran, and Algiers. In strictly military terms, establishing the bridgeheads depended on the courage and discipline of the assault parties—composed, nonetheless, of men new to the business, and hazards, of war. *Consolidation* of the bridgeheads depended on support for the assault parties from within the three cities—above all, Algiers, where the overall and specific risks were greatest.

Murphy's "great leaders" might, at the last moment, promise an unopposed landing, but only brave youngsters in the "patriot groups" were likely to ensure it or, failing that, to limit the risks as the TORCH assault parties left the relative security of escorting forces and headed for an unknown shore. The SOE directive's political element—recruiting courageous and intelligent agents—was directly related to its operational requirement. The priorities that SOE laid down are summarized here because they show, as little else can, the enormous responsibility demanded of patriots of no experience and scant resources. The operational directives were written by SOE for anti-Vichy "patriot groups." The directives were not written for Murphy's conspirators, and Murphy had no part in their composition.

The directives were written primarily for operations in and adjoining Algiers, although similar directives applied in principle to Casablanca and Oran. Those summarized here are confined to Algiers. Between $D-1$ and $D+1$, OSS "patriot groups" were to: cut all power cables and telephones; mark beaches; seize Blida and Maison Blanche airfields; demobilize armored fighting vehicles (tanks and armored cars); seize radio stations and telephone exchanges; seize the docks; provide guides for assault force beach parties; prevent key roads from being blocked and bridges blown; release "United Nations" prisoners; seize key—but unspecified—personnel.

These were formidable requirements, and that Eddy was confident of their being met is a tribute to his optimism rather than his sagacity. Eddy's only doubts concerned the two airfields, the release of prisoners—that is, those confined in Vichy concentration or internment camps—and the docks. Eddy said that the airfields could "probably" be seized; prisoners "probably" released. The docks could not be seized. Eddy's response to the directives was, in fact, guesswork. He was not directly in

touch with "patriot groups," and his assessment of their intentions, methods, and capacities was based on his subordinates'
reports. Moreover, the priorities reflected the most optimistic
of five possibilities, ranging from best case to worst case.

These five possibilities ranged, in code-name terms, from
PEACE to STRAFE. The best case was a clear indication that
TORCH's assault forces would be welcomed; the worst case,
in the SOE assessment, was Axis intervention in Tunisia, not
French resistance in the harbors, on the beaches, throughout
the cities, or the hinterland. SOE's planning staff, although
small, consisted of officers trained to consider the wider possibilities. In their appreciation, the objective of establishing a
base for offensive operations in North Africa—necessary as it
was for SOE operations in the Unoccupied Zone of France
and elsewhere—would be most thoroughly frustrated by an Axis
riposte in Tunisia, not by Vichy opposition and resistance to
the assaulting forces. Even if these forces made an unopposed
entry on the North African stage, a rapid Axis reaction could
still render TORCH a most hazardous operation.

One might well suppose that Baker Street's appreciation
was confined only to support of the assault parties. Not so. Six
additional requirements were established by 12 October:

(1) Destruction of petrol supplies if the Commander-in-
Chief desired this;
(2) Promotion of pro-Allied demonstrations by natives;
(3) Release of Allied prisoners-of-war at Laghouat, giving them instructions for operations;
(4) Elimination of members of German and Italian Armistice Commissions;
(5) Release of Polish and Spanish [Republican] political
prisoners, giving them specialised tasks;
(6) Elimination of pro-Axis Frenchmen.

These requirements are as deliberately anti-Vichy in concept
as one could find.

But—by mid-September Eddy got cold feet. That element

in "this great tangle of TORCH," much else apart, explains why Eisenhower's questions of 10 October remained unanswered—except in terms dictated by Robert Murphy. Moreover, during September and October, Brigadier General Lyman Lemnitzer, Eisenhower's operations officer, was only in touch, rather than in close and continuous communication with Guinness and Eddy. There was no intelligence liaison. There was belated awareness in AFHQ that SOE existed, and had a role; Brigadier General Alfred Gruenther, a member of Lemnitzer's staff, visited Gibraltar in mid-October, and the AFHQ directives that resulted bear an obvious resemblance to those written by Guinness. In particular, "guides"—from the "patriot groups"—were to ensure that the Eastern Task Force assault parties reached their first objectives. But—and this is an absolutely critical point—RYGOR's intelligence that Maison Blanche and Blida airfields could be seized without difficulty, would indeed surrender to the Allies without a shot being fired, was not distributed to AFHQ. The essentially political role of the "patriot groups"—to mount an anti-Vichy *coup*—was unknown to AFHQ.

RYGOR's intelligence about Maison Blanche and Blida was reliable, as later events proved. AFHQ preoccupation with the airfields, together with Murphy's insistence in London—when masquerading as "Colonel McGowan"—that Eddy and his "patriot groups" would *not* play a decisive role ensured that the night of 8 November and the early hours of the 9th witnessed Darlan's triumph, the defeat of Frenchmen who believed in the Allies and liberation. By mid-October, with D-Day less than three weeks distant, AFHQ could find no time for the role of young Frenchmen who might save Allied lives.

PART TWO

Operation
TORCH

4

———◆———

On the Eve

I

In late December Guinness wrote a report that stated the British case regarding clandestine operations in an ostensibly Allied campaign: "SOE is a new aspect of warfare. Its potentialities and method of working are hardly yet realised by the military authorities and were certainly a closed book to the Americans. SOE must itself bring pressure to bear so that conferences can be called with the Force Commanders or their representatives and targets discussed. We must be quite honest with the Force Commanders and point out how little can be achieved unless our representatives in the field can get a reasonably early warning, and, on the other hand, the dangers to security involved in giving too early a warning.

"Unfortunately, in TORCH, for political reasons, all action in the field was put under Mr Murphy's control. He was made

judge of the timing of the preparations and the date after which
OSS representatives could reveal details to their agents. Mr
Murphy was not a member of OSS and I feel this must have
had a very adverse effect on what could have been achieved,
especially as he withheld disclosing D-Day and H-Hour to OSS
representatives at Casablanca, Oran, Algiers and Tunis until
24 hours before the assault.

"I feel however that it should have been the duty of either
Eddy or Colonel Brien Clarke [SOE head of station in Gibral-
tar], when they knew that this was happening to get AFH[Q]
to telegraph Murphy authorising him to give this warning earlier. I consider this was a cardinal error that probably vitiated
all our carefully laid plans."

Guinness's judgment on Murphy's actions is, ironically,
weakened by his assumption that common objectives were to
be sought. Guinness further assumes that Eisenhower could
tell Murphy what to do when in fact, as we know, the latter
was responsible and answerable only to Roosevelt. Murphy was
not fully in the AFHQ operational picture; he knew D-Day
and H-Hour (8 November; 0300) only in late October. Nor, as
we have seen, was Baker Street fully in the AFHQ picture—
indeed, hardly in the frame. Murphy was allowed to indulge
in "political maneuvering" not only because of Roosevelt's orders
to him, but also from the lack of genuine liaison—and understanding—that characterized the actions of so many engaged
in planning TORCH.

Murphy was carrying out his president's orders. Murphy
put pressure on Eddy to support him, not SOE. By 12 September, Murphy and General George Patton—designated as the
Western Force commander—had strictly forbidden Eddy to
undertake the six tasks that SOE intended adding to its two
main directives. Eddy's signals to London between this date
and 4 October indirectly reveal the conflict between Murphy's
and SOE's objectives. Eddy "would gladly arrange for the
elimination of the members of German and Italian Armistice
Commissions, but thought it most inadvisable to become

involved in the political quarrels between the French." Eddy
begs the question: elimination of members of the commissions
was an essential preliminary to serving notice on the Vichy
administration that collaboration with the Axis was to be
destroyed by clandestine Allied action. It was for this prime
reason—although there were others—that Guinness so directed
Eddy. Baker Street argued for drastic, undiplomatic, action.

Eddy claimed that "the more notorious collaborationists
would be taken care of by French patriots without any effort
on our part." In effect, Eddy was not prepared to argue with
Murphy when the latter made it plain that the Vichy administration was to be maintained with full American support.

The essence of Eddy's changed attitude becomes clear from
the following: "As was expected Murphy was to play a very
important part. He was to carry out preliminary negotiations
with the French leaders in North Africa and the success of
these might greatly reduce, or even make unnecessary, the tasks
assigned. As he alone would have firsthand knowledge of the
progress of these negotiations, Eddy was to take directives from
him both as to the timing of OSS preparations and as to any
modification in them that might be needed.

"Murphy might even find it convenient to control subversive operations in Algeria and Tunisia himself. If he did he
would keep Eddy informed. He was to direct the OSS representatives in Casablanca, Oran, and Algiers as to the date after
which they could start disclosing plans to their agents. This
should be postponed as long as possible and depend on the
reliability of the individual agent and the time needed by him
to make any preparations. Eddy would be informed verbally
by Colonel Gruenther of D-Day and H-Hour, and Murphy
would tell him when he could release that information to his
OSS representatives."

Thus the SOE War Diary for 14 October, a week after
Mack's appointment—one subject to Murphy's "political
maneuverings," as directed by Roosevelt. However, the War
Diary assumes that Murphy intended to commit the patriot

groups in conformity with Guinness's directives. This assumption is the key factor in the eventual conflict between the United States and Britain about the basic *political* objectives of TORCH. Baker Street, in October, assumed that Murphy and Eddy were fighting the same war. They were not. Baker Street also assumed that the various Combined Chiefs of Staff and AFHQ directives of 6 October gave Eisenhower supreme command over all forces and individuals engaged in TORCH, including Murphy. But Eisenhower's comments about Murphy's responsibilities show this to be a false assumption.

In particular, Eddy's apparent subordination to AFHQ, indeed to Mack, was no more than an exercise in fudging. The SOE archive reveals that Eddy was in touch with Murphy—although they rarely met—but that the former was reluctant to assert authority. By 18 October Clarke in Gibraltar was sufficiently aware of this factor to inform Hambro:

> As regards the big thing, Eddy, Gruenther, Guinness and I worked on the details of Eddy's instructions, and we had a meeting with H.E. [Lieutenant General Sir Noel Mason-Macfarlane, governor of Gibraltar] after lunch. The big point which H.E. makes is one which I expect you all in LM [LONMAY, code name for the overall SOE role in TORCH] agree with, namely that if Murphy is successful in his negotiations there will not be a great deal which Eddy's people will be required to do, with the exception of Tunisia. If Murphy's negotiations are non-productive, then Eddy's friends must do their best, but it cannot be a great deal compared with the boys that have to do the actual fighting.

In short, when Clarke sent this message, neither SOE nor AFHQ—at the *operational* level, concerned with TORCH's assault phase on D-Day—knew that Murphy was in touch with Darlan. Murphy had not only made contact with Darlan, but had also been ordered by Roosevelt to offer him rewards that would entrench him in North Africa—prospectively in France—and enable anti-Vichy opposition to be eliminated.

II

Murphy was consistent in his innate hostility to the "patriot groups." In his own words, emphasized by his actions, such groups consisted of "restless and even dangerous men and women, most of them anti-Nazi, but also anti many other things . . . What would these mixed-up people do if French Africa should become a battleground? The answer, it seemed to me, was that only French administrators already familiar with the complexities of these variegated local situations could possibly maintain the order in French Africa which an Allied Expeditionary Force would require."

Yet it is clear from the American diplomatic archive that, in the eighteen months between Murphy's arrival in Algiers and the Anglo-American landings in North Africa, he conspicuously failed to establish the basis for effective, pro-Vichy collaboration. Murphy failed to establish such collaboration with Weygand; he failed to do so with "French administrators already familiar with the complexities of these variegated local situations." Murphy knew that Pétain's influence in North Africa precluded collaboration with the United States; Pétain *might* favor collaboration personally—but not to the point where North Africa became a battleground, political or strategic. *Attentisme* would also dominate individuals and groups in North Africa, an attitude only modified by strong pro-Axis sympathies. Murphy reported these factors to Washington, but neither he nor Roosevelt drew the right inferences, let alone made the right decisions. What Murphy's supposed collaborators demanded was rewards, not risks. What Darlan sought—and gained— was power.

Murphy could neither define nor interpret what he was trying to do. The key figures remained noncommittal. The "intelligent moment" had not arrived. On 2 January 1942, Jean Rigault told Murphy: "At the present moment there does not exist in French Africa a civilian official or an army officer who has the prestige or the authority to undertake the initiative to place the country in a state of defence . . . these decisions must be provoked." Murphy could not oblige. General Emile Béthouart (commanding the Casablanca Division) on whom Murphy placed hopes, quickly backpedaled when pressed.

In April, however, the month of shifting trends, an entirely new dimension was added to conspiratorial hopes. General Henri Giraud, who had commanded the French Seventh Army in 1940, escaped from imprisonment in Königstein Castle. By July, Giraud, who always proclaimed "I am a soldier; I don't play politics," had provided for various contingencies. He at once signed a declaration of loyalty to Marshal Pétain; after being contacted by an official of the U.S. embassy at Vichy, who brought a message from Roosevelt, Giraud began to plan a role that was intended to rival, then supplant de Gaulle. Darlan, who had marked *his* card also, does not seem to have entered Giraud's thoughts. Darlan, busy considering what North Africa might have to offer, ignored the apparent attractions to Roosevelt—and Murphy—of the most senior French officer on hand. Giraud ostensibly—and prospectively—placed himself at the Allies' disposal.

Giraud's "escape" was, in fact, contrived by British and French agents. Murphy may be forgiven for not knowing this; or that Giraud pledged his loyalty to Pétain; *or* that, in order to tempt Giraud, Roosevelt promised that "French sovereignty would be restored in full." Murphy, a middle-rank diplomat, was not really in Roosevelt's confidence, and this fact explains much of his inability to tell the latter candidly that fomenting conspiracy in North Africa was more of a gamble than Washington collectively was disposed to accept.

By the early summer of 1942, the political stakes regarding North Africa had been raised to the point where if Murphy could not foment conspiracy on his own account he must find a "leader" who could. Murphy remained dazzled by men in, apparently, high places. When Giraud started sending smoke signals about his availability for conspiratorial purposes, Murphy was not slow to respond. He also renewed his overtures to senior members of the French armed forces in North Africa. But—"The French officers deep in conspiracy with Robert Murphy in North Africa . . . urged that the technique of ultimata and debarkation [sic] without prior accord and without someone controlling an effective organization inside the country is costly and may prove disastrous in this area [French North Africa]. They continue to plead for our cooperation in organizing an effective coup d'état *in advance of any military intervention*" [writer's emphasis].

Murphy could not meet these demands. Murphy was not "deep in conspiracy"; he was desperately trying to be. Giraud, a catch, if rank and reputation meant anything, might take Murphy to the right places. Unfortunately for this notion, some of those with whom Murphy was already attempting to conspire were "right" in another sense. Lemaigre-Dubreuil and his kind were of the extreme right wing politically; although Giraud's views echoed theirs, they saw no role for him except as he might serve their ends. These can also be simply defined, although they were never simply expressed: a Cagoulard France. The "group" to whom Murphy refers were in fact what later became known as "The Five." This was not the "patriot group" with whom Eddy was involved, but men who sought their own advantage—once, as Murphy's 6 May wire to Hull so clearly reveals, it was clear they would be the beneficiaries of any collaboration.

In short, Murphy, remaining convinced that the people with whom he dined were the keys to his conspiracies, sought assurances from the three echelons in North African Vichy who were, in fact, least likely to commit themselves unless assured of personal or corporate advantages: entrepreneurs; high officials; and the senior and middle ranks of the armed forces. These echelons were respectively out for themselves; *attentiste;* anxious to preserve the identity of the armed forces despite defeat, armistice—and Vichy. In London, Eisenhower made bricks without straw; in Algiers, Murphy cultivated men of straw.

Neither entrepreneurs, officials, nor soldiers had much time for Giraud—as events, for him, were cruelly to prove. But in the months preceding Darlan's covert October demand, Giraud appeared to be the man to bind disparate elements together. As a soldier he was, and undeniably, a man of stature. During these months of anxious preparation, and as the German High Command awoke to the prospect of an Allied invasion, Giraud was touted as the man of the hour. Jacques Lemaigre-Dubreuil, traveling freely between North Africa and the Unoccupied Zone in legitimate pursuit of his business interests, was Giraud's point of contact with conspiracy. Lemaigre-Dubreuil was in regular touch with Murphy. Both conspirators set out to woo the "nonpolitical" general. Giraud might rally North Africa in defense of French—or Vichy—interests; he might issue a call to arms that would pledge French armed forces there to the Allied cause.

Thus, by April 1942, Murphy, while still conspiring to right and far right, had been forced to the conclusion that Giraud must be cultivated—yet Darlan should be regarded as the real key to the whole business. Darlan's position in the Vichy regime became precarious from the beginning of 1942, as Laval, returning to office on 18 April, regained influence over an ailing Pétain. In the long, disingenuous, retrospective letter that Darlan wrote to Leahy on 27 November he declares that, in January "I yielded to the Germans on some minor matters . . . my only intention [was] to prevent them coming to Africa . . ." Darlan then adds: "Last April, Marshall Pétain strongly insisted upon my staying as a member of the Government. I replied to him that I preferred to retire completely."

Darlan then compounds these deceits. The minor matters on which he yielded to the Germans concerned deportation of Frenchmen—Jews and Gentiles—to Germany. Darlan was in fact sacked from Pétain's government at Laval's, and Hitler's, instigation. But Darlan knew how to swim. His letter to Leahy continues: "He [Pétain] then declared to me: 'If you go, I shall also go.' I answered: 'Your departure would mean disaster. I shall stay then as 'dauphin' and as military chief, but I refuse to form part of a Cabinet the ideas of which concerning home as well as foreign policy are not mine.' "

Decoded, Darlan's message is clear enough; he had changed sides. There was no future for him in Laval's France; there might be one for him in Vichy North Africa, supported by, albeit dependent on, Roosevelt's *Pax Americana.* Leahy's return to Washington in April and Giraud's escape provide counterpoint to Darlan's calculated move. Laval's patent, genuine commitment to Hitler and a fascist Western Europe secure against "bolshevism" differed in no ideological sense from anything that Darlan espoused.

The difference between Laval and Darlan lay in personality: Laval clung to his beliefs, such as they were, conscious of the support he enjoyed among the French right, and quite passionately convinced that fascism was a creed for which one might die. Laval was Cagoulard; cultivation of him by Noguès and others was only to be expected. Darlan, aloof, and alone, other than his following in the French armed forces' hierarchy, saw in the America he knew through Leahy a solution to his dilemma. Laval genuinely believed Hitler would triumph; Darlan certainly convinced himself that the United States would prove omnipotent.

Murphy had no conception of the drama, the tragedy of France under the harrow of occupation, and Vichy. Murphy was aware—if unwilling to stress when reporting to Washington—that no "great leader" in French North Africa had committed himself to the Allies. Roosevelt had sent Murphy to Algiers in April 1941 so that an American sphere of influence might be established. Murphy had failed to do this. Now, with his country embroiled in global war, Murphy was compelled to establish a base for offensive operations in North Africa. The "great leaders" might still prove responsive to the American spoils system, provided a figurehead could be produced. Between April and the eve of Cherchell, Murphy doggedly tried again. He marked his card for five principal conspirators who, in their own interest or from conviction—never, be it said, in any form of genuinely collaborative enterprise—might be induced to prepare the way for a coup, which would deliver North Africa into Roosevelt's hands.

The "Five," as they came to be known, lacked even the common denominator of regard for Murphy as Roosevelt's agent in place. None regarded him as a plenipotentiary. The "Five" fluctuated in composition—Van Hecke of Les Chantiers de la Jeunesse, a Vichy youth organization; the elusive journalist Jean Rigault; and a career diplomat, Tarbé de Saint-Hardouin, all claimed membership, later. But, in Murphy's book those who mattered were two soldiers, Generals Charles Mast and Emile Béthouart; the quintessential entrepreneur, Jacques Lemaigre-Dubreuil; the totally equivocal figure of Henri d'Astier de la Vigerie, *Chantier*, Vichy official—and apparent Gaullist; and Colonel Jean Chrétien, Juin's Director of Military Intelligence. But of comparable importance—or irrelevance—we should note Admiral Raymond Fenard, who can only be described as Darlan's agent in Algiers, Admiral Esteva in Tunis having the dubious honor of being his representative at the exact point where an Axis riposte might be expected.

Major General Mast was a regular soldier with few ideas beyond maintenance of the status quo. In May 1942, when he first "entered into touch with Murphy" (as a British Foreign Office report rather coyly puts it), Mast was commanding the Algiers Division of the French North African Army. Mast was Giraud's agent from the time of the latter's escape and, after the manner of a true subordinate, clove to him only. Béthouart, commanding the Casablanca Division, deluded Murphy into the belief that he would "immobilise" Noguès on the eve of an Allied landing, but, in fact, refused to commit himself to positive action until 5 November—too late. Lemaigre-Dubreuil, undoubtedly resourceful after a fashion, appears to have enjoyed political conspiracy for its own sake, exaggerating his role as the link between Murphy and Giraud, keeping an eye always

on the main chance. Chrétien marked *his* cards for Darlan—
and played them on the eve of Cherchell.

Fenard, as Darlan's man, could not be ignored—but would
not be committed. Darlan, from April 1942, set his sights on
French North Africa, but kept his counsel, determined that his
prospective collaborators would make the first move. While
Giraud bided his time, Darlan waited. Thus Fenard and
Esteva—whose careers had been made by Darlan—rose to none
of Murphy's lures. Murphy notes that Fenard came to see him
on 6 May with the specific purpose of discerning the former's
interest in Darlan. Murphy claims that Darlan's "discreet
overtures" followed. In fact, Murphy was forced to make
promises before Darlan would respond.

D'Astier is a more interesting, and a more important,
character in this curiously Shakespearian drama of ambition
and frustration. *Les Chantiers,* from its establishment in July
1940, had provided cover for patriots, namely those who were
neither collaborators nor *attentistes,* but awaited the moment
to fight again for France. But Pétainists who enrolled, in order
to form cadres instructing youthful recruits, were also converted into Gaullists by the absurdities of camp life dedicated
to impossibly Spartan ideals and neo-Nazi beliefs. The nature
of Vichy made converts. D'Astier fits neither category. His two
brothers, François and Emmanuel, were committed Gaullists
from June 1940; however Henri, apart from an indication of
Royalist leanings, defied—and eludes—simple definition.

D'Astier's actions on the night of 7–8 November remain
inexplicable. The malaise afflicting even resourceful men and
women in Vichy North Africa may have clouded both principles and judgment. One wonders what d'Astier thought of
Murphy. But when d'Astier left *Les Chantiers* in the summer
of 1942 to join the police department in Algiers—a transition
explicable only in terms of intrigue—Murphy found an opportunity to convince himself that Algeria's administrative and
security system had been penetrated by an essential collabora-

tor. One also wonders whether Murphy, trapped in a web of his own making, would have understood Jacques Soustelle's comment: *"D'Astier était monarchiste—il l'a dit lui-même vingt fois—d'un monarchisme romantique, mais surtout amoureux de l'action."* Certainly, d'Astier was not a man of the left. Did d'Astier betray the Algiers group because some were, allegedly, communists?

Murphy did not delude himself that Yves Châtel, the Governor General of Algeria, would conspire in support of the Allies, although he was known to be in touch with Giraud. Juin remained politely noncommittal. Washington could not grasp these implications. On 15 May Murphy merely reported that Juin could not be relied on for "independent initiative." Yet Murphy for long entertained hopes about Noguès. Not until 8 June when Noguès said "Morocco is very favourably disposed to the United States, but we shall resist any effort which may be made to attack us," did Murphy accept that Casablanca's seizure by force of arms or capitulation through what he most oddly calls his "fifth column" posed extreme difficulties. Murphy might also have pondered Consul Childs's note: "Resident-General Noguès expressed his satisfaction with Laval's appointment as Chief of Government. Noguès intends to give Laval his wholehearted support."

Not until 4 September did Murphy know the (October) TORCH D-Day; he was never fully in the AFHQ operational picture about Algiers as a reluctant American concession to Churchill and the British Chiefs of Staff. As the long, weary summer weeks dragged by, Murphy was, nevertheless, forced to realize that Algiers lay at the heart of all conspiracies, any coup, the whole of Roosevelt's Vichy gamble. Algiers was the scene for intrigues that became more dangerous as they multiplied. We read Murphy's telegrams torn between irritation and sympathy. Murphy, who was given to generalization, noted: "There is a struggle going on in the minds and hearts of many French Army officers who are tormented by doubts as to where their duty lies." There was, however, no collective struggle, expressive of widespread doubt; if there had been, the SOL would have stifled it.

Roosevelt's Vichy gamble required that Vichy remain in being. Murphy's conspirators, and others on whom hopes were set, knew this. With the possible exception of d'Astier, the "Five," that fluctuating faction, wanted a clear sign from Murphy that Vichy in North Africa would remain in being, come what may. The prospect of fighting against Axis forces took second—or third—place to the perceived necessity to maintain the status quo. Roosevelt's ostensible, proclaimed reason for invading North Africa—to prevent the Axis from doing so—never cut any ice with the conspirators or the patriot groups. The former looked to their future; the latter saw Vichy and the Axis as equally evil.

Eddy went about such business as did not directly conflict with his subordination to Murphy. Once Eddy had been given SOE's directives (only nominally counterpointed by Mack's appointment), he was convinced that "immobilizing" Algiers must be the first priority. But, as we have seen, even this task was vitiated by Eddy's subordination to Murphy. Giraud, Darlan, and Murphy began to maneuver around one another, a circus in which Murphy was neither ringmaster nor clown, merely an ingenuous participant. By early July Giraud had caused Mast to deliver the following fiction, duly reported by Murphy: "Mast states the opinion that we could count on the co-operation in French North Africa of at least 14 divisions composed of French officers and French native troops."

Murphy was induced, on 8 July, to compound his naïveté: "Giraud ('our friend') hopes to become the pivot of resistance in Europe and Africa." This kind of wishful thinking, encapsulated in telegrams, was distributed throughout Washington. Conclusions, of a sort, were drawn. Leahy, writing to Admiral Ernest King on 17 August, argued that resistance by fourteen divisions could well jeopardize TORCH from the outset.

Juin did not command fourteen divisions. On paper, Juin commanded *eight* divisions. Numbers apart, the divisional structure in French North Africa was maintained for administrative purposes. Juin's forces were, in fact, garrison troops, with all this implies in potential for disaffection—and inability to act swiftly and cohesively. It was this factor that led to the SOL being reinforced. London, collectively, had a better grasp of operational issues than Washington, but the intelligence problem remained. Giraud's advent, such as it was, further complicated a situation that regularly drove Eisenhower to distraction.

We reach the month before Cherchell with a sense of bewildered fatalism. Giraud, loitering in the Unoccupied Zone, dreams of glory. Darlan—whether "dauphin" or not, certainly commander-in-chief of the French armed forces, and quite determined to exploit that residual power—arrives in Oran on 2 October on a prolonged "tour of inspection." Satirical comments from Consul Felix Cole in Algiers—"The Admiral, despite a carefully maintained photogenic smile, utterly fails to influence the masses; Weygand had prestige, Darlan none at all"—cannot alter the fact that Darlan had timed his tour in terms of what Churchill was later to call "a strange and formidable coincidence." Murphy, after being marooned in Washington and London, reports hastily from Algiers on 30 September: "There is substantial reason for them [Giraud's confidants] to be reassured. There is cause for the greatest optimism."

But, by 15 October, Murphy, using Chrétien as his intermediary, had embarked upon conspiracy with Darlan. During his contacts with Murphy, Giraud had made conditions magnificent in their futility. Not only did he demand the arbitration of "resistance in Europe and Africa." He also insisted that the economic, not merely the political, future of North Africa be placed in his hands. Murphy was thus forced into contact with Darlan, the one "great leader" who could, or might, deliver certain goods. Chrétien made Murphy bell the cat: "Please inform me at once how far I may go in replying to Darlan's representative who, in effect, asks (i) would we be willing to co-operate with Darlan and (ii) if so, would we be able to do so quickly on a large scale here *and/or* in *Europe* [writer's emphasis]. I urge that we encourage Darlan, and believe this would be reconcilable with eventual co-operation with Giraud, about whom I shall telegraph encouraging news tomorrow. Darlan is expected here [again] next week. Please inform Leahy and Eisenhower."

This telegram, undated, but from internal evidence sent to Hull on 12 October, namely before Darlan left Oran for Dakar on the 21st, reflects the latter's determination to seize *political* leadership in North Africa as a prelude to succeeding Pétain in Vichy. Darlan did not waste time during his tour. The authorities were forced to bribe crowds to cheer for him but, ignoring this factor, Darlan privately began briefing the civil and military administration of North and West Africa about his intentions. There should be public defiance of the United States, but a conspiracy would ensure an "occupation" by American forces committed to maintaining Vichy in power. We should not be surprised to learn that Darlan, returning to Vichy after this tour, prepared to bring his family with him on the next visit to Oran and Algiers.

Darlan, according to Chrétien, was convinced that German occupation of "Le Sud" (ATTILA) would be initiated once an Anglo-American force invaded North Africa. Darlan appears to have been equally convinced that if Roosevelt was prepared to give him political leadership in North Africa, a future awaited him in France. Darlan, through Chrétien, stated his explicit terms—that implicit element came later: to be commander-in-chief of all French forces in North Africa. In return, the French fleet at Toulon might be "entrained" for the North African shore. Darlan put all his demands positively but left his terms for collaboration in the conditional tense. Darlan gave no positive assurance about the Toulon fleet, and refused to be drawn concerning Esteva's response should the Axis move troops into Tunisia.

Darlan insisted on "immediate large-scale matériel and economic supplies to North Africa." Chrétien concluded this stark demand with admirable brevity. If these conditions are met, "there is a strong possibility that Darlan would undertake such co-operation. If he did so, the military and naval forces in Africa [that is, in *West* Africa also] would undoubtedly obey his command." Darlan knew that Dakar ranked with Casablanca—or Algiers—in Roosevelt's strategic, and economic, perceptions. Childs in Casablanca radioed: "Noguès was obviously concerned to use Admiral Darlan's visit to fortify his own position."

Noguès also hedged his bets. Despite his contact with Laval, Noguès had been forced by Darlan to consider the implications of American forces invading his Moroccan fief. But Darlan had also forced *Murphy*—in effect, Roosevelt—to choose. Murphy radioed Leahy on 15 October: "Mast told me that Giraud contemplates that we deal with him and not with Darlan. Mast has learned that Darlan is seeking to climb on the bandwagon but in his opinion Darlan cannot be trusted."

Yet Murphy knew, at last, what he had to do—unless he listened to Eddy, and SOE. In a further communiqué of 15 October, Murphy states: "I replied [to Mast] that we hoped that the French would demonstrate some unity, that Darlan is Commander-in-Chief of the French armed forces, that the French fleet has its importance, and that the Admiralty (Fenard) commands the forts and coastal batteries in French North Africa." Mast clearly disliked this belated rejection of Giraud and asserted, "Giraud will command the Army which is loyal to him and not to Darlan. The Navy in French North Africa [whose most senior officer, in fact, was Admiral François Michelier, a committed opponent of conspiracy] would fall into line with the Army." Murphy, a child among these men of Vichy, concludes this communiqué by a veritable *cri de coeur*:

"Are you able to suggest a happy formula which would leave the command essentially with Eisenhower but permit the French to regard the operation as theirs . . . Mast asserts that Giraud's command will give us entry practically without firing a shot."

Murphy received his answer soon enough. On 17 October, according to his own later account, he received from the President, through Admiral Leahy, full authorization to enter into any arrangement with Admiral Darlan which would, in his opinion, assist military operations; concurrently, at Eisenhower's headquarters considerable thought was given to devising a formula enabling Giraud and Darlan to work together. In short, "There was no thought in the minds of American war planners that a Darlan deal would not be acceptable to Washington."

The Eisenhower papers confirm the accuracy of these statements so far as he is concerned. But AFHQ as such did not know the secret details and commitments of Murphy's "political maneuverings" with Darlan. Eisenhower's staff thus remained ignorant, as did SOE, of what Murphy had been ordered to do in order to maintain Vichy in North Africa through collaboration with Darlan. Eisenhower's questions to his staff of 10 October were thus in no sense answered a week later. Clark departed for Cherchell in a state of some confusion. Eisenhower ordered Clark to avoid discussion of Darlan's prospective role, but gave no indication of what should be done if Giraud's spokesman insisted on doing so. Darlan, however, held cards that Giraud could not match. From various sources, Darlan disclosed that the Axis was preparing to counter any Allied move into North Africa—preparations that the ENIGMA confirmed. Darlan fueled these fears by hinting to Murphy that the Axis riposte would take the form of "an invasion of French North Africa through Spain."

This was precisely the kind of rumor that gave Darlan status in American eyes. Darlan's renewed, adroit references to the possibility of a Hitler-Franco axis only made Eisenhower the more determined to use Clark's journey into the unknown for easing assorted burdens, of which quite the most obvious was doubt about the French Army's attitude to Allied invasion. But this burden proved impossible to ease, or shift. Vichy in North Africa defied all attempts to pose questions, much less answer them.

III

During the late evening of 21 October 1942, eight men prepared to land on the beach at Cherchell, forty-two miles west of Algiers. A group of senior American and junior British officers were, in the early hours of the 22nd, paddled ashore from a British submarine, *Seraph* (Lieutenant N.L.A. Jewell, R.N.), lying, and during daylight, submerged five miles offshore. Then began an episode on the eve of the Anglo-American invasion of North Africa three weeks later that, in its fated combination of duplicity, guesswork, farce, and sheer confusion was to prove characteristic of the weeks and months that followed. The origins of the episode at Cherchell reveal similar confusion between ends and means.

The principal figure in the group of Allied officers was Mark Clark, a tall, bad-tempered, ambitious major general, Eisenhower's deputy commander in the field. Clark's knowledge of France was confined to a brief period of service there in 1918. Clark spoke no French capable of either cementing conspiracies or conducting negotiations; he was armed with only one conviction: that the French in North Africa would welcome the Stars and Stripes or, if they did not, would nevertheless be forced to salute it. French North Africa, October 1942, was entirely—and inevitably—beyond either the imagination or comprehension of a newly promoted, forty-six-year-old major general whose entire career to this point of crisis had been spent in the straitjacket of the American military caste.

Consider the situation, and the facts, and reflect on the mood—of Clark and his compatriots, stepping ashore to a strange rendezvous on a cool North African night, forty-eight years ago. Consider also the mood, the temper, of the conspirators whom Clark expected rather than hoped to meet. Among the two or three hundred young men and women in and around Algiers who were "mostly Jewish and left wing," the echo of resistance could be heard. *Combat* stirred conscience, posed questions, sowed the seed for a later, Gaullist flowering. But these were not the Frenchmen whom Clark was about to meet.

Henri Rosencher, a member of this Jewish and left-wing group, wrote: *"C'est après ma sortie de prison que le miracle se produit. Je suis contacté par un étudiant en médecine, José Aboulker, pour entrer dans un réseau de Résistance nommé 'Combat.' "* We have met Aboulker and will find Rosencher again. As *Seraph* headed for the beach at Cherchell, these young men and their fellow prospective résistants—against *Vichy*— were still trying to escape ". . . *les atrocités françaises sont ultra-pétainistes . . .*" All told, throughout North Africa, there were, perhaps, six or seven hundred such prospective résistants, too few to constitute an anti-Vichy movement, unless outside support was provided. SOE had tasked Eddy accordingly; Murphy was to ensure that Eddy failed to provide it.

Sympathy must be accorded Clark as his foldboat steers for Cherchell's rocky shore. Clark's task was to discover what the hell was going on in terms of Murphy's collaboration. Murphy's telegrams had been pondered in AFHQ, rather as men use seaweed to forecast the weather. The telegrams crackled disturbingly, but interpretation proved difficult. Murphy code-named Giraud "Kingpin"—Mast was "Flagpole." But surely there was only one kingpin—Admiral Jean François Darlan, commander-in-chief of the French armed forces, whom the British collectively detested, but whose potency they could hardly ignore.

Clark's journey to Cherchell was imposed on him by sheer

force of circumstance. Eisenhower could not go; no officer junior to Clark would do. *Somebody* had to find out what, if anything, lay behind Murphy's telegrams. The entire episode, not least its substantial element of farce, reveals that Roosevelt's Vichy gamble was in the hands of Murphy, a poker player with very poor cards and a diminishing belief that he could avoid being called. Or, rather, the cards might not be so bad if Murphy could only decide which hand to deal. Eisenhower, a bridge player, reckoned that Murphy, whose preferred game actually was poker, "dealt all his cards at once."

By mid-October, Murphy was "urgently looking for French assistance in every direction." To compound this confused signal for historians, Murphy wrote, retrospectively: "By that time we had secret sympathizers in every military headquarters, in various governmental and police establishments, the youth organization, and a tight little group of ardent civilians." Murphy is here referring to the Algiers Aboulker Group. Murphy could never bring himself to name the group, but it is a fact that by the eve of TORCH he had come to accept that effective "immobilization" of Algiers was beyond his capacity. Initial seizure of Algiers as the assault parties of the Eastern Task Force reached the shore must be entrusted to those who had no intention of sustaining the Vichy of Noguès and Juin, Châtel and Esteva.

On 20 October, Murphy radioed the War Department in Washington that Juin remained hesitant, Darlan noncommittal. The same day, Murphy also communicated with Leahy about Darlan's son, Alain, who had acted as an occasional go-between in Algiers. Alain was seriously ill with poliomyelitis, and Murphy sought American help. Darlan was responsive to the offer, but remained silent on what he would do as the invasion fleet closed in on the shore. Clark would not have seen these telegrams, nor known about Murphy's failure to make progress with Juin. Yet, at H-hour, Juin was going to be a more important figure in the North African hierarchy than anybody else. But Clark had seen enough for disquiet.

An OSS Report of 2 September stated: "General Juin, Commander of French armies in North Africa, is friendly to the Allied cause but he cannot be expected to take any favorable action that is not authorized by the French Government." The report continued, clinically: "Noguès, Resident General in Morocco, is not expected to be of any use to us, and is expected to comply, insofar as he finds it possible, with orders received from Vichy. Admiral Esteva, Resident General in Tunisia, while hopeful of Allied success in the war, will carry out any orders received from Darlan. Vice-Admiral Fenard, Secretary-General of North Africa, probably will be of value to an Allied effort if properly approached and if he is satisfied that French sovereignty in the Colonies will be maintained." So much for conspiracy. The OSS Report was not made more palatable to those who believed in the Vichy gamble by describing Châtel as one "who may be of assistance to us."

What *did* AFHQ know? Casablanca was, perforce, left to Patton. Since it was all but certain that the French Navy would fiercely resist the Allied invasion, Patton's troops were to be escorted by a strong naval force, whose commander, Vice Admiral Kent Hewitt, had orders to destroy all opposition. Casablanca, therefore, in terms of H-hour and D + 1, was not a consideration to AFHQ. Operations there would succeed, or fail, by force of arms. On the eve of TORCH Roosevelt ensured that assorted proclamations stressed pacific intentions; Casablanca and the French fleet were another matter, and would remain so even if General Béthouart was prepared to "immobilize" Noguès. The directives issued at the end of September to the naval task force commanders for TORCH defined "hostile French action" in very broad terms. *All* submarines and vessels under way, for example, were to be treated as hostile whether or not their movements suggested resistance.

Algiers, however, was the key to unlock North Africa. Clark's mission to Cherchell was concerned with asking one direct question: "Would the French Army and Air Force oppose an Allied landing?" Murphy had failed even to ask that question, let alone get an answer because, while radioing optimistically about Giraud, he had entered into a one-sided collaboration with Darlan. Mast resented this move, and thus remained ambiguous about his compatriots' intentions. Murphy could produce no officer more senior than Mast to meet Clark. Thus the vital, implicit question might be posed, but could not be answered. In the event of an opposed landing, who would prove responsive to offers on the eve of TORCH? Darlan? Juin?

To what end would such an armistice lead? Clark was forced to pose—or, at least, consider—these questions, but, like Murphy, was neither empowered, nor able, to ask them directly. Murphy's conspiracy was too fragile for candor. The house of cards would collapse if anyone blew on it. Mast—a mere major general—genuinely committed, moreover, only to Giraud, was equally irrelevant as a participant in political negotiations, or deals more closely resembling ward politics than the conduct of grand strategy. Roosevelt ordered Clark not to disclose the date of D-Day, nor provide any intelligence that an active conspirator—and Mast was one, in the sense of commitment to Giraud—could utilize so that Algiers would be "immobilized." On 22 October, Giraud was still in limbo, although plans had been made to move him to Gibraltar in that valuable craft *Seraph* as one who might prove useful, somewhere, sometime.

José Aboulker has claimed that his group was privy to the Cherchell meeting and its deliberations. This claim is true to the extent that Murphy had become, temporarily, dependent on patriots whose notions of "immobilization" were political, not merely confined to the execution of Eddy's SOE orders. But Aboulker's claim is invalid in the sense of the group's participation in the Cherchell meeting. Mast was accompanied by Murphy—who appears to have enjoyed dodging about the rendezvous, an empty farmhouse, while local customs officials became increasingly suspicious of flashing lights and the frequent oaths of anxious men from the sea, slipping and stumbling on unfamiliar ground—and a collection of staff officers from Juin's headquarters, and elsewhere. Henri d'Astier is said to have met Clark at Cherchell, but neither Clark nor surviving participants corroborate this.

Mast, with Murphy in attendance, hoped to convince Clark and his subordinates that he and his compatriots represented conspiracy in effective military form. What, in fact, Mast wanted was not only the date of D-Day, but also positive assurances from Clark that if given time—or thus given room for maneuver—the Algiers Division might lay down its arms, only to pick them up again in the Allied cause without fear of recrimination or reprisal. Murphy's plea to Mast on 15 October that the "French should show unity and accept Darlan as Commander-in-Chief" had a curiously unreal note to it a week later.

Mast repudiated the plea at Cherchell, and remained loyal only to Giraud's pretensions during the following, critical fortnight. So far as one can tell from the sole survivors of this farmhouse dialogue of the deaf, Murphy insisted that Darlan's role was crucial to success. Mast refused to agree, indeed was quite unable to do so. All the published accounts of this lamentable episode ignore or skate over the real issues. Clark, never the most genial or relaxed of men, met those who were prepared to conspire—on their terms. Clark had been ordered by Eisenhower to keep quiet about Darlan. Murphy insisted on talking about him. Indeed he had little choice. Clark, out of his depth, heard Murphy, the eternal optimist, assure Mast that Giraud had a role to play, vital, unspecified, indeterminate.

Given these absurdities, it seems only fitting that the meeting concluded with low comedy. The customs officials decided to investigate, supposing that smugglers were about. The visiting conspirators hid in the farmhouse cellar. Murphy and Mast managed, by a sort of mime, to suggest a meeting between bored soldiers and ladies of the town. The *ruse* succeeded. Twenty-four hours later, the coast clear, Clark and his baffled, shaken party scrambled down to the beach. Murphy

urged haste. Confusion resulted. In worsening weather, the three
foldboats headed for *Seraph.*

Clark, for a reason best known only to himself, stripped,
leaving his uniform trousers on the beach. The name tag had
not been removed. One foldboat swamped; weapons sank
beneath the waves; classified papers floated, emblematic of
uncoordinated hazard. *Douceurs* in the form of gold (Canadian
dollars, the equivalent of $18,000 U.S.) disappeared without a
trace. Clark, at last, was hauled aboard *Seraph* and sought
comfort below.

IV

On 23 October, the second battle of El Alamein began. Ten
days later, the Afrika Korps began its long retreat to the Tunisian
redoubt. The Allies were poised to clear the Axis from North
Africa. The Fighting French "flying column" in General
Montgomery's Eighth Army was small, but tested by battle, a
welcome, honored element in the British camp. On that same
hard-fought day of 23 October, Patton's Western Task Force
cleared the East Coast of the U.S. and headed out into the
Atlantic. The troops were told "You will be welcomed as guests."
There was no suggestion that hard fighting lay ahead. TORCH
had been set in motion, and all now rested on time and chance.
Eisenhower reported to Marshall on a tour of troops stationed
in Scotland, destined for North Africa: "Most of them did not
know exactly what was expected."

In Tangier, Eddy sat down to consider the implications of
his most recent sojourn with Brien Clarke in Gibraltar. The
patriot groups were to be armed with modern weapons, not
dependent on antique Lebel rifles. On 11 October, AFHQ had
directed *Murphy* to ensure that "each task force will be supplied with a stock of rifles and ammunition." The intended
recipients were not named in this ambiguous directive, but only
the patriot groups needed weapons. A week after the AFHQ

directive had been sent to Murphy, Guinness and Eddy decided
that the patriot groups should receive the weapons from them.
The reader can draw his own conclusions, merely noting that
subsequent failure to deliver on time what the patriot groups
needed was, in Murphy's opinion, due to "lapses" by SOE.
There is another explanation, as we shall see.

Two SOE missions, MASSINGHAM and BRANDON,
prepared to establish themselves in the Algiers area immediately after D-Day. BRANDON would also be responsible for
running the weapons and munitions from Gibraltar to the groups
in Algiers on D-5. Communications problems were tackled in
Gibraltar, and the BBC was alerted to broadcast the action signals on D-1, *but only to the groups,* as the Center and Eastern
Task Forces (Oran and Algiers) cleared the straits and closed
the shore. Whatever Murphy, Mast, and other conspirators
failed, or refused, to do at the critical hour, the "anti-Nazi"
French citizens of North Africa were to be given all the support
that OSS and SOE could afford.

Brien Clarke noted in his report of December 1942, "In
the course of the previous few months, approximately 600 tons
of special stores had been accumulated at Gibraltar for eventual distribution in North Africa—special flares for airborne
operations, and offensive and defensive weapons of all kinds,
to be distributed to *the French Résistance elements with whom
OSS had been working"* [writer's emphasis]. Mast and his
compatriots did not need this matériel. Moreover, OSS had
nothing to do with Mast, nor other conspirators about whom
Murphy entertained hopes. Although the bulk of the matériel
was intended for BRANDON, the initial delivery (twenty tons)
was specifically intended for the patriot group in Algiers. A
converted fishery protection vessel (HMS *Minna*) was selected
for the task and, by late October, was secreted within the mole
at Gibraltar.

This sequence of events would appear to suggest a combined operation, in which each had his appointed role. Darlan,
the real kingpin; Giraud, the embodiment of soldierly virtue;

the "Five," indicative of zeal for the Allied cause—whatever that, or their aims, might be; the "Group," ready, willing, and able, in Murphy's words, to "occupy fort and city of Algiers." Some of the contradictions inherent in this mishmash of egos and principles have already been exposed, but fundamentally different objectives can only be understood if the differing fortunes of the individuals involved in such contradictory interests are narrated, and compared. We turn first to the "Group" because, while Darlan stalled and Giraud sulked—thus reducing their respective henchmen to an impotence rendered all the more pernicious from lack of true initiative or clear, positive aim—young French citizens bestirred themselves.

The hazards of the coup were very considerable: on the one hand, possible betrayal from within the groups; on the other, possible betrayal by those who, in fact, regarded them as one element in a comprehensive conspiracy to put the TORCH assault parties securely ashore as prelude to a major political stroke of an entirely different persuasion—*maintenance* of Vichy.

Henri d'Astier took overall command of the main patriot group once he moved from *Les Chantiers* in Oran to the police department in Algiers. Whatever d'Astier's motives for switching from an organization based on ideology to one depending on law and order, he became better placed to foment conspiracy. Algiers was the key to North Africa. One could argue, indeed, that d'Astier's move was a perfect example of the OSS January 1942 recommendation to build conspiracy around officials rather than "the great leaders." But d'Astier was no ordinary official, or conspirator. His motives for joining *Les Chantiers* were never discerned; he was no ordinary policeman. D'Astier, in a sense, was his own man: conspiracies breed conspirators, serving their own ambitions.

The conspiratorial factor is peculiarly relevant to the situation of increasing tension that developed as D-Day approached. José Aboulker, who among many others may be regarded as the most active member of the Algiers Group, the embodiment of one who was "young, left-wing, and Jewish"—

or, in Murphy's words, "anti-Nazi but anti many other things"—was prepared to see d'Astier take command because of apparently shared ideals. Moreover, throughout 1942, the Aboulkers, father and son, were under police surveillance. D'Astier, by contrast, provided—or appeared to provide—the cover needed for the coup to succeed. D'Astier knew all the people who counted, and developed the knack of being in touch with most of them. D'Astier's newfound compatriots in the administration—Achiary, "*Commissaire de la Brigade de Surveillance,*" Rigault, and the like—were, doubtless, enthusiastic conspirators. They were prominent by their absence on 7 and 8 November, conspicuous by their adhesion to Darlan thereafter. Achiary, however, remained a member of RYGOR.

If the Aboulkers and their Algiers Group had stuck to the OSS connection, trusting only themselves and their American compatriots, a genuine anti-Vichy coup might well have succeeded. But Murphy, Mast, and d'Astier between them ensured that the coup failed, and the OSS report of 28 January 1943, (together with José Aboulker's eyewitness account) makes that fact abundantly clear.

D'Astier knew that Mast, commanding an internal security force rather than one of the "fourteen divisions" with which he had beguiled Murphy, was the man who could make or break a coup. If the Group succeeded in executing Eddy's directives from SOE, Algiers could be seized, "immobilized." But the Group, however bold and resolute, could not hold Algiers if Mast was unable or unwilling to play his part by deploying his forces in its support. The SOL, backed by armored elements in the Algiers Division known to be immune from conspiracy, would be able to strike back at the Group. Modern weapons would not enable the Algiers Group to withstand the SOL. The weapons were intended as an expression of moral support—and to assist in the elimination requirement established by the Guinness directives—not as the means whereby a group of youngsters could take on a gang of toughs.

The AFHQ operational orders for "immobilizing" Algiers

required Allied troops assaulting the mole to link with the Patriot Group by 0300 on D-Day. This timetable was based on the supposition of a landing that, even if opposed, would not fail. But, given the manifold uncertainties of landing on an unknown shore, the Group's role could only be regarded as a preliminary stage. Mast—with Juin's approval *and* Michelier's support—had then to declare further resistance useless, thus actively supporting the landing parties in consolidating their bridgehead. We shall now see how, during the fortnight preceding D-Day, events conspired to frustrate the coup, thwart Eisenhower, confuse Murphy—and thus play comprehensively into Darlan's hands.

Admiral Darlan arrived in Rabat on 26 October, imposing further equivocation on Noguès. Murphy radioed Eisenhower that Giraud, thwarted in pursuit of his grandiose pretensions, had nevertheless indicated through Lemaigre-Dubreuil that he was willing to consider some role in the great events that were about to unfold. Eisenhower in London, but rather apprehensively preparing to set up his staff in Gibraltar, joined yet again in the chorus of derision that had greeted Giraud's strategic notions, but was unable to throw him over entirely. On the 25th Eisenhower had told Marshall, "If his [Giraud's] decision is favorable his evacuation [from Southern France to Gibraltar] must take place not later than 1 November."

But Giraud refused to move. While *Seraph* lurked in the Gulf of Lyons, tasked to collect this recalcitrant political opportunist, Murphy reported that Mast also refused to commit himself unless and until he received word from his master. By the 27th, Mast was driven to ask Murphy when the landings would take place. Mast had been denied this information at Cherchell—"four days' advance warning" being Murphy's reply—and had left that rendezvous apparently convinced several weeks, or more, would elapse before the invasion fleets appeared off the North African coast.

Murphy told Mast he was prepared to give him the exact

date of D-Day on 4 November. There was still time to collect
Giraud, land him in Gibraltar—and hope he would provide an
acceptable, amenable military facade for an American political
adventure. But, within a matter of days, Mast had to do more
than "sign orders" for the patriot groups (which is about the
extent of his direct involvement with those ardent youngsters).
Mast had to decide whether or not he would take the risk of
actively fomenting conspiracy to the stage where, *if* all went
well, the Algiers Division would welcome the invaders. Such a
welcome was dependent on cooperation with those responsible
for naval defenses and airfields. A virtually unopposed landing
also required the SOL to remain in barracks.

Despite the names that are tossed around so liberally in
Murphy's reports and AFHQ's directives, there were only two
senior officers who were committed to conspiracy—to *mutiny:*
Mast and Colonel Louis Jousse, the Algiers garrison commander. But their commitment was dependent on Giraud, and
might even then fail if Juin exerted authority, or the formidable SOL turned on the Algiers Division. Mast could appreciate
these factors a great deal better than Murphy. It is some measure of the latter's inadequacy that he did not even attempt to
understand that whether or not the French military caste was
divided in loyalties, its senior members were uncertain of their
objectives and their own capacity to attain them.

Eisenhower reverted to depression as the waiting days
passed and the prospect loomed of being incarcerated on the
supposedly inhospitable Rock while ineffective conspiracies were
spun about his hapless head. Murphy continued his exchanges
with Giraud—they only agreed on the latter's point that "dissident elements," namely actual and prospective Gaullists,
should be excluded from conspiracy or its aftermath—but
Eisenhower was driven to note some stark realities. On the
29th, Eisenhower admitted to Marshall: "There is no question
that General Clark's visit to North Africa did much good, even
if it resulted in nothing more than the acquisition of a lot of
information."

TORCH's commander-in-chief continued in the same vein:

"The opportunity we had hoped for of getting Giraud and Darlan together went glimmering [did not work], at least so far as General Mast is concerned. He believes that Darlan is not to be trusted, and that Giraud will have nothing to do with Darlan." But, despite this bleak view of the situation—underlined by Darlan's arrival in Algiers on the 28th in order to brief his agents and adherents—Eisenhower could as little disown Mast as he could wholly abandon Giraud.

November—a cold month in North Africa, a foreboding time for raw Allied troops—was ushered in by Murphy's transformation. Until the last days of October Roosevelt's man on the spot had remained buoyant, optimistic, sanguine. By 1 November, all was changed. Giraud continued to haggle over such less-than-vital matters as the value of the French franc in relation to the American dollar. Murphy was loath to abandon Giraud; Darlan continued to wait. He could afford to do so. Giraud's adherents might fail in their tasks as H-hour approached; if they saw their leader ditched and Darlan again propositioned, their commitment to the Allied cause would be suspect, probably worthless. On the 1st, Murphy, in what can only be called, objectively if unkindly, a state of panic, appealed to Roosevelt. Could the invasion be "postponed"?

Murphy's communiqué tells all: "I am convinced that the invasion of North Africa without favorable French High Command will be a catastrophe. The delay of two weeks, unpleasant as it may be, involving technical considerations of which I am ignorant, is insignificant compared with the result *involving serious opposition of the French Army to our landing*" [writer's emphasis].

Murphy's appeal reveals much about his ignorance of TORCH as a major operation of war. TORCH convoys, at acute risk if detected by U-boats, could not simply sail somewhere else. Gibraltar, crammed with ships and aircraft, proclaimed invasion with every passing day and each new arrival. Roosevelt's reply was swift and crushing: "The invasion must proceed; it cannot be delayed." Eisenhower, whose arrival in Gibraltar was expected hourly, delivered his own rebuke: "It is inconceivable that Murphy can recommend such a delay." SOE in Gibraltar, reporting to Baker Street, transmitted these messages via Clarke, thus enlightening him as to the burdens thrust on the patriot groups.

Murphy, despite tacit, total reliance on Darlan as the one real kingpin, was forced to offer Giraud and Mast verbal concessions. Eisenhower was driven to compose for Giraud a flattering message: "Because of your brilliant reputation and of the great esteem in which you are personally held throughout the Allied world and the French Empire I feel that nothing could be so effective in assuring collaboration between French North Africa and the Allied Forces as your immediate arrival in that country . . ." In plain English: "For God's sake, stop haggling; come over; tell Mast to get cracking."

Giraud finally agreed to be picked up by *Seraph* on the 4th, thence to meet Eisenhower in Gibraltar; that same day, Murphy gave Mast the date of D-Day. Giraud, whom no rebuke ever mollified, was, within four days of D-Day, convinced he was the man of the hour, in North Africa, in France. Roosevelt's Vichy gamble, concocted in political terms, had acquired the atmosphere of a casino.

V

Some among this ill-assorted collection of collaborators and résistants kept their heads, and spirits. On the night of 2 November *Minna* made its first attempt to land weapons for the Algiers patriot group. The operation was code-named LEOPARD. *Minna* sailed from Gibraltar as directed by Murphy, arriving off Cherchell at dusk. The required signals were not made from the beach. The two following nights, *Minna* again arrived off the coast. Once more, no signals were given.

Minna's commander and crew, like their compatriots in *Seraph*, were experienced in clandestine operations. Radio links between SOE in Gibraltar and OSS in Algiers were satisfactory. There was no doubt about the alternative rendezvous—twenty-five kilometers *east* of Algiers—or of the recognition signals. These were to be "a steady white light with a steady blue light alongside." The second and third attempts to land weapons reflected a belated awareness by SOE and OSS that a rendezvous close to Cherchell made little sense.

The Algiers group was not tasked to take direct delivery of the weapons. D'Astier and Mast were responsible for receiving the weapons, and for their subsequent distribution. The whole point of the "immobilization" plan was that it should be executed by patriots who could lie low—or continue with their daily activities—until the last possible moment. The group was given D-Day on the 3rd—a day *before* Mast extracted this from Murphy—thus enabling final preparations to be made. A "premature uprising" would not only have alerted the security forces but might well have tipped the balance against a coup. The Algiers Division and, which is more to the point, Juin's headquarters would then have been faced with a genuine conflict of loyalties. Given Mast's equivocations—accurately reflecting his desire and that of his brother officers for a coup on Giraud's terms, *attentisme* as it were masquerading as decisive action—the group's only chance of executing Eddy's SOE directives lay in bold, ruthless action as darkness fell on 7 November.

The January OSS report states: "The AIM of the Fighting Groups was to disorganize the Military and Civil High Command in order to allow the first landing parties to reach Algiers without fighting. The main idea of the operation was to cut off all telephonic communications, military, official, and public. Superior officers and official personages were to be arrested." Among those earmarked for arrest we should note senior officers of the SOL and members of other extreme Vichy organizations. Given this formidable list of requirements, twenty tons of Sten guns and other automatic weapons might have provided more than a moral boost. Elimination would have been messy, but effective. The weapons did not arrive. Murphy alleges lapses by SOE, but failure to deliver was because those responsible for collection and distribution had other ideas.

By 4 November Murphy was wholly dependent on whatever Mast chose to do before and during the landings—much as he was to be subject to Darlan's dictates after them. *Before* conceding the date of D-Day to Mast, Murphy radioed the War Department in Washington: "Flagpole states that he is prepared to cooperate in one of two ways. He will seize command in Algiers. His superiors are Juin and Koeltz. In that case he would require four days before TORCH to make preparations. If we are unwilling to give 4 days' notice he will be unable to seize command. In that case we must be willing to risk combat resulting from orders given by General Juin but Flagpole will facilitate an entry to the best of his ability." Readers will note the marked contrast between what the patriot group was going to do, and what Mast might do.

The essential point to grasp here is that Mast, four days before D-Day, had done nothing to ensure an unopposed landing. For many weeks, Mast had known about TORCH, and since the Cherchell meeting, knew how much depended on him. Yet Mast had refused absolutely to commit himself. Mast and Murphy were united only in their willingness to rely on the Algiers patriot group for actual "immobilization." Roosevelt's and Giraud's agents, their conspiracy all but dissolved, would also unite in abandoning the patriot group to Darlan's tender mercies. "Four days' notice" was a condition known to Mast since late October. Over a week later, he was still watching how events would develop.

Mast was given the four days' notice—but did nothing positively to assist the imminent Allied landings. Mast knew, simply as an experienced regular soldier whose current appointment imposed particular responsibilities on him, that the patriot group could not deal with the SOL. No steps were taken by Mast to coordinate operations with the patriot group in order to preempt any move by the SOL—Darlan's Praetorian Guard. On the 5th, Darlan arrived in Algiers from Oran. Churchill's "strange and formidable coincidence," the origin of a "a base and squalid deal," could no longer be disguised. Giraud was aboard *Seraph*, a difficult, even a contumacious guest of the Royal Navy. Béthouart in Casablanca declared for the Allies—secretly and uselessly. Juin tells Murphy that Darlan is ready to "come over." The hinge of fate swung slowly, deliberately as the Allied armada sailed through menacing seas. The raw troops aboard little knew what awaited them.

Juin added an oracular but telling comment: "Darlan repeated his statement made to Admiral Leahy in 1941 regarding his desire that the United States talk to him when he was able to provide large-scale assistance." Darlan's late, forcing bid left Giraud at sea in more senses than one; made Mast a spectator; put every onus on the patriot group to strike in the Allied cause. Murphy was immobilized; YANKEE, his radio net to Gibraltar and beyond, virtually went off the air. Giraud was at sea; Murphy, figuratively, in the air. Darlan's time had come.

One is now forced to sympathize with Murphy; to see Mast's point of view; to wonder, as the Algiers patriot group, frustrated by lack of modern weapons, prepared to act, whether a concerted American effort to back youngsters who neither vacillated nor bargained would not have transformed TORCH from a political gamble to a feasible operation of war. On the night of the 5th and 6th, *Minna* made a third attempt to land weapons, again balked by lack of recognition signals. On the 6th, Darlan's particular confidant, General Jean-Marie-Joseph Bergeret, arrived in Tunis from Vichy, en route to Algiers and his role as Fernand Bonnier's executioner. The stage was all but set.

The Foreign Office in London noted: "Algeria is now a part and the only part politically of Metropolitan France which is neither directly nor indirectly under Axis control. It follows that even though political arrangements deriving from a collaboration in Algiers have, for the present, a strictly military purpose, it is impossible to prevent their being examined by Frenchmen everywhere in the hope of discovering from them some shadow of things to come. Frenchmen everywhere are looking for a new centre of authority."

This coded plea for a Gaullist "centre of authority" was shortly to be met with a counter-coup. On the eve of TORCH, Darlan made his final dispositions. He was in Algiers; his family came with the baggage. Bergeret, a former Vichy minister for air, was at hand. Juin was in attendance. Murphy was busy, but futile. He was like YANKEE, whose traffic had to be limited for fear of disclosure. The more Murphy said, the less his words counted. On the eve, conspiracies and conspirators alike dissolved in the fevered air of an event in history both contrived and heroic.

The patriot groups remained undaunted. The BBC prepared to broadcast *"Ecoute, Yankee Robert arrive, Robert arrive."* The OSS and SOE had done their best. Now everything depended on courage, and fate. José Aboulker and his comrades rallied, in garages and cafés, private houses and apartments. *"Chaque heure qui s'égrene augmente notre impatience. Enfin, le 7 novembre au matin, on nous alerte: c'est pour ce soir. Enfin, nous allons combattre."* Henri Rosencher, heeding the call to arms, had lost family to the gas chambers, was hungry and penniless. But youth and ardor came to his aid.

Giraud arrived in Gibraltar on the 7th. His meeting with Eisenhower was a painful affair, perhaps better recorded than dissected. Giraud could not rid himself of a certain innate arrogance, the notion that, on the eve, he would become "head of all French Civil and Military affairs in North Africa," as Eisenhower, in a fulsome welcome letter of 4 November had rashly indicated. A few minutes in Eisenhower's temporary headquarters sufficed. The real commander-in-chief, on edge with the anxiety of his president's gamble, cut short Giraud's demands. A faked Giraud broadcast on the 6th had been received coldly throughout North Africa. This was no time for fooling. Giraud remained on the Rock, an enforced guest, prisoner of his illusions. On the eve of TORCH, the stage was set for the gamble to succeed triumphantly or fail ignominiously.

5

Darlan's Triumph

I

Allied troops went ashore in Morocco and Algeria on 8 November 1942 without the faintest idea about the reception that they would meet. From generals to private solders, and whether American or British, no man in the invasion force knew if he would have to fight, be welcomed, or participate in the charade of a token resistance to the invasion of French colonial and metropolitan territory. After eighteen months of plots and plans, conspiracies and calculations, Robert Murphy and his American colleagues in North Africa remained unable to say what would happen at H-Hour on D-Day, and afterwards. Eisenhower's subordinates were forced to make their own, quasi-political assessments. "The Eastern Assault Force plan for capturing Algiers did not rely on possible assistance by friendly French elements but was based on an analysis of the terrain and the defenses" is fair, official comment, retrospective, but right.

Churchill had some inkling of the real situation, but his commitment to a Mediterranean strategy—and reluctance openly to quarrel with Roosevelt—led him to see North Africa as a prize that might be secured by a swift blow. On the eve of TORCH, and during the anxious days that followed, Churchill bowed to Roosevelt's dictates. But Churchill was to make ample amends, confronting Roosevelt once Darlan seized power in North Africa with arguments that were rejected, but could not be ignored. Neither Roosevelt, nor his colleagues, advisers, and subordinates even began to understand that Darlan, Giraud, and all others involved in conspiracy might be honorable or not—by some abstract definition—but were governed in practice by self-interest, not support for the Allied cause. This was the truth that Churchill hammered home.

Frenchmen who sought an alternative to Vichy lacked authority and cohesion. Although imbued in most cases with the ideal of restoring democracy to France, members of patriot groups in North Africa also lacked effective leadership. The American and British clandestine services could not provide this leadership before and during the invasion, because they had neither cemented effective conspiracy with anti-Vichy groups nor established a clear chain of command and liaison with their political and military masters in London and Washington.

Both OSS and SOE were, broadly speaking, anti-Vichy in composition and outlook. OSS, however, although in a better position than SOE to establish an anti-Vichy network in North Africa, lacked the latter's bitter experience of Résistance—and Vichy repression—in France, and did not perceive that the task of supporting patriot groups meant recourse to violent means, including assassination. The directives that were written for Eddy and the patriot groups reflect the evolution of doctrine about war in the shadows to the point where, as Colin Gubbins, SOE's Director of Operations, made plain, those who got in the way "were to be killed, quickly."

The net result of confusion between objectives and methods was that, as we have seen, AFHQ failed to establish or maintain an intelligence or operational liaison with OSS and SOE, and hence with the patriot groups, above all in Algiers. The further result of such confusion was that neither AFHQ, nor OSS and SOE, let alone the patriot groups, grasped that fundamentally different objectives were sought by Murphy on the one hand and anti-Vichy elements on the other. Murphy sought to do Roosevelt's bidding—to maintain North African Vichy in power. Some in AFHQ, the clandestine services, and the patriot groups respectively supposed, believed, or knew that Vichy would never cooperate wholeheartedly with the Allies. Thus they remained ignorant of Roosevelt's objectives and Murphy's intentions until Darlan seized a political position of great power and potential. Then, reaction was swift, and positive.

II

Algiers is the stage where the Vichy gamble must be witnessed. Eisenhower realized that initial failure in Tunisia would make the Vichy administration throughout North Africa think twice about giving his forces outright support. TORCH was designed by Roosevelt as "a military promenade." Eisenhower was rather grimly aware that it might turn out to be nothing of the kind, and would be something worse than a fiasco if his forces' lines of communication were threatened by opposition from the very people with whom he hoped to collaborate.

Eisenhower and his staff were in the dark about the political situation in the Algiers area and Tunisia, and thus unable to give clear orders to the Eastern Task Force commanders. To further confuse the issue, the Eastern Task Force suffered from divided command. A force of no more than 10,000 in the initial phases (4,000 American, 6,000 British) would be commanded successively rather than jointly by the American Major General Charles Ryder and the British Lieutenant General Kenneth Anderson.

Roosevelt did not intend that Americans should have to fight the Axis in Tunisia, and the planned commitment and deployment of Allied forces in that territory reflects this determination very clearly indeed. As planned, by D plus 23 (1 December), the Eastern Task Force would comprise 102,000 British, 10,000 American troops. Algiers and Casablanca would be American fiefs, Vichy therein an acquiescent satellite. This deployment did, in fact, occur, as Roosevelt intended. Apart from detachments from a parachute battalion, no American troops were committed to Tunisia from the Eastern Task Force until 19 November.

General Ryder was ordered to capture Algiers with the Eastern Task Force. Once Algiers was in Allied hands, General Anderson's "First Army" was to take such steps as might be appropriate for occupying Bône, Philippeville, Bougie, and Bizerta as preliminary to the capture of Tunis by D plus 46— 24 December. The tactical objectives, however, were given a higher priority than the strategic or, insofar as AFHQ understood what was being conspired elsewhere, the political objective. Ryder and Anderson were ordered to seize or take control of airfields before all else, Maison Blanche and Blida in the Algiers area, any others that could be secured farther east. BRANDON, its initial task completed, was to be attached to First Army with the objective of recruiting those who would assist with sabotage and other irregular operations.

The tactical priority given to airfields is understandable, but posed as many problems as it was designed to alleviate. Even if French armed forces in the Algiers area welcomed the Eastern Task Force, Ryder was ordered to put Maison Blanche and Blida firmly under his control before occupying Algiers.

The assault parties directed on the docks area of Sector B would, if successful—either in the welcome they met or the opposition that they overcame—proceed to occupy the center of Algiers. But no provision had been made by AFHQ to cooperate directly with the Algiers patriot group in order to effect a coup. General Lemnitzer, as Eisenhower's operations officer, had ordered the Eastern Task Force assault parties to establish contact with the Algiers patriot group once ashore, but there were crucial differences between this kind of contact and that envisaged by SOE and OSS.

Establishing contact in Algiers itself required not only that the Eastern Task Force assault party directed on the dock area succeed quickly and comprehensively in quelling or neutralizing opposition, but that the Algiers patriot group be supported by Murphy. *AFHQ*, moreover, had directed Murphy not only to provide anti-tank mines, but also to liaise with both the assault parties and the Algiers patriot group. This was a task for which Murphy was, ostensibly, the only choice. But the distribution of weapons to the Algiers patriot group was also partly Mast's responsibility. We know now that Murphy and Mast neither complied with their directives nor honored their pledges. Murphy was, as Eisenhower tersely expressed it, responsible for "political maneuvering"; once Giraud left France, Mast was committed to Giraud and to him alone.

We can see, therefore, that attainment of Eisenhower's objectives regarding Algiers and Tunisia, and the execution of his staff's order by Ryder and Anderson, depended on factors that included contradictory, indeed conflicting, political and tactical elements. An Allied force of initially no more than 10,000, well supported at sea but inadequately so in the air, afflicted moreover with all the defects of divided command, was to land on beaches and a mole without knowing what to expect. Aside from the coast defenses and docks—which, we must recall, Eddy had said were beyond the Algiers patriot group's capacity to seize—the defense of the Algiers area was in the hands of over 15,000 regular troops. These troops could be rapidly reinforced by the SOL—backed by armor—and a force of Gardes Mobiles.

Although SOE and OSS had a definable objective for the Algiers patriot group—to seize control in Algiers, not merely to "immobilize" the operations of its defenders and the internal security forces—it was one doomed to failure through lack of an agreed Allied political objective, and the necessity for the Eastern Task Force to concentrate on ensuring its own survival. Given these factors, Darlan's triumph was all but inevitable.

III

The curtain rises off Casablanca. Ashore, Noguès was not yet sundered from Laval; but offshore, Admiral Hewitt, on 7 November, was ready to support Patton's troops with all the force at his disposal. There is a certain irony in contrast: Noguès as representing perfectly the Vichy so strongly espoused by Roosevelt, and the impending destruction of French warships, a one-sided conflict more bloody than Mers el-Kébir. Hewitt's strength lay not only in numbers and firepower—three battleships and eight heavy cruisers—but also in being able to maneuver at will against one battleship, a cruiser, and lightly armed destroyers.

There is a political dimension to events at Casablanca, but it is interesting only in relation to what occurred in Algiers. Defeat by American firepower, not compromise or bargains, forced Noguès to switch from outright opposition to calculating compliance. Noguès maintained contact with Laval—but, by 11 November, had turned up in Algiers as Pétain's "representative" in North Africa. This legerdemain rendered Noguès suspect rather than potent, but does illustrate the nature of Vichy on the eve of Darlan's coup. Béthouart's hesitations, by contrast, precluded effective conspiracy, for whatever purpose.

On 5 November, Eddy's assistant at Tangier, Captain Hol-
comb, and David King, the OSS station officer in the U.S. consulate at Casablanca, sent detailed assessments to AFHQ of
what Béthouart had, finally, promised, and what he hoped to
achieve: neutralization of all French forces in Morocco.

The details of this belated adhesion to the American cause
need not concern us because, apart from the fact that even at
this eleventh hour Béthouart asked for the presence of an
[American] "staff officer of sufficient rank and authority . . ."
to keep him in countenance, Murphy had decided that support
from patriot groups in Casablanca might risk the kind of "anti-
Nazi but anti many other things" coup that he was determined
to prevent in Algiers. This decision was conveyed to Béthouart
by none other than Jean Rigault, and was hardly calculated to
stiffen the former's resolve.

Béthouart, in effect, was abandoned by Murphy through
the device of giving him complete, solitary responsibility for
seizing Noguès and his subordinates pending either an American assault or a sufficient show of force. Béthouart was not
the man to strike a swift, decisive blow. He lacked standing;
was isolated from Algiers; all too aware that Noguès and
Michelier represented Vichy as "a psychological basis [for
actions] which went beyond official habits of obedience to a
legitimate central authority." Moreover, as Béthouart himself
said: *"La mystique de Pétain est épouvantable."*

King, in compliance with directives similar to those issued
to Eddy by SOE, had prepared sabotage plans. Denied the
opportunity to execute them, King, on 7 November, nonetheless alerted the Casablanca patriot groups to the imminent
arrival of an all-American invasion force. King could have saved
his breath. Béthouart fumbled; Noguès—and Michelier—
reacted swiftly; staff of the U.S. consulate were surrounded by
a detachment of the SOL, and removed to a disagreeable desert
location, Kasbah-Tedla.

The patriot groups stayed underground. Noguès, despite
a personal appeal from Roosevelt, intended to resist the inva-

sion initially; Michelier to fight. Leaflets with photographs of Roosevelt and a message from Eisenhower appeared on the streets. Noguès retaliated by announcing that "a state of war had been declared officially between France and the United States."

"The battle of D-Day" on 8 November, as King's colleague Stafford Reid described it, demonstrated the truth that Patton's virtually independent command would be exercised by undiplomatic methods. Throughout the months preceding D-Day Patton had been skeptical of the elaborate preparations for unopposed landings. "Why give the other guy a chance to draw first?" he asked. Patton believed that blowing *Jean Bart* out of the water would be a better inducement for Vichy to change sides than recourse to conspiracy and bargains.

The American landings at points some distance from Casablanca immediately ran into difficulties and opposition, forcing Hewitt to riposte. Provided with strong air cover, the battleship *Massachusetts* and supporting vessels closed the harbor at Casablanca and opened fire at 0640, engaging *Jean Bart* at 0704. The latter had already opened fire, but the point is academic: the poker cards in Roosevelt's Vichy gamble were replaced by the arbitrament of war. The battle was not entirely one sided. *Jean Bart* was supported by shore batteries, and the cruiser *Primauguet*, accompanied by seven destroyers, cleared the harbor and engaged the U.S. Navy at close range.

But although "These French destroyers did indeed put up a fight that commanded the admiration of all," the issue was decided by 1400. *Jean Bart* was out of action; *Primauguet* and the destroyers sunk or disabled. Although resistance continued at sea and on land for another two days, war had come to Vichy North Africa in a form that few Frenchmen expected. Late on the evening of the 8th, Darlan ordered Noguès to proclaim a local cease-fire. Noguès refused, loath to abandon Laval prematurely.

As always, the plain folk paid for the "great leaders' "

ambitions. One eye-witness of this tragic Sunday battle recalls "a beautiful blue-and-gold autumn day, a smooth sea. Sea gulls with black-tipped wings were skimming over the water apparently unconcerned by these strange antics of the human race." Stafford Reid saw French sailors clinging to rafts in the harbor mouth. "This spectacle is heart-breaking." Two days later, Noguès was all smiles on meeting Patton, and Michelier's subordinates more than helpful towards their Sunday enemies. But Reid also remembers two young widows of the D-Day battle, "bowed in deep grief." Reid, a veteran of the Argonne, evokes futility: "The light was reflected on their black dresses and white kerchiefs. No hour of joy and liberation could atone for their loss. What a tragedy."

The D-Day assault on the mole at Oran was a tragic affair also. Murphy did not even cancel plans for a coup. There were none, of any worth, to cancel. Mast, sufficiently equivocal over Algiers, was totally so concerning Oran. *Les Chantiers* remained unresponsive to overtures. The garrison produced no Béthouart, no Jousse. The assault parties of the Center Task Force were sacrificed in attacking defenses too strong for heroism to overcome.

At 0300 hours on 8 November 1942, HMS *Walney* and *Hartland* reached the Oran mole, wearing the White Ensign and the Stars and Stripes. Bunting made no difference. As at Casablanca, and when no conspiratorial complications fouled the air, the French armed forces belied all the optimistic forecasts that Robert Murphy had made to anxious men in Washington and London.

By 0400 *Walney* and *Hartland* were well ablaze. "Bodies were piled two and three feet deep on the decks." By 0410 *Walney* was sunk, *Hartland* abandoned. Mers el-Kébir had, in some sort, been avenged. Meanwhile, an entirely American force landed against slight opposition west and east of Oran, and began a flank march into the city. Force of arms was barely necessary, but, as we turn to the situation in Algiers, neither Casablanca nor Oran was in Allied hands.

Apart from a comparably futile direct assault on the docks, no scenes of carnage and few of heroism illuminate the Algiers stage. Murphy enters right at 2200 on 7 November and, with Darlan and Juin, occupies the center for much of the next twenty-four hours. A dress rehearsal for the consummation of conspiracy, for the maximum appeal to Darlan whatever else was in the works, had been held three days earlier. Despite his hopes for Mast, and delegation of sabotage details to that deeply puzzled follower of Giraud, Murphy knew that the Vichy gamble depended for success on Darlan. Ignoring Mast's intermittently expressed unease, Murphy had continued to cultivate Juin. On 5 November the two met again. Juin remained noncommittal, but Murphy, seemingly more at home with "great leaders" than backstairs conspirators, saw him as still open to offers.

Enter left nervous, excited members of the Algiers patriot group, unaware that at 1500 on the 7th, Darlan had postponed his return to Vichy, had, via Chrétien, given Murphy one more day to confirm Leahy's offer of 17 October: leadership in North Africa *and* "Europe." Courage was abundant among the group—although poltroons failed to muster, or deserted, leaving fewer than four hundred at their posts—but leadership other than in personal terms was wanting. So too were twenty tons of Sten guns, and other arms, including those that AFHQ had charged Murphy to deliver. The Aboulkers and their compatriots trusted Henri d'Astier and Jean Rigault, both in close contact with Murphy. The seeds of failure lay in that misplaced trust, not only in the workings of Darlan's clear and orderly brain.

At sea, the assault parties of the Eastern Task Force completed their preparations. A cold, misty night, with but a slight swell cloaked movement and eased taut nerves. The deception plan for the Eastern Task Force at sea took all vessels well to the east of Algiers; the assault parties had a long, cold, ride ahead as the leading elements left the security of the big ships and headed for beaches and mole. With the exception of the crews and troops aboard *Malcolm* and *Broke*, whose task was to secure the docks, neither commanders nor men had much care for what might be conspiring in Algiers. Unlike the Allied forces directed at Casablanca and Oran, the Eastern Task Force as a whole knew that the real enemy lay to the east. Securing Maison Blanche and Blida, possibly against stiff French opposition and Luftwaffe attack, was an objective that concentrated all minds in Ryder's force.

By 0200 on D-Day the curtain has risen. One figure leaves the stage. General Mast, loitering in the wings for so long, had conferred with Murphy (and Henri d'Astier) at 2200 on the 7th. Mast indicated, no more, that all was in motion: but Mast is not specific—about anything. He chooses not to, or fails to warn members of the Algiers patriot group of prospective danger from the Gardes Mobiles and the SOL; he certainly does not say to his subordinates and to the gendarmerie forces: "Lay down your arms." Mast's dilemma can be, must be understood: he knew D-Day, but not H-Hour; he had no notion of whether "Robert" would arrive in overwhelming force or as a mere raiding party. Murphy was unable to provide concrete information, reliable detail. Caution, hesitation, *attentisme* finds its clearest expression in Mast. All Mast's want of resolution must be understood, not merely accepted, if what followed is to be seen in its true historical perspective.

By 0200 on the 8th Mast had wandered off into the night, not to be seen for hours. The Algiers patriot group had occupied many buildings; cut some telephone and radio / telephone links; rounded up assorted, enraged commanders and staff officers; carried out the first part of their orders. The group then awaited support—which never came. The group was doomed to have its anti-Vichy coup frustrated—in the dark hours of 8 November. D'Astier, at police headquarters, kept his own lines open, to his advantage.

"Bonjour de Gaulle." Roosevelt and Churchill bring two reluctant French-men together at the Casablanca Conference. Left, standing, is General Henri Giraud, High Commissioner of French Africa; at right, standing, is General Charles de Gaulle, then President of the French National Committee in London, leader of the Free French.

Admiral Darlan's funeral procession to Algiers Cathedral. British and American troops march past the coffin. The ceremony was attended by Generals Eisenhower and Clark, President Roosevelt's emmissary, Robert Murphy, and other dignitaries.

Lieutenant General Mark Clark, right, on the speaker's stand in Casablanca with French General Noguès—May 1943.

Marshal Pétain and his then heir apparent, Admiral Jean-François Darlan.

The facade of unity. Darlan flanked by General Eisenhower and General Clark.

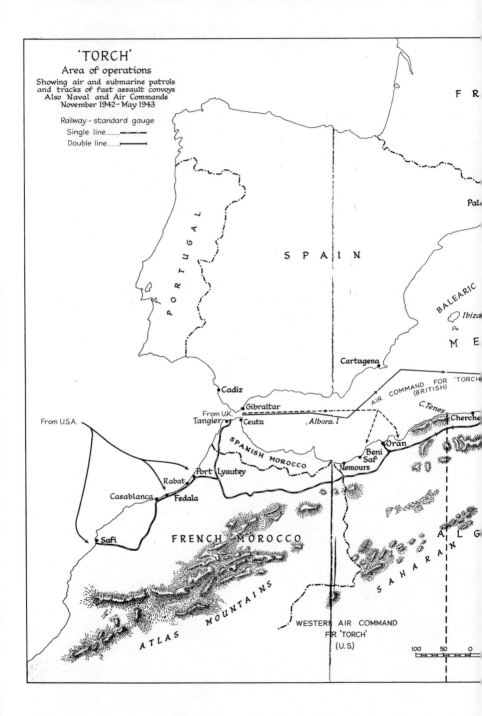

'TORCH'

Area of operations

Showing air and submarine patrols
and tracks of fast assault convoys
Also Naval and Air Commands
November 1942 – May 1943

Railway – standard gauge

Single line........

Double line........

FR

Pal

PORTUGAL

SPAIN

BALEARIC

Ibiza

ME

Cartagena

Cadiz

Gibraltar

Tangier

Ceuta

Albora. I

AIR COMMAND FOR 'TORCH
(BRITISH)

C. Tenes

Cherche

From U.S.A.

SPANISH MOROCCO

Oran

Beni
Saf

Nemours

Rabat

Port Lyautey

Casablanca

Fedala

Safi

FRENCH MOROCCO

ALG

SAHARA

ATLAS MOUNTAINS

WESTERN AIR COMMAND
FIR 'TORCH'
(U.S)

100   50   0

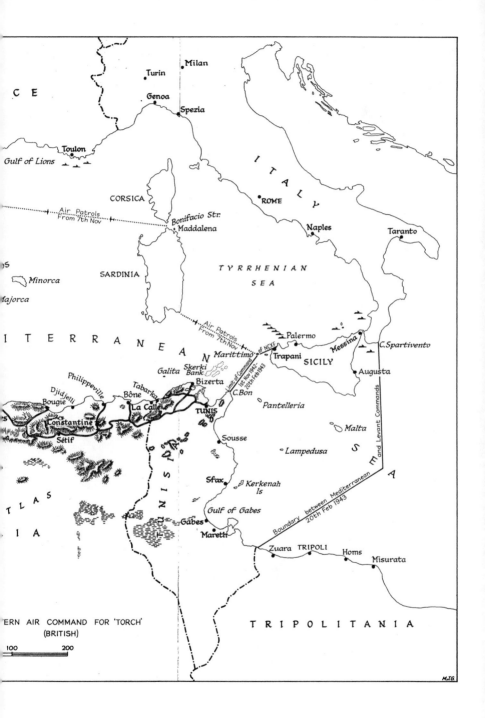

CE

Turin
Milan
Genoa
Spezia

Toulon
Gulf of Lions

CORSICA

Air Patrols
From 7th Nov

Bonifacio Str.
Maddalena

ITALY

ROME

Naples

Taranto

TYRRHENIAN
SEA

Minorca

Majorca

SARDINIA

Air Patrols
From 7th Nov

Palermo

Messina
C. Spartivento

MEDITERRANEAN

Philippeville

Djidjelli
Bougie

Constantine
Sétif

ATLAS

IA

Galita

Tabarka
Bône
La Calle

Skerki
Bank

Marittimo

Bizerta

C. Bon

TUNIS

Sousse

Trapani
SICILY

Augusta

Pantelleria

Malta

Lampedusa

Sfax

Kerkenah
Is

Gulf of Gabes

Gâbes

Mareth

Zuara
TRIPOLI

Homs

Misurata

Boundary between Mediterranean
20th Feb 1943

and Levant Commands

Limit of Command of NCXF
1st Nov 1942–
20th Feb 1943

ERN AIR COMMAND FOR 'TORCH'
(BRITISH)

100   200

TRIPOLITANIA

M.J.G.

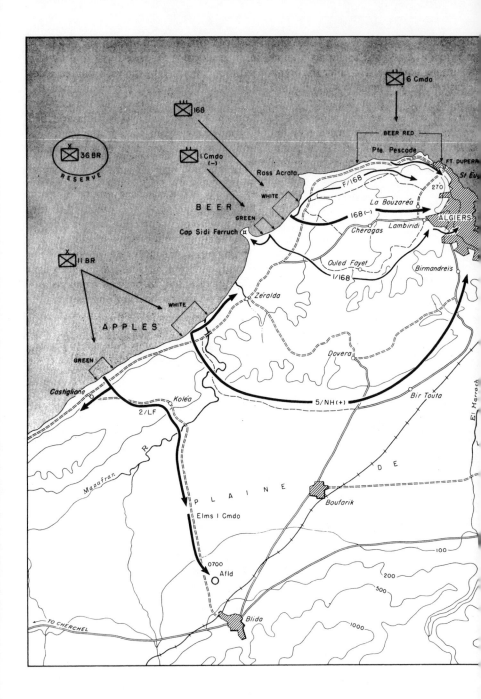

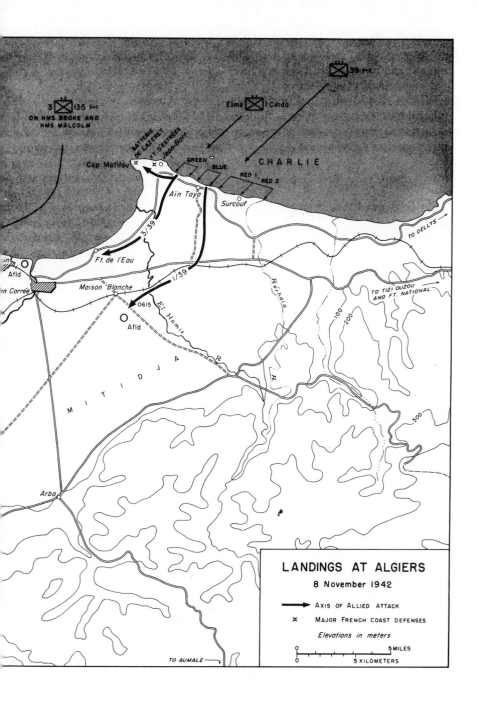

LANDINGS AT ALGIERS

8 November 1942

→ AXIS OF ALLIED ATTACK

✕ MAJOR FRENCH COAST DEFENSES

Elevations in meters

De Gaulle's kingmakers: Anthony Eden,
Winston Churchill, and Harold Macmillan.

The face of an assassin? Fernand Bonnier,
age twenty.

"Torch" beaches near Algiers. British weapons and
equipment being landed from Landing Craft
Mechanized (LCMs).

Two faces of Vichy—opportunism and patriotism. On the eve of the Allied landings, Admiral Darlan is met, on arriving in Algiers on October 28, 1942, by, left to right, Generals Juin, Koeltz, de Biosboissel, and Mast.

Admiral Darlan pins the insignia of Grand Officer of the Legion of Honor on General Henri Dentz for his defense of Syria against British and Gaullist forces.

But the Algiers patriot group did attempt its anti-Vichy coup at one dramatic moment. Murphy seeks Juin—and Darlan. Bernard Pauphilet arrests the two clear embodiments of Vichy, and does so at d'Astier's instigation, with Jousse's support. The act, and its motive, is less significant than Murphy's inopportune arrival as witness of it. Murphy is forced to choose, to play all his cards at once. Murphy must choose, not merely play the Darlan card on his master's behalf, disowning the "anti-Nazi but anti many other things" young patriots in the process. Juin, angry at being arrested—in his pajamas, *sans des plumes*—is a spectator of Darlan's first meeting with the representative of America at war. What follows is still preliminary to genuine drama.

Juin, deprived of positive action but determined to hedge his bets, dismisses Mast, and appoints General Jean Roubertie in his place. (Roubertie, with other senior officers, had been arrested by the Algiers patriot group, but was soon at liberty.) Juin also orders the forces under his nominal command "to maintain contact [with the invading troops] without aggressivity." This was no call to arms, but *attentisme* given idiosyncratic expression. Darlan, with all the time in the world but with a hand containing only two good cards—Esteva and Count De La Borde, the admiral commanding at Toulon—deals discards: he sends telegrams to Pétain, and orders a temporizing cease-fire.

Much has been made of these telegrams: they are really of no great account. Darlan, Laval's political victim, was not in Algiers to represent Pétain, however much he invoked his name when convenient in the following days. Darlan had come to Algiers to change sides, and gain his own laurels in so doing. The cease-fire was a mere gesture, rejected by Noguès, ignored at Oran, irrelevant at Algiers. Yet the situation at Casablanca and Oran establishes a bond between Murphy and Darlan. The threat of continued conflict, or renewed resistance, the prospect of sustained American casualties, would, later, justify

Murphy's approaches to Darlan. In fact, Darlan was given another good card to deal.

By sunrise (0400), the gamblers can be seen at their play. Essential drama—France's future and Roosevelt's way of war—remains disguised by elements of tragedy and chance. *Broke* and *Malcolm* are disabled or sunk, but British troops in Sector A and American in Sector B are ashore and marching toward Blida and Maison Blanche. French Army resistance is negligible, owing little to Mast, much to force of arms. The French forces in the Algiers area knew by 0400 that this was no commando raid. "Force H" and Vice-Admiral Sir Harold Burrough's covering force—battleships, aircraft carriers, cruisers—had closed the shore observed by French aircraft; such strength meant invasion.

This winter Sunday, breaking bright and clear after the misty night, is an odd one. The SOL and Gardes Mobiles are on the streets, bundling dazed members of the Algiers patriot group into a miserable captivity. A few shots are fired, the odd death may be recorded. Vichy in Algiers had only to pit tanks and half-tracks against antique Lebel rifles, and all hopes of an anti-Vichy coup dissolved, for the present. The Algiers patriot remnant was not, however, abandoned. By D plus 1, BRANDON was ashore, and immediately took the remnant under its wing.

By mid-morning, and while Hewitt's ships pulverize the French Navy at Casablanca, men of the Lancashire Fusiliers wave at families bound for mass in Algiers. On 25 April 1915, the fathers of these men went ashore at Y Beach, Cape Helles, Gallipoli, there to be slaughtered. A pilot of the Royal Naval Air Service flying over the scene remembers "the sun shining brightly, the sea red with blood." No such carnage awaited the sons in the orange groves of Kolea and Boufarik. The airfields were taken without a fight, before noon.

The Eastern Task Force assault on the docks had failed, thus precluding any hope of timely Allied support to the Algiers patriot group, but so far as General Ryder and his troops were concerned, the fog of war had lifted. Algiers would be theirs once fully encircled. By 1500 on the 8th, American troops were in the city. Ryder was ashore, in touch with Murphy, and Darlan.

Whatever might transpire in Juin's house or elsewhere in Algiers, the Eastern Task Force had established a bridgehead, and the British element was preparing for its major objective : Tunisia. Fighting continued at Casablanca and Oran, but the issue was not seriously in doubt. One issue, above all, had been resolved : a major invasion had been met by gallant, but ineffectual, resistance from the French Navy. The French Army was neither willing nor able to fight with prolonged determination. Yet it is precisely at this point, on the afternoon of the 8th, and as Eisenhower on the Rock begins to breathe again, that Darlan takes the initiative—and retains it thereafter until his death.

General Clark's arrival in Algiers from Gibraltar on the afternoon of the 9th has been described as if Caesar were dealing with the Gauls. The *record*—of negotiation in Algiers and from the positive flood of signals that Clark sent to Eisenhower— lies in front of the writer, convincing new evidence of the essential purpose behind Roosevelt's Vichy gamble. The gamble not only prevented Clark from wringing any concession from Darlan, but also delayed the march into Tunisia. But hitherto received versions of events would have us believe that Clark laid down the law to a cowed, beaten Darlan. We are told that Clark banged the table, that he threatened Darlan with arrest, and worse. This was braggadocio, credible as a reflection of Clark's character, distasteful as coming from a senior officer, irrelevant to a poker game.

At no time in these days, as fighting at Casablanca and Oran slackened and ceased, but continued intermittently in and around Algiers, did Darlan concede anything. As before, time was on his side, his alone. Time was Clark's enemy. On the 9th, and at Laval's request, the Axis began to occupy Tunisia. On the 11th, and as Anderson's First Army—a token force—began the sea-borne move into Tunisia, ATTILA commenced. Darlan had all the time in the world—but not in France. To innate cunning and vaulting ambition one must add fate.

Darlan had nowhere else to go. If Darlan was to realize his ambition of supplanting Laval, he must first become Roosevelt's surrogate in North Africa. But Darlan was in no sense Clark's prisoner, literally or figuratively. Admiral Royer Dick, the sole survivor of the two days' negotiations, puts the case exactly: "At times we did not know who was prisoner of whom."

Clark had many cares, to be sure. Giraud arrived in Algiers on the morning of the 9th; was at once disowned by such compatriots as he had the misfortune to encounter; proceeded thereafter to sulk in his tent. Giraud's behavior in these days suggests a man out of touch with reality. Darlan is reality, and can assert it. Patriots and conspirators leave the stage. The spotlight falls on Clark, not yet educated by his bruising experience at Cherchell into an understanding of what was at stake for France, her troubled soldiers and citizens. Murphy sits and listens. He is superfluous also.

Clark was explicitly required to seek French authority for the maintenance of law and order, civil administration, lines of communication. All the hostages to misfortune that lay behind Roosevelt's concept of occupying North Africa as if this were merely a business deal were present to Clark's mind. The French Army might be supine, but a hostile, a sullen, an uncooperative administration and *colon* population would prove a bigger problem to an untried U.S. Army than the Axis in Tunisia or the French fleet at Toulon.

IV

The British government strongly disliked Roosevelt's determination to present TORCH as an all-American affair. Churchill, his colleagues, and much of Whitehall were frequently at odds with de Gaulle, but loathing for Vichy and dislike of Roosevelt's assertive ways resulted in outright disagreement between London and Washington. On 26 October Roosevelt had, and not for the first time, rejected de Gaulle's overtures for participation in TORCH. Throughout late October, but with scant success, Churchill attempted to dissuade Roosevelt from communicating with Pétain. On 5 November Churchill asked Roosevelt when, not whether, de Gaulle should be told about TORCH. Churchill had reluctantly agreed with Roosevelt that de Gaulle and Fighting France should be excluded from TORCH as such. But he was determined that this concession should be redeemed by the strongest expression of support for one to whom, as he said to the president, "I have exchanged letters of a solemn kind in 1940 recognising him as the Leader of Free Frenchmen."

Churchill then proposed to Roosevelt that he should tell de Gaulle of TORCH on the evening of the 7th. Roosevelt point-blank refused, but Churchill, simmering, saw de Gaulle at midday on the 8th. Roosevelt's rejection was discourteously worded. Not only that, but the communiqué in no sense allayed Churchill's fears that Roosevelt's prime motive for TORCH was to reestablish Vichy in North Africa for the furtherance of entirely American strategic objectives, let the cost to France be what it might. Churchill's fears were not allayed by Roosevelt's gratuitous comment of 5 November: *"Admiral Leahy agrees wholly with [my] thoughts."*

Churchill, accompanied by Eden (now a committed Gaullist), repeated his pledges to de Gaulle on the 8th; declared that he saw him as "a unifying leader"—a phrase also used in writing to Roosevelt, on whom it made no impression whatso-ever; and then let de Gaulle have his say. "I cannot under-stand," said de Gaulle, "how you British can stand aside so completely in an undertaking that is of such primary concern to Europe." Churchill and Eden could only agree. Their agreement was confirmed on the evening of the 8th, when de Gaulle broadcast in terms that directly opposed Roosevelt's policies.

Ever one to reinforce success, de Gaulle on the 9th declared to Admiral Stark: "I should like to send a mission to Algiers. I request the Government of the United States to take the necessary measures so that this mission may reach its destination." Stark gave the kind of assent inseparable from an underling's role, convinced that no such mission would be allowed if Roosevelt ruled against it.

De Gaulle, equally aware of Roosevelt's opposition to such a mission, virtually demanded from Churchill that support be given. De Gaulle was sure of Eden's support. Even before Darlan began dealing the aces to Clark, SIS reported from Algiers on 8 November: "It has to be recognised that the role given to Admiral Darlan has perturbed and is still liable to perturb, a considerable number of Frenchmen who, sometimes at great personal risk, and, in many cases, of danger to their lives and property in France, have decided to throw in their lot with the Allies."

This oblique reference to the Algiers patriot group is not only evidence of prospective British support for an anti-Darlan front in North Africa, but is emphasized by an early MASSINGHAM assessment: "The coup had as one of its objects the removal of the whole of the collaborationist group who were in power." In London, Vichy collaboration with Murphy was viewed not only with alarm, but also with skepticism. Such collaborators kept a foot in the Axis camp also, none more so than Darlan.

René Pleven, Colonel Pierre Billotte, and General François d'Astier (three of de Gaulle's closest associates in London) were told to stand by: de Gaulle's mission to Algiers would need British support; the object of the exercise would be "the removal of the whole of the collaborationist group." At an emotional Gaullist rally in London's Royal Albert Hall on 11 November none present were left in any doubt that de Gaulle's passionate plea for the unity of France meant that the destruction of Vichy in North Africa must first be achieved.

Roosevelt's depth of commitment to Darlan also demanded a response—from General Clark, and very quickly. Clark was at the end of a long line of communication from Washington, London—and Gibraltar, where Eisenhower remained until his arrival in Algiers with Admiral Sir Andrew Cunningham (the most senior British officer at Eisenhower's side) on the 13th. Clark was faced with a double problem—to meet Roosevelt's political and strategic requirements; thereafter to tackle the immediate operational requirements of cease-fire, Tunisia, and the Toulon fleet. There is no doubt that Darlan saw Clark's dilemma quite clearly, and turned it to his advantage. Yet Darlan's success in outwitting Clark led inevitably to his death. The power that Darlan seized and the arrogance with which he exercised it intensified reaction against him. Clark's surrender to Darlan did more than create Gaullism in North Africa; Frenchmen there rallied to the cause of a united France.

But none of this could be known as Clark and Darlan began their two days' gambling session. Clark sat down to play with one more card filched from him. On the evening of the 9th Clark and Giraud met for a brief, pointless exchange. Giraud again demanded the role of commander-in-chief of all French forces in North Africa. Clark, his eyes open, refused. Giraud returned to his tent. Clark was left with the uncomfortable fact that he could no longer deal Giraud to Darlan. Cordell Hull's spirited, and public, defense of Roosevelt's Vichy policy on the 9th was tantamount to giving Darlan yet another card, all the more valuable in that he could deal it more than once. In the draft armistice agreements which had been drawn up in Washington during October as the basis of a deal with Vichy in North Africa, control of the press and broadcasting was to be vested in the Allies. But almost before Darlan put the first meeting with Murphy behind him he ensured that Radio Alger and the local press would remain firmly in his hands. Hull's message was broadcast. Clark sat down to play with the cards stacked against him.

Clark had to deal; he could not call, or pass. He needed Darlan's authority for a cease-fire throughout North Africa that not only would hold firm, but also would allow for unopposed Allied occupation. But, of equal importance, Clark needed Darlan's collaboration over Esteva in Tunis and De La Borde at Toulon. Clark needed collaboration, quickly. A skilled negotiator would have eased the pressure of time by appearing relaxed. Clark was never relaxed. He showed his hand. Moreover, although Darlan was indeed "an astute and bloodless calculator," he was not immune from insult. There is little doubt that the courteous Eisenhower could have played the cards a great deal better than his deputy. Yet even Eisenhower could not have escaped from his president's policies.

Roosevelt sent Esteva a personal message on the 9th. There was no answer. So much for Tunisia. Roosevelt's hopes for the Toulon fleet had been expressed to Churchill in January 1942. In effect, Roosevelt said: If Darlan brings us the Toulon fleet, we can do business with him. Roosevelt, with much else on his mind, saw no reason to doubt that, in return for an unspecified role within the American orbit, Darlan would put the necessary pressure on a couple of admirals who had risen through the French Navy by his favors and influence. Clark's efforts on the 10th and 11th were therefore concentrated almost entirely on browbeating Darlan to contact Admirals Esteva and De La Borde. If Darlan would collaborate on these crucial operational requirements, a deal was possible.

Darlan refused to be drawn. He wanted to know precisely what he would get in return for collaboration. Darlan refused to commit himself to a comprehensive cease-fire—Clark's first demand of the 10th—not only because he was bidding for the highest stake left to him, but also because he knew that Roosevelt had never specified what a deal with Vichy in North Africa actually meant in terms of personal power and political perquisites. Clark certainly had no mandate to say what Darlan's actual reward for collaboration would be. Eisenhower had no authority.

Murphy was not even part of the poker session, a grim enough one for the future of France. Darlan refused to order Esteva or De La Borde to collaborate; he merely hinted that he might attempt to contact them. By the 10th, Darlan had finally been repudiated by Pétain—in effect, by Laval. Although this move was inevitable, it forced Darlan to bid high. In turn, Clark was forced to bid for favors. By the 11th, Clark was driven to consider what he could offer Darlan, at almost any price.

Clark's telegrams to Eisenhower, and the latter's to Washington and London, together with the only record of the negotiations with Darlan that can be regarded as accurate, provide abundant evidence of what actually happened. The messages are a revealing account of tension and frustration. The record of negotiations provides not only the essential background to Clark's and Eisenhower's communiqués, but also clinching evidence of what Darlan demanded—and seized. This was nothing more nor less than that "Admiral Darlan would become the political head in France." Roosevelt's mid-October pledge was thus confirmed.

But the record is also essential for setting the scene. "The paramount necessity of pushing on eastwards as rapidly as possible to forestall German movement in Tunisia, which was even then starting, put the Allied forces into a position which necessarily had a dominating effect on the subsequent negotiation. Hence our hands were tied in negotiating, by the initial necessity of ensuring that our forces were not robbed of the fruits of the rapid successful landing which had been achieved." The record continues, with considerable understatement: "Admiral Darlan was at liberty and all the leading French authorities were in a state of indecision and not one of them could be regarded as reliably attached to our cause."

Clark reported to Eisenhower on the 10th that "Kingpin and his gang" had ceased to be of much account. Clark continues: "I pleaded with Darlan to order FRENCH FLEET here. He replied that his order would no longer have effect. I therefore asked that he make a plea to the French Fleet. He replied that he could not." This admission by Clark is all the more revealing if we turn to the record. Clark had attempted coercion earlier in the meeting. Darlan had asked for a recess. This granted, and Clark's temper presumably under some control as a result, Darlan agreed to a compromise—but one that in no sense committed him. The record states: "Admiral Darlan announced that he would issue an order to all the ground, air and naval forces in North Africa, including Morocco and Tunisia, to discontinue hostilities immediately." Darlan accordingly issued the following statement:

1. Our engagements having been fulfilled, and the bloody battle become useless, order is given to all land, sea and air forces in North Africa to cease the fight against forces of America and their Allies, as from receipt of this order, and to return to their barracks and bases and to observe strictest neutrality.
2. In ALGERIA and MOROCCO, Commanders-in-Chief will put themselves in liaison with local American Commanders on the subject of terms for the suspension of hostilities.
3. I assume authority over North Africa in the name of the Marshal. The present Senior Officers retain their commands and the political and administrative organisations remain in force. No change will be made without a fresh order from me.
4. All prisoners on each side will be exchanged.

Darlan's order not only concedes him an implied authority beyond his role as commander-in-chief of the Vichy French armed forces, but also is revealing in its language. Darlan achieved two objectives: By assuming "authority over North Africa in the name of the Marshal" he not only asserted his own authority over those French armed forces about which Clark was so anxious, but he also moved toward the stage where he could demand power in return for concessions concerning the French fleet and Tunisia. We should also note that the order, as issued, belies Darlan's pledge to order French forces in *Tunisia* to "discontinue hostilities." One can argue that "North Africa" is comprehensive enough, but what Clark needed was Esteva's positive collaboration. Such collaboration meant resistance to the Axis. Darlan made no commitment on that score.

So much for the 10th. In a later message to Eisenhower that day Clark conceded that "a most difficult position had been reached." Clark admits that "Darlan [is] obviously playing for power." Further evidence of this fact is furnished by the latter's continued refusal to bestir himself over Tunisia. Clark asked Darlan to urge his "Commanders" to "facilitate his [Anderson's] unopposed movements by sea tonight to BONE BOUGIE DJDJELLI." Clark and Anderson had come to a rapid, mutual detestation, but the former knew that unless some Allied troops moved quickly into Tunisia all the elaborate political scheming that lay behind TORCH would simply be junked as so much waste paper and hot air.

But Darlan continued to hold his hand. The commencement of ATTILA on the 11th was a major psychological shock to Juin and his compatriots throughout North Africa. Giraud, a rather forlorn figure by this time, commented: "We are at the end of our rope. It is time for FRENCHMEN to get together." But Darlan, the only member of this Algiers poker game with prolonged, deep—and recent—experience of Pétain's Vichy, grasped at once how the psychological shock could be turned to his advantage. Darlan had long been prepared for ATTILA; indeed his plans had partly been laid in expectation of it. North Africa would now be isolated from Vichy. Darlan could carve out his own fiefdom—"in the name of the Marshal."

Evidence of this fact was at once apparent. Eisenhower urged Clark on the 11th to "plead" yet again with Darlan regarding the Toulon Fleet, and to "telephone at once to Tunis urging Admiral Esteva to denounce the Axis personnel, and to declare himself for us." Clark did as he was bid. The 11th was, indeed, a day of reckoning for Clark. He removed the guard from Admiral Fenard's house, where Darlan was staying in what he drily called "protective custody," and sought in other ways to conciliate him. Admiral Dick recalls a series of rather absurd handshakes, and an atmosphere of contrived *bonhomie*. Clark assured Eisenhower, "For the present believe we are holding our own," but this statement only reveals that Darlan held the cards.

At the first meeting on the 11th, Darlan refused to telephone Esteva, but sent De La Borde a "please yourself" message: "I invite you to direct the Fleet towards *West* Africa" [writer's emphasis]. With that, Clark had to be content, unaware that Darlan said to Dick after sending the telegram: "I am afraid they will not come." But the truth is that "they" had neither been ordered nor requested to come—to *North* Africa, which is where Eisenhower and, above all Cunningham, wanted them. Admiral De La Borde's refusal was tersely expressed: *"Merde."*

Anderson finally managed to see Darlan on the 11th, but the harassed British commander found his quarry unresponsive. Darlan was increasingly sure he could wring concessions from Clark. Darlan was in a mood to boast. "I have repeatedly told Hitler and Goering that to win the war they must hold North Africa and so complete their mastery of the Mediterranean; they wouldn't listen to me; and now you have come I am quite certain that you and your Allies will win in the end. The difference between Laval and myself is that he has always been certain that Hitler would be victorious, but I have always had my doubts." Darlan knew Anderson was only a British soldier. He could thus afford to say what he skillfully avoided saying bluntly to Clark: Let me run North Africa and you will have no problems.

This was not what Anderson had come to hear. Darlan's observations were no help to Anderson who, on D plus three had a mere 23,000 troops under command with which to commence operations in Tunisia. By this date, the Axis had already committed over 30,000 troops, and further reinforcements were arriving with neither protest nor opposition from Esteva. Anderson knew that Clark—"who neither liked me personally nor approved of my conduct of the advance into Tunisia"— had no intention of dispatching American troops in any strength to support First Army while the situation remained confused. Yet occupation of Tunisia was Eisenhower's operational priority once the three bridgeheads of Casablanca, Oran, and Algiers had been established. Clark could ignore Anderson, but not the commander-in-chief.

Throughout much of the 11th Clark was again reduced to pleading with Darlan in the hopes that he would not merely telephone Esteva but give him orders. Darlan did telephone— but would give no orders. Anderson was forced to act on his own initiative. By the evening of the 11th Algiers was quiet— and British Military Police were directing the traffic. But in winter cold and dark, lacking their greatcoats (due to loss of a freighter at sea) Anderson's minute force opened the Tunisian campaign. On paper, in November, Allied troops were due to occupy Tunis after six weeks' bloodless campaigning. In the event, Tunis was captured after six months' hard fighting, and considerable casualties.

Clark was trapped by the very nature of the Vichy gamble. Murphy was at Clark's side, a spectator of this unequal duel, but in the unique position of being able to meet Darlan's demands. Leahy's offer—Roosevelt's bribe, in fact, lacking the prize of the Toulon fleet—was duly, inevitably made. The record of the negotiations states:

> Meanwhile, during the afternoon [of the 11th], further agreement was reached that Admiral Darlan would become the political head in France, and General Giraud would be the military commander of all French forces in North

Africa. A public announcement was decided upon for the next day, emphasizing the unity of all factors for the combined effort. Admiral Darlan and General Juin telephoned Admiral Esteva to tell him to resist the Germans.

But even this combined approach to Esteva failed: the call was made too late to affect events in the Allies' favor, and moreover, lacked all conviction. The record notes: "Admiral Esteva, over the telephone said 'I have a tutor by my side' so it would appear that he was not free."

Esteva's lack of freedom reflected pressure from his subordinates rather than threats by the Axis, but whatever the circumstances, Darlan was indifferent to the fate of his creatures. Esteva's subordinates had no desire to fight against, or with, British troops—nor did they do so. The subordinates had even less desire to fight against Axis troops, and were of several minds about collaborating with them. Darlan provided neither guidance nor authority on these hard choices, although, by 11 November, he was fully aware that military success for his new masters depended on a rapid, decisive occupation of Tunisia.

Darlan thus finally seized power from an American major general whose role as Roosevelt's emissary was simply too complex and tortuous for political success to attend it. Darlan, as we shall see, not only seized power from Clark and Murphy—and hence Eisenhower, and Roosevelt—but also proceeded to exercise it on a scale that not even the most ardent exponent of the Vichy gamble could, for long, approve.

V

Agreement between Darlan and Clark was put into writing on the 13th; signed on the 14th; and published, in a form from which all the real terms had been expunged, on the 22nd. Between the 11th and the 22nd Eisenhower and Cunningham justified their support for the deal to Washington and London;

Roosevelt justified it to Churchill; and de Gaulle reproached Churchill in language magnificent in its scorn—and truth. In North Africa, and behind the *attentiste* slogan of "business as usual," citizens of France set their hands to several distinct, divergent, opposed choices.

Darlan lost no time asserting and proclaiming his power. Once his objective was attained, Darlan knew that time was no longer on his side. Opposition to Darlan began, and grew swiftly even before Clark conceded defeat. As some of the truth leaked out, opposition intensified, to the point where rage, fear, ambition, and conspiracy were subsumed in the need to "eliminate" Darlan. The word is that used by the British Foreign Office, not by any purveyor of the sensational and melodramatic. Meanwhile in Tunisia, Axis forces consolidated a sound defensive position beyond Tunis and inflicted painful defeat on Allied troops.

By 14 November Eisenhower had conceded that "local sentiment [in North Africa] did not remotely resemble prior calculations." Nevertheless, Eisenhower sent a series of signals to Churchill, the Combined Chiefs of Staff, and the British Chiefs of Staff on the 14th which are more indicative of special pleading than an accurate summary of recent events. Eisenhower's argument comes to this : Darlan secured a cease-fire—but can repudiate it; if we repudiate him, we lose the Toulon fleet and Esteva's collaboration. Pétain's prestige in North Africa is utilized by Darlan, a factor that we cannot ignore. Darlan will support our Tunisian campaign; Giraud recognizes Darlan's authority, and will subordinate his own interests to it. Darlan's authority in North Africa relieves us from the burden of military occupation—"in Morocco alone General Patton calculates that it would take sixty thousand Allied forces to hold the tribes quiet." Finally, the "de Gaullists" should welcome Giraud's assent to the Clark-Darlan Agreement.

Eisenhower attempted to ensure a welcome for his misleading—and, in certain respects, inaccurate—messages by admitting that there might be "a feeling at home [the United

States] that we have been sold a bill of goods." Eisenhower
went further: "If the two Governments [United States and Brit-
ish] after analysis are still dissatisfied with the nature of the
Agreement, a mission of selected British and United States
representatives, including the Free French if deemed advisa-
ble, [should] be immediately dispatched to this Headquarters,
where in ten minutes they can be convinced of the soundness
of the moves we have made." Considering that Eisenhower,
on the 14th, had also told Washington and London that "Murphy practically lives in Darlan's pocket," it is difficult to believe
that ten minutes would have done more than convince any open-
eyed visitor that Darlan was omnipotent, and would please
himself on all major issues.

Neither Eisenhower's concession nor suggestions can mask
the fact that he was confused, and that he failed to substantiate
his argument. Darlan as "a temporary expedient" might have
been justified on strictly practical grounds. But Darlan's actions
between 9 and 11 November, let alone thereafter, reveal that
he was prepared neither to impose his authority on Esteva and
De La Borde nor to support the Allies in Tunisia, or elsewhere
in North Africa. The Vichy gamble had succeeded to the extent
that the Allies had established a bridgehead in North Africa
with only slight casualties. The gamble was threatened by failure to the extent that Axis forces were on the offensive in Tunisia. Of even graver importance was the fact of Darlan's
arrogating power to himself on a scale that threatened Anglo-
American relations—and, above all, menaced the survival of
French Résistance.

Admiral Cunningham's telegram to the Admiralty, also of
14 November, appears to support Eisenhower's argument.
Within days that support had been withdrawn. Cunningham
was not the bluff sailor of anecdote but, like Anderson, a Scot
of bleak perception. As commander-in-chief of the Mediterranean Fleet for most of the preceding three years, Cunningham had endured triumph and disaster, but with more of
the latter as his daily portion. Cunningham was relatively

indifferent to political conspiracies, but knew that Darlan could neither *guarantee* the Toulon fleet's arrival in North—or West—African waters, nor would impose his will on Esteva. But Cunningham forced himself to dissemble.

Cunningham hated all that Darlan represented—he was later to call him "a skunk"—but, in these troubled days, when TORCH remained a gamble at the strategic level, declared: "I understand the agreement reached yesterday at Algiers, which includes Darlan in the setup, has caused some perturbation at home. I wish to emphasise strongly that unless Darlan is accepted, we should have to proceed to immediate occupation of the whole of North Africa with all that entails and probably a renewal of hostilities with the French. If we reject Darlan we lose all chance of an early occupation of Tunisia. Kingpin's influence on the French is practically nil. I believe that Darlan has honestly tried to bring out the Toulon fleet. Nobody likes having him, but he is the only man who has the necessary following, particularly amongst French officialdom throughout the region."

Darlan was certainly not, as Eisenhower said in his communiqués, "the one leader in North Africa whom all elements in North Africa will recognize." If this had been the case, all would have flocked to his standard. Within days, and despite issuing proclamations "in the name of the Marshal," opposition to Darlan took a distinct, definable form. By no stretch of the imagination could Darlan, to quote Eisenhower again, be said to lead "a provisional government." Eisenhower, unconsciously emphasizing Roosevelt's determination to create a satellite administration, ignored the political reality that government implies either consent or coercion. Darlan was about to "govern" North Africa on the basis of his opportunism—backed by an autocratic, indeed punitive, Vichy administration.

VI

Eisenhower was certainly right about "feeling at home." Reaction to the 14 November agreement was swift and strong. But the reaction was much stronger in London than Washington. This was true not only because de Gaulle's Fighting France—civil and military—was based there, but also due to the fact that Darlan's seizure of power pushed Churchill, finally, into support for the former's *political* ambitions in terms of French Résistance.

Churchill hesitated for months before he consummated this crucial change in British policy, but the first step was taken even before the Clark-Darlan Agreement was publicly announced. The agreement finally concentrated British minds about Vichy, disposing of residual doubts, providing de Gaulle with his political bridgehead in North Africa, preliminary to establishing himself in France. Churchill responded to this concentration of argument, and emotion; these influences were all the more powerful in stemming initially from the man on the spot, none other than Admiral Cunningham. He remained in Algiers after Eisenhower's return to Gibraltar, and despite the 14 November telegram supporting the latter's exercise in wish fulfillment, decided, "in ten minutes," that Darlan was extremely bad news for the Allies, and should be kept in his place.

Cunningham never minced words. He was particularly concerned that Darlan's appointment of Giraud as "Head of the Armed Forces" was coupled with repudiation of de Gaulle. Darlan was determined to assert himself: "I have expressed an intention that de Gaulle will not be recognized here, nor will any of his Government." Cunningham was incensed by Darlan's arrogation of power, and alarmed at its implications. Cunningham concluded his 15 November message by stating: "I immediately instructed Clark to inform Darlan of my strong disapproval of this reference to de Gaulle. What we must avoid at all costs, although we do not admit this here, is the taking over of the whole region under military government. This would be the result of repudiation of [the] Darlan gang."

It is no exaggeration to say that, within hours rather than days, Churchill, his ministers, and Whitehall were reacting adversely to the implications of the agreement—and to Cunningham's implied warning: If Darlan is not confined, he and his "gang" must be repudiated, even eliminated. Cunningham knew that his words would be heeded in London. On the 14th, Eisenhower had told Churchill: "Please be assured that I have too often listened to your sage advice to be completely hand-cuffed and blindfolded by all of the slickers with which this part of the world is so thickly populated." Eisenhower was trying to convince himself that his judgment was sound, that bridge was a better training for backing political gambles than poker. Cunningham could understand Eisenhower's dilemma, but had little faith in his judgment. Cunningham's 15 November communiqué, so far as it related to Darlan and de Gaulle, was intended to start a chain reaction.

Yet Churchill faced mounting problems in dealing with Roosevelt. Churchill, for all his antique, dedicated imperialism, was a cultivated European, who instinctively believed that de Gaulle meant what he said. De Gaulle utilized low cunning on occasion, but he never attempted to flatter Churchill, or treat the issues that were common to both as other than urgent and serious. Churchill, for all his frequent irritation with de Gaulle, respected him as a man, one who shared equivalent values. With Roosevelt, by stark contrast, Churchill was driven to blandishment, and seemed not insensible to flattery in return. As the war progressed, this unequal relationship evolved to the point where Churchill was driven to inconsistency, fulsomely grateful to Roosevelt one day, animated by pride and conviction the next. De Gaulle saw all this, and did not hesitate to take advantage of Churchill's dilemma.

In the early hours of the agreement, Roosevelt set out to flatter. He told Churchill on the 11th: "I am very happy with the latest news of your splendid campaign in Egypt [heading doggedly for Tunis, Montgomery's forces had just recaptured Tobruk], and of the success that has attended our *joint* landing in West and North Africa. This brings up the additional steps which should be taken when and if the south shore of the Mediterranean is cleared and under control. It is hoped that you with your Chiefs of Staff in London and I with the Combined Staff here make a survey of the possibilities including forward movements directed against Sardinia, Sicily, Italy, Greece and other Balkan areas, including the possibility of obtaining Turkish support for an attack through the Black Sea against Germany's flank."

This was heady stuff, which Roosevelt hoped would be strong enough to distract Churchill's attention from the immediate and urgent issue of whether or not Darlan should rule the roost in North—and West—Africa. Although Churchill must have known, even in the midst of his temporary euphoria, that Roosevelt did not mean a word of what he said about Greece, the Balkans, and Turkey (as events throughout 1943 and 1944 were comprehensively to prove), his reply of the 13th was effusive. The British Chiefs of Staff would immediately be summoned to discuss Roosevelt's momentous conversion to a Mediterranean strategy. Meanwhile, TORCH and "the splendid campaign in Egypt" were certainly occasions for rejoicing. On Sunday the 15th, the sound of church bells was heard over English fields and cities for the first time since the fateful summer of 1940.

Yet, on 13 November, a mere two days after Roosevelt tempted Churchill with strategic fables, the British governing establishment mounted a counterattack on the Clark-Darlan Agreement which was sustained with growing determination until, six weeks later, Fernand Bonnier emerged from the shadows. This counterattack was sustained in London, Washington—and Algiers. The strength and consistency of this British opposition—preceding, then complementing Gaullist

objectives and intentions—can only be understood if the vigor
of protest from Algiers to London, and London to Washington, is appreciated.

Anthony Eden provided the first response to the 8 November SIS warning from Algiers, and to de Gaulle's demand that
day for a mission of investigation. Eden was frequently, one
might almost write habitually, dominated by Churchill on major
foreign-policy issues. Nothing is more significant, therefore, in
considering the British counterattack on the Clark-Darlan
Agreement than Churchill's determination to give Eden overall command of operations. By the 13th Eden had sent Mack—
in Algiers—a long, detailed telegram which not only questioned the agreement's essentials, but also requested Eisenhower to accept a mission from the French National Committee.

Darlan's "inclusion in a French administration in North
Africa, even with General Giraud's consent, would cause more
trouble than it would be worth." Eden, having ordered Mack
to have no direct dealings with Darlan, further instructed him
to emphasize to Eisenhower that "we owed allegiance to General de Gaulle [who] had been with us through all the dark
days." Eden also told Lord Halifax (the British ambassador in
Washington) to convey the same message to Cordell Hull.
Neither Eisenhower's nor Cunningham's messages of the 14th
deflected attention in London from the central political issue:
Darlan's seizure of power. Indeed, as we have seen, Cunningham's communiqué of the 15th alerted Whitehall in general and the Foreign Office in particular to the deeper
implications of that seizure: not merely exclusion of de Gaulle
from a place in arbitrating the future of France, but rejection
and extinction of Fighting France, above all if it attempted to
establish a political base in French North Africa.

On the 16th, Churchill stated plainly to Roosevelt "that he
could not regard the arrangement [agreement] as permanent
or healthy." Churchill added, "We feel sure you will consult
us on the long-term steps, pursuing always the aim of uniting
all Frenchmen who will fight Hitler." Churchill also urged

Roosevelt to keep the agreement secret. Roosevelt ignored the implied reference to British support for de Gaulle, and the request for secrecy. Cunningham's warnings about de Gaulle had, however, been repeated by him to Eisenhower. Although once again a prisoner on the Rock, Eisenhower ordered Clark to remove any slighting references to de Gaulle from Darlan's public pronouncements. After only one day of Darlan (the 13th), Eisenhower had sensed that the agreement might well "cause more trouble than it would be worth."

De Gaulle again saw Churchill on the 16th. De Gaulle has given his own account, but forbore to state that Churchill exclaimed "Darlan should be shot." De Gaulle reported this outburst to Jacques Soustelle, but it may be added here that the robust Churchillian sentiment was echoed throughout Whitehall as the counteroffensive gathered momentum. "The base and squalid" deal had not yet received the full force of Churchill's condemnation and opposition, but de Gaulle's great protest to him struck home:

> You invoke strategic reasons [for the Clark-Darlan Agreement], but it is a strategic error to place oneself in a situation contradictory to the moral character of the war. We are no longer in the Italian Renaissance when one hired the myrmidons of Milan or the mercenaries of Florence. In any case we do not put them at the head of a liberated people. Today we make war with our own blood and souls and the suffering of nations.

De Gaulle pressed home the attack. Although the agreement's details were not officially known in London until 21 November—and then only in anodyne form—de Gaulle had his own sources. Even had no source supplied damning detail, de Gaulle's instinct and suspicions drove him to cast Darlan as a threat not merely to France but to Europe as well. De Gualle produced messages from the French Résistance. "They show that France is plunged in amazement. Imagine the incalculable consequences if France came to the conclusion that for the Allies, liberation meant Darlan."

Churchill hardly needed de Gaulle's messages from France, résistant, or otherwise. Baker Street had already expressed collective "horror" at the agreement. Lord Selborne, SOE's Ministerial head, was fully informed. Colin Gubbins saw Selborne on the 18th—the very day, coincidentally, that Bonnier, at BRANDON's Cap Matifou headquarters, drew the short straw for Darlan's assassination. Gubbins warned Selborne "of the extreme danger of the present situation in Algiers." A SOE report also stated: "The Agreement with Darlan has produced violent reactions on all our subterranean organizations in enemy-occupied countries, particularly in France, where it has had a blasting and withering effect." Protest—and fear—was not confined to SOE. Mere mention of Darlan's name produced strong reactions. "The staff dealing with France in PWE and the BBC resigned almost to a man." Before 8 November, SOE and its clandestine confrères elsewhere in the Whitehall labyrinth rarely gained Churchill's direct attention. Darlan's apotheosis opened up channels of communication that had been blocked for two years.

But Roosevelt had made a deal with Darlan. Churchill's words to de Gaulle on 16 November must be read in the context of this bitter realization. "Darlan has no future. You stand for honour. Yours is the true path, you alone will remain." Churchill then again gave de Gaulle permission to broadcast on the BBC so that he could "let France know he opposed the present dealings." De Gaulle left Number Ten Downing Street more than ever inflexible—but convinced, with the instinct of a born politician, that Churchill would now commit and deploy all his formidable resources in the rejection and destruction of the Clark-Darlan Agreement.

Such, indeed, proved to be the case, although protest alone could ensure neither rejection nor destruction. The counterattack was an operation that combined the majesty of Churchill's rebukes with the persistent questioning of Eden and colleagues. But it was an operation that depended for final success on recourse to violence. Churchill's message to Roosevelt of the 16th does, however, mark the first phase of the battle:

> I ought to let you know that very deep currents of feeling are stirred by the arrangement with Darlan. The more I reflect upon it the more convinced I become that it can only be a temporary expedient, justifiable solely by the stress of battle. We must not overlook the serious political injury which may be done to our cause, not only in France but throughout Europe, by the feeling that we are ready to make terms with the local Quislings. Darlan has an odious record. It is he who has inculcated in the French Navy its malignant disposition by promoting his creatures to command. It is but yesterday that French sailors were sent to their death against your line of battle off Casablanca, and now, for the sake of power and office, Darlan plays the turncoat. A permanent arrangement with Darlan or the formation of a Darlan government in French North Africa would not be understood by the great masses of ordinary people, whose simple loyalties are our strength.

Roosevelt's reply of the 17th took the form of a press conference, during which he said:

> I have accepted General Eisenhower's political arrangements made for the time being in Northern and Western Africa.
>
> I thoroughly understand and approve the feeling in the United States and Great Britain and among all the other United Nations . . . The present temporary arrangement in North and West Africa is only a temporary expedient, justified solely by the stress of battle.
>
> The present temporary arrangement has accomplished two military objectives. The first was to save American and British lives, and French lives on the other hand.
>
> The second was the vital factor of time. The temporary

arrangement has made it possible to avoid a "mopping-up" period in Algiers and Morocco which might have taken a month or two to consummate. Such a period would have delayed the concentration for the attack from the west on Tunis, and we hope on Tripoli . . .

Admiral Darlan's proclamation assisted in making a "mopping-up" period unnecessary. Temporary arrangements made with Admiral Darlan apply, without exception, to the current local situation only.

Roosevelt chose a press conference to mislead Churchill and to conceal from him that Darlan was to be "political head in France." Roosevelt was playing a long suit, his cards close to his chest. "In his private talks he [Roosevelt] made it clear he would use Darlan as long as he needed him." Darlan took the point. Clark ordered Darlan to broadcast Roosevelt's "temporary expedient" statement on Radio Maroc and Radio Alger. Darlan refused—and was successful in his refusal. Darlan, in practice, and with few exceptions, controlled and censored the North African press and radio from the time he seized power. Darlan was aided and abetted in censorship by none other than Jean Rigault, who, by 24 November, had become "Secretary for Internal Affairs and the Press" in a North African administration more repressive and racialist than anything manufactured by Pétain and Laval.

Roosevelt ignored isolated State Department protests about the Clark-Darlan Agreement, but he was, at all times, sensitive to American public opinion. Congress was in no mood to question the Clark-Darlan Agreement, but the press had become increasingly Gaullist in sympathy as certain correspondents discovered facts for themselves. America's most famous newspaperman, Walter Lippmann, is a case in point. Lippmann, although a Jew, had hitherto been lukewarm about Darlan and his ambitions. But Lippmann wrote to Hull on 17 November in words designed to enrage both the recipient and his president. "I urge you to dispel any idea that we should recognize and uphold Quisling governments. Darlan has joined the Allies

only to maintain Vichy's authority in France's overseas territories. American policy should be to force him out of all the
favors he is capable of doing for us and [to] liquidate any political authority he might claim. He is in our power and we must
firmly insist on not letting him put us in his power." Lippmann
concluded by criticizing Murphy for "miscalculation in the
political preparations" for the Allied landings in North Africa.

Lippmann went public on the 19th. Hull, "whose vanity
was matched by a ferocious temper"—and was also an old,
tired man—immediately berated Lippmann for attacking "the
record of the American Government." Lippmann replied by a
further criticism of Murphy which in view of impending and
subsequent developments in North Africa, should also be quoted:
"He is a most agreeable and ingratiating man whose warm
heart causes him to form passionate personal attachments rather
than cool and detached judgments. American policy is in the
hands of naive and gullible men."

Eden was well aware of this conflict in the American mind.
On 17 November, Eden stressed to Halifax: "It's a question of
Darlan or de Gaulle. We can't have both." A Foreign Office
note of the same date states the case more bluntly: "The questions (i) how to apply this policy [that of the 'temporary expedient'] so long as Darlan is in authority, and (ii) at what point
and by what methods Darlan is to be eliminated must be governed by military considerations. But as soon as the military
situation permits it would be desirable to get rid of Darlan, and
policy meanwhile should be shaped, so far as possible, with
this object in view."

Eden endorsed the note, and did so to Halifax with the
addition of a double reminder: "We are fighting for international decency, and Darlan is the antithesis of this. It should
be possible to find [in North Africa and France] men who, even
if they have not openly come out on our side in the past, were
not 'contaminated by Vichy' and had not actively cooperated
with the enemy. These men could form, not a Government,
but a Provisional Administration under which we should hope

to unite all 'resisting Frenchmen,' including those who had joined Fighting France.'' De Gaulle could not have wished for a more positive expression of British support than the convictions—*and* course of action—encapsulated in Eden's endorsement and reminder.

VII

By late November, British officials and senior commanders in North Africa were all but openly opposed to Darlan. Anderson noted in his diary: "The 'old gang' [Darlan and his adherents] assumed that a change of coat was enough and that a change of heart was unnecessary. It is a fair criticism to say this was not appreciated sufficiently quickly and that too many Vichy sympathisers were left in positions of authority too long." Not until 8 December—by which time the situation in Tunisia had deteriorated alarmingly—did Eisenhower reach the same conclusion, and draw the unavoidable inference: "If things go on like this [continued defeat for Allied forces in Tunisia] Darlan will change sides again."

Anderson's comments were based on his visits to First Army's forward units. Despite the overall failure of Allied airborne operations at this stage of the campaign, Bone had been captured by 12 November, denying Axis forces both port and airfield. Anderson immediately pushed his few thousand troops east and southeast, hoping to seize Bizerta, then attack Tunis from the north and west. But Axis counterattacks quickly halted British troops in ideal defensive terrain south of Tamera and east of Beja. The race for Tunis was lost, and Anderson was forced to cling to what had been won. He was hard put to do this, and his problems were accentuated by the attitude of Darlan's protégés—Vichy French civilian and military authorities in Tunisia.

Anderson wrote in his *unpublished* dispatch:

When, acting under instructions from General Eisenhower, I began the eastward move from Algiers, the attitude of the French forces and population in the area between Constantine and Tunis was completely unknown, and the omens were not too propitious. For General Barré, the French Commanding General in Tunisia, was definitely reported to be negotiating with the German Commander in Tunis, and, as we pressed forward this information was repeatedly confirmed. Many mayors, railway station and post-masters and other key officials with whom we had dealings as we advanced were lukewarm in their sympathies and hesitant to commit themselves openly, while a few were definitely obstructive or hostile.

I can safely generalise by saying that at this period : in the Army units we encountered, senior officers were hesitant and afraid to commit themselves; the junior officers were mainly in favour of aiding the Allies; and the men (mainly native troops) would obey orders. Amongst the people the Arabs were indifferent or inclined to be hostile, especially within the borders of Tunisia; and French civilians were in our favour but apathetic; and the civil authorities were antagonistic as a whole. If our affairs prospered all would be well—but if not?

Anderson's troops could do no more than hold on in Tunisia: the Allies were wholly on the defensive. The British government, preparing to dispatch substantial additional forces to this new, complex theater of war, intensified the diplomatic offensive. But an open breach between London and Washington—in effect, between Churchill and Roosevelt—was to be avoided if at all possible. Even Eden, de Gaulle's champion, saw the necessity to rely on diplomatic pressure—unless it should prove useless. Such reliance gave Darlan time to consolidate his power base.

Darlan did not waste the time he had gained. By mid-November Eisenhower knew that only Darlan could order French affairs in North Africa. Meanwhile, the round-up of those who were "anti-Vichy and anti many other things" continued. Anti-Semitism in the press was actively encouraged by

Rigault. Henri d'Astier, as Darlan's police and security commissioner, knew whom to threaten. The night of 8 November
had not only given Darlan his chance; events that night had
revealed that Résistance to Vichy faced many perils.

Pétain, asserting an authority that, after ATTILA, existed
only in name, had "stripped Darlan of public office" on the
16th and, on the 18th, gave Laval full power. On the 16th,
de Gaulle and FNC had publicly dissociated themselves from
"negotiations with Darlan." These rather artificial declarations provide an ironic counterpoint to Darlan's establishment
on 24 November of a "Conseil Imperial," whose members
consisted of Giraud, Noguès, Châtel—and Boisson, governor-
general of French West Africa. Bergeret, while remaining as
Darlan's chief of staff, became the Counseil's secretary-general.

Radio Morocco, reporting the advent of the Conseil, stated,
doubtless on good authority, that Darlan, as high commissioner, "would exercise the functions and prerogatives of Head
of State." Such an announcement made nonsense of Roosevelt's assertions that he could dispense with Darlan anytime
he wished. The same was true of Eisenhower's claim—also on
the 19th—that the high commission was confined to purely
administrative tasks in support of the Allies.

Eisenhower's "mandatory optimism," as he characteristi-
cally called it in a letter to General Clark of 15 November, was
of short duration—by the 18th he was privately stressing Darlan's "crookedness" to his chief of staff, Bedell Smith. But, in
the weeks immediately following D-Day, the commander-in-
chief was so immersed in the minutiae of promotions and favors
that he found little time for the real issues, political or military.
Anderson, in Eisenhower's opinion, was doing "a grand job"—
but he remained isolated and exposed nonetheless. Cunningham, by contrast, although burdened with comparable
command problems, was determined that supporting Eisenhower did not preclude questioning the wider implications of
Darlan's seizure of power. Neither Mack nor the Political

Warfare Executive team attached to AFHQ functioned effectively until late November; in terms of immediate British opposition to Darlan's ambitions, Churchill personally and Whitehall collectively relied to a great extent on Cunningham's acrid running commentary about the situation in Algiers.

Even today, doubt remains about what Churchill really knew of Roosevelt's most far-reaching intentions concerning Darlan. There is no doubt, however, that once Churchill awoke to the true nature of "the base and squalid deal" he utilized all means within his power to destroy it. On 14 November Eden had instructed Mack to prepare for the visit of a FNC delegation to Algiers. This was a premature move, foiled by Mack's lack of authority and Eisenhower's "mandatory optimism." The commander-in-chief said no. But Cunningham's communiqué of the 18th, in which he commented that "Darlan sees himself as the natural successor to Pétain" alerted London to wider considerations, and raised the British diplomatic counterattack to a new level of intensity.

Darlan boasted of his successor role to Eisenhower and Cunningham. By mid-November Darlan's proclamations as high commissioner had acquired a sinister tone of arrogance. On the 19th the understandably confused subjects of Pétain's successor were told: "I intend to maintain French unity and sovereignty. I shall exact from everybody the strictest obedience and most perfect discipline. I ask you to lift your hearts together with me towards the Motherland which suffers and its revered chief. Being certain of the ardent support and the ardent aspirations of the majority of Frenchmen in the Motherland, we Frenchmen and Mohammedans in Africa will continue our efforts to achieve in order and discipline the aim we have set ourselves—the liberation of France through the Empire." *Attentisme* was, officially, at an end. Personal rule replaced it.

Eisenhower defended Darlan—also on 19 November—in a report to the Combined Chiefs of Staff. Eisenhower reported that Darlan was "doing all he could to resist the Axis." But in

London such mandatory protestations were ceasing to convince, or to assuage doubt. Darlan's real objectives were becoming plain. In invoking and repudiating Pétain as it suited him; in asserting an unwarranted role as "Head of State"; in demanding "obedience"; above all in appealing to the twin goals of unity and empire, Darlan was going well beyond anything even remotely envisaged by Eisenhower and Clark. Darlan was raising Leahy's offer—in reality, Roosevelt's—to become "political head in France" by the process of establishing not merely a North African but an imperial political base from which no Allied diplomatic effort was likely to remove him. Darlan's protest to Eisenhower on 21 November that "I am only a lemon which the Americans will drop after they have squeezed it dry" is a wonderful example of mendacity.

By 21 November the Foreign Office had received copies of the Clark-Darlan Agreement, due for publication the following day. But neither Eden nor his subordinates were much interested in the agreement's formal provisions, fine print, or unpublished details. A Foreign Office note of the 21st stated that "the existing French Administration in North Africa may be equated with Vichy in general and Darlan in particular." The note further stated: "The status, command, functions, employment, rights and privileges of French land, sea, and air forces will remain under French direction." But these comments merely reflected an accurate assessment of what Darlan had achieved. Neither the Foreign Office nor, indeed, the British government and Whitehall as a whole, believed Eisenhower's protestations. What, then, was to be done?

The collective British view was expressed by Cunningham, who stated on the 18th that "the Agreement will not repeat not be accepted in its present form." British staff officers at AFHQ read of the agreement's provisions with "dismay." At SOE headquarters in London the reaction of "horror" was soon to be intensified as "shoals of messages" from British-supported Résistance circuits throughout France came pouring in to Baker Street, all of them expressing detestation at the idea of Allied deals with Darlan, and foreboding as to what might follow.

In such circumstances, and with Darlan striving to establish an impregnable position for himself, the British government's queries to Washington on the agreement's published provisions failed to sound a warning note. Neither Churchill nor Eden was able to hint at Darlan's elimination by robust means; indeed, no thought in London had yet been given to that ultimate solution. Roosevelt was able to take the queries in his stride. He assured Churchill that "he did not want to elevate Darlan to the position of a national plenipotentiary." Neither Churchill nor Eden was inclined to accept this statement, but the latter's riposte on 21 November nevertheless remained studiedly diplomatic: "The terms of the Agreement were unnecessarily favourable to Admiral Darlan."

Churchill who, unlike Roosevelt, appreciated the fact that TORCH as a military operation was in danger of becoming the fiasco that Whitehall had feared, was loath to badger Washington again directly. The president would only send a temporizing message to Eisenhower, who would thus waste time in devising misleading replies when he should be fighting the Axis. Nevertheless, Eden instructed Halifax on 21 November to inform the United States government that the British government accepted neither the agreement as a whole as other than a purely provisional arrangement, nor Darlan's assertions as to the authority vested in him.

Halifax was also instructed to remind Hull that most of what Darlan asserted "appeared to be in conflict with the president's intention [as given in his 17 November press conference statement] that the arrangement with Admiral Darlan should only be temporary and local." By 22 November, Churchill, Eden, all who mattered in London knew the reality of the problem: Roosevelt and Darlan in combination, indefinitely. In these circumstances, the diplomatic counterattack would lose momentum if outright rejection of the agreement and an open breach with Roosevelt only forced the latter into an even closer association with Darlan.

Churchill's and Eden's tactics were to sustain the counterattack by maintaining steady pressure. But hopes of success were decreasing as the agreement was published. By 22 November, the British counterattack was being seriously considered in terms of the third element : clandestine operations. A British intelligence summary at this time noted: "The President [Roosevelt] was inclined to think of French North Africa as conquered and occupied when a formal Agreement had been signed with the French."

The collective British view was that the president had to be proved wrong. Sir Alexander Cadogan (permanent under secretary at the Foreign Office) noted in his diary for 14 November: "We shall do no good until we have killed Darlan," thus echoing a conviction to which Churchill had first given expression on the 9th. A fortnight later, the conviction was becoming the basis for an unavoidable necessity. It was not until 8 December that Mack in Algiers actually stressed to the Foreign Office: "Darlan must be got rid of : the question is when." Thus the issue had become one of when, not whether.

VIII

At Ain Tya, some twelve miles east of Algiers, BRANDON gave seventy young Frenchmen the protection of British uniforms. These résistants came from various quarters—*Les Chantiers*, the Algiers patriot group, the French Army. Several had participated in the abortive coup of 8 November, others, *aspirants* in more than one sense, believed the French Army would only be worthy to fight again when the stain of Vichy had been expunged. All were threatened by Darlan. Attachment to BRANDON—if not, strictly speaking, recruitment by that mission—ensured not only protection but pay, and rations. The

résistants were issued with pay books, and borne on BRAN-
DON's ration strength. The Cross of Lorraine was worn as a
shoulder flash. In all other respects, Henri Rosencher, Philip
Ragueneau, Fernand Bonnier, Gilbert Sabatier, and their
compatriots were under British comand. "These were the people who would have helped us" recalls a former member of
BRANDON. "All we could offer them was immunity from persecution."

True—yet this group of résistants to Vichy as such, to Darlan in person, were not only prospective Gaullists but retained
links with others in Algiers who had also been active on 8
November. By the time Bonnier drew the short straw a unit
was forming in Algiers, armed with British weapons, intended
to be the cadre for "special services." The Corps Franc d'Afrique,
later commanded by General Goislard de Monsabert—one of
the few senior officers in Algeria to commit himself immediately after the Allied landings—collectively saw Giraud as their
man; in doing so, the Corps Franc attracted Frenchmen who
opposed Darlan without espousing de Gaulle. Henri d'Astier
kept an eye on the Corps Franc, as he did on most things.

The murky air of Algiers was not breathed at Ain Tya or
Cap Matifou. A battle was raging in Tunisia : BRANDON,
reinforced by *aspirant* Frenchmen, prepared to move east in
support of First Army. On the evening of 18 November, four
of the *aspirants* sat in a barn, and, almost on impulse, agreed
to draw straws for Darlan's assassination. Patriotism strengthened the impulse into resolve; bitter resentment at Darlan's
seizure of power transformed resolve into a fateful, fatal decision. Fernand Bonnier, twenty, intense, rebellious, drew the
short straw, to his horror. Philippe Ragueneau, older, tougher,
offered to take Bonnier's place. This chivalrous gesture refused,
Bonnier was tied to fortune's wheel.

On the 19th, BRANDON moved east, in support of the
First Army. Bonnier was left in charge of Gilbert Sabatier,
Matifou's camp commandant; then he returned to Algiers, and
to MASSINGHAM. Weapons training at Cap Matifou had been

rudimentary. Henri Rosencher recalls: "Firing on the range with rifles was about the size of it." MASSINGHAM was prepared to remedy that deficiency, in its own rather distinctive fashion. Bonnier was ordered to attend a course in small arms and sabotage, preparatory to the task of training agents for operations in "Le Sud." Bonnier was accommodated at the Corps Franc camp adjoining MASSINGHAM's headquarters, Le Club des Pins.

Thus the environs of Algiers provided sanctuary for résistants. In Algiers itself, Darlan's seizure of power had not only led to the revival of *Combat* but the appearance of posters on the walls of Algiers and other cities proclaiming "Darlan to the gallows!" and like sentiments. The Aboulkers, father and son, had gone underground. A prospectively Gaullist movement was conceived. But genuine resistance to Vichy was born only after 8 November. José Abouiker catches the truth: "Before the landings, Murphy and I were Bob and José. Now he doesn't know me." An American journalist catches the mood: "The army brass hats and the people of the Prefecture whom we arrested hate us," one of the younger men said. "They hate us because we know what cowards they are. You should have seen how miserably they acted when they saw the tommy guns, the brave Jew-baiters. The chief of the secret police, who has been of course restored to his position, kneeled on the floor and wept, begging one of my friends to spare his life. Imagine his feelings toward the man who spared him! Another friend, a doctor, is to be mobilized—in a labor camp, of course—under the military jurisdiction of a general whom *he* arrested."

Darlan had seized power. His punitive authority, by late November, seemed absolute. But fate stalked him nonetheless. A senior British officer, serving on the staff of Churchill's War Cabinet, paid a visit to North Africa in early December. He noted in his diary: "It is difficult to lay on an efficient assassination." Difficult, but not impossible.

6

"The Urgency
of Elimination"

I

Algiers, late November 1942, was a city where rumor, intrigue, repression, and expectation flourished in the corrupting air of Darlan's regime. The only signs of war were in the port and roadstead. There, the Royal Navy and Allied merchant shipping lay bow to stern, targets for the Luftwaffe, virtually defenseless against sustained attack. But the real war had gone east, to the Tunisian front; air raids on Algiers were few and ineffectual.

The Luftwaffe, flying from all-weather airfields adjoining Tunis and Bizerta, struck daily at Anderson's sodden troops, achieving a mastery of the skies that was to last well into the New Year. The Royal Air Force and the United States Army Air Force, operating from dirt strips in the forward areas or from good, but distant, airfields in the rear, could do little but wait for the rain to stop. The rain did not stop. In Tunisia, it rained, and rained, and rained. Anderson was code-named GROUCH by his American compatriots. Anderson had something to grouch about.

Eisenhower was perplexed, intermittently optimistic, frequently depressed by a situation in which, as he said on 4 December to an old friend from West Point days, "I think sometimes I am a cross between a one-time soldier, a pseudo-statesman, a jack-legged politician and a crooked diplomat." Darlan, ensconced in the Palais d'Été, assessed Eisenhower's predicament accurately, and exploited it ruthlessly.

Darlan was master, and only with his death could Eisenhower assert himself. Eisenhower's instinct was to propitiate Darlan in the hope, if hardly the conviction, that he would thereby not desert the Allied cause, whatever reverses might be suffered in Tunisia. Harold Macmillan believed that Darlan, "once bought, stayed bought." Not so, not at all.

Darlan, his admiral's uniform exchanged for dark suit and homburg hat, recreated Vichy in Algiers. The SOL, officially disbanded after the Allied landings, but at once resurrected, was Darlan's Milice; the Gardes Mobiles, his private army. Darlan was quite content to let Giraud play soldier, and was adroit in using the latter as a means of pleading with Roosevelt for the French Army in North Africa to be rearmed with American weapons. Darlan was playing for higher stakes than anything Giraud could envisage.

Darlan's regime functioned. Children went to school. Taxes were collected. The trains did not run on time, because even Darlan conceded something to the Allies' military needs, and there was not enough coal. There was not enough coal, even though Spanish Republican prisoners were forced to dig it. Protests to Murphy at this continued incarceration, worsened by forced labor, were met with a rejoinder that revealed how completely he lived in Darlan's pocket: Murphy "smilingly explained that, whatever the justice of the procedure might be, it was important that they be kept working because they were digging coal."

Eisenhower was not only trapped in a political dilemma, he was also surrounded by advisers whose inexperience, or indifference, led them, with honorable exceptions, either to ignore or deny the nature of a fascist administration. Noguès exceeded Darlan in his persecution of Jews, or indeed anyone who stood in his way. Protests were also made to Murphy at Noguès's absolute control of the press and radio; his support for the SOL in Morocco to the point where it even furnished a guard of honor at a French-American military ceremony; the distribution of antidemocratic books and pamphlets; the continued appearance of *La Voix Française*, an avowedly Vichy publication, which ranted interminably about "the Jewish peril, the Bolshevik peril, and the Democratic peril." Noguès's hatred of the Blum government and the Popular Front had been common knowledge. Murphy allowed that hatred to fester in an atmosphere where any profession of democratic belief was dangerous.

Percy Winner of the Office of War Information reported to Robert Sherwood that Murphy ignored Noguès's repression; he lived in his pocket also. Winner stated, with some understandable bitterness, that Murphy was no longer "at home" to members of the Algiers patriot group. Winner reported: "These young men are not of the stamp of the persons with whom Murphy now deals. Some are Jews. Some are Democrats. Some are merely brave persons who hate tyranny, including the present French tyranny. Murphy has not taken the trouble to track down rumours that some of them are still in jail or have been sent back to jail."

But Darlan would not be eliminated by reliance on emotional Gaullism, by some vague surmise that "the street" must arise and demand liberation from the yoke of a fascist regime. Darlan would be eliminated by diplomatic pressure—or by other means. "Darlan is Vichy, and Vichy is the rule of the same wealthy and selfish interests which have ruined France. There may have to be civil war before the Darlan regime goes under. Darlan must go some time." René Capitant in *Combat?* No. A reasoned protest by honest Frenchmen? No, or not quite, and not yet. The sentiments, toned down before being sent to London on 7 December, are those of the British Political Warfare Executive Team in Algiers, endorsed by Harold Mack.

Mack, in Eisenhower's messages to Churchill and the Combined Chiefs of Staff of 14 November, was to be one of those "capable men who will cooperate with Darlan." Mack, behind his Irish charm and humorous acceptance of life's absurdities, was a capable man who had not the slightest intention of cooperating with Darlan. On 26 November, Eden had categorically instructed Mack to avoid Darlan, to accord him no recognition, to demonstrate, civilly but unequivocally, that, as the Foreign Office representative in Algiers, he and Darlan had nothing to say to each other.

II

Eisenhower and Murphy were committed to a policy of propitiation. Excepting those who had joined MASSINGHAM and BRANDON or continued to act in secret, anti-Vichy elements in North Africa had changed sides, gone underground, or were bemused. Mack and his colleagues, by complete contrast, were free to urge Darlan's elimination, not only because the British government demanded it, but also because their own observation and convictions complemented what Whitehall collectively came to believe as a fact: Darlan threatened the campaign in Tunisia; he menaced the campaign of Résistance in France.

Eden and Mack gained a powerful ally in Cunningham. He was among the first in Algiers to warn London of a third danger to British interests from Darlan, one that matched Tunisia and France in gravity. Darlan's wider ambitions have been mentioned earlier in the context of the Conseil Imperial, and his arrogation of a role to which he was in no sense entitled: "Head of State." On 2 December, Eisenhower rather feebly told Marshall: ". . . I do not see how I can prevent this group [the Conseil] from using any label for themselves that they desire."

Yet Eisenhower was aware that the Conseil posed dangers for Allied unity. Eisenhower was opposed to Darlan's plan of establishing a "French Imperial Federation." Even Roosevelt jibbed—while, at this time, offering Darlan all possible medical facilities in the United States for treating his son's infantile paralysis. Roosevelt may have made a compassionate gesture; his real interest was to keep Darlan in play. Eisenhower knew, because he was told, that the British Chiefs of Staff were strongly opposed to Darlan's pretensions. But Eisenhower did nothing to curb them.

During the last week of November, Darlan and Boisson concocted in Algiers a scheme, masked by the Conseil Imperial and the "Imperial Federation," whereby a new version of Vichy would be established at Dakar, in Martinique, at Jibouti— where de Gaulle's troops were on the point of displacing the administration. Darlan also began writing to French diplomatic missions that retained links with Vichy and, in some sense, still represented France overseas beyond the imperial ambit.

Darlan was careful not to write to the Vichy embassy in Washington, but if we look at his extreme activity during this period but one conclusion is possible: Conscious not only that the tide of events in Tunisia could turn against the Allies, but also that Roosevelt and Eisenhower might then see him in his true colors, Darlan strove to establish a base in North Africa in which he could not only entrench himself, but from which he could extend his influence. Darlan knew himself to be a potential victim of fate, but was determined to play out the game to the last card.

Darlan exploited all Eisenhower's credulity in order to attain his objectives. On 24 November Eisenhower assured the Combined Chiefs of Staff that "Darlan has stated to me that he will conduct the affairs of North Africa on a liberal and enlightened basis." This extraordinary assurance was given just at the moment when not only was Churchill's diplomatic counteroffensive gaining momentum and receiving reinforcement from all that Mack, the PWE, and SOE were reporting from Algiers, but also as British public and political resentment at Roosevelt's deal with Darlan reached a crescendo.

> On November 26 questions were asked in the House of Commons about Admiral Darlan. When this traitor and arch-enemy of England was first recognized by General Eisenhower as the Government of North Africa at the beginning of the campaign, the public had with some hesitation accepted the plea that the step was one of purely military expediency which seemed to justify itself by its results. Now, however, that the Admiral was commencing to arrogate to himself almost dictatorial powers the British public was becoming very uneasy over the matter, nor was it entirely reassured by President Roosevelt's statement that the arrangement was only temporary.

This strongly restrained summary—from a quasi-official source—reflected Eden's conviction that Darlan not only threatened British interests but, as Macmillan commented, "tarnished" Britain's reputation as a nation that had gone to war in 1939 because fascism could no longer be appeased but must be destroyed. Eden was not only foreign secretary, and in close although frequently discordant—when not unwillingly subservient—relations with Churchill. From the beginning of November 1942 Eden had also been Leader of the House of Commons. Although this additional burden was unfortunate in two ways—Eden's health, never good, was taxed; he was not "a House of Commons man," bonhomous and buttonholing— the experience revealed how MPs thought and what the British public instinctively felt.

Loathing for Darlan was widespread in Britain—and not

least because admiration and support for de Gaulle and the Fighting French were strong, and consistent. On 25 November the *Washington Post* reported that "the British public was shocked by the Darlan deal." The *Post* was loyal to Roosevelt, but perceived, as did an increasing number of Americans, that the British public was not only shocked, but disturbed, at Britain's collaboration in a deal that appeared to be engineered exclusively in the service of American interests. On 2 December Eden told the House of Commons: "Darlan's actions are the unilateral expression of himself. They do not bind the British Government in any way." But Darlan's actions were also the expression of Roosevelt's objectives and Eisenhower's enforced acceptance of them.

On both 2 and 3 December, Darlan used his censored press to announce that "he proposed to issue an ordinance where, in the absence of a head of State who is a prisoner he assumes the prerogatives of a head of State as the repository of French sovereignty." Darlan, dealing high, banked on residual respect for Pétain among the colons, officials, and senior officers to give him the trick he had to win: an assertion of political authority. Darlan needed this authority before de Gaulle mounted *his* counteroffensive. Darlan announced, with revealing magniloquence, and with that use of the third person so characteristic of deceit: "His present purpose is limited to the establishment of a French African Authority which he hopes may eventually include other Empire elements such as Martinique."

By 4 December Eden knew about "Darlan's detailed rationilazations [*sic*] for setting up a government independent of Marshal Pétain's authority." Eisenhower did his best to keep Eden in the picture, but Mack, the PWE, and the clandestine services were a more reliable—yet an undeniably committed— source on the implications of what Darlan intended to do. Eden did not for a moment believe Darlan's assertion that "a government of France can only be established when the people of

France are free to make their choice." Eden stuck to the conviction that he had expressed to Halifax on 17 November: "It's a question of Darlan *or* de Gaulle."

Eden's support for de Gaulle did not blind him to the likelihood of the latter seeking outright political power in North Africa, subsequently in a liberated France, whether or not the people were "free to make their choice." But Eden—and his colleagues—intended that de Gaulle, not Darlan, should be the arbiter of French fortunes; that intention rested on detailed appreciations of British interests, and a conviction that Britain was fighting an ideological, clandestine war to a degree quite comparable with one fought for the preservation of the United Kingdom and the empire.

Eden would have agreed with de Gaulle's spokesman in Washington, Adrien Tixier, who on 28 November stressed to Adolf Berle of the State Department: "If Darlan ever entered France, especially at the head of a French army equipped by Americans, there would be civil war at once." For a month preceding this exchange, de Gaulle and his assorted emissaries in and to Washington had been urging Roosevelt, Hull, Sumner Welles, and anybody else they could see to understand the dangers of the Clark-Darlan Agreement. Roosevelt remained obdurate, his advisers insensitive. On 20 November, Welles had noted, testily: "Neither Frenchman [Tixier and André Philip] showed the slightest gratitude or recognized the liberation of North Africa by American forces, but insisted over and over again that the administration of North Africa must be in their own hands [that is, of the French National Committee] not later than two or three weeks—'which will give you time to occupy Tunis.' "

De Gaulle's emissaries failed to budge Roosevelt's subordinates and, in a sense, we can see why. De Gaulle had no leverage so far as Roosevelt was concerned, because whatever the truth of his assertions, he had no demonstrable or obvious following in North Africa. Even if de Gaulle had established a political base for himself in North Africa, this would not nec-

essarily have affected Roosevelt's views about French Résistance. Roosevelt did not accept the British view that de Gaulle
was the symbolic leader of that Résistance—and, prospectively, its real leader also. Roosevelt was lukewarm about resistance movements in general and de Gaulle in particular.

"On November 26 Mr Eden wrote a minute to the Prime
Minister in which he pointed out that the French authorities
in North Africa were not following the lines laid down in the
President's statement [of 17 January]. Admiral Darlan, in a
letter of November 21 to General Clark, had made it clear that
he interpreted the term 'temporary,' in relation to his own
appointment, as meaning 'until the liberation of France.' We
could be sure that the Admiral would use all his skill to fortify
himself in his present position . . . Mr. Eden . . . felt that there
were grave *military* [writer's emphasis] risks in continuing to
deal with Darlan and his associates . . .

" 'We are dealing with turncoats and blackmailers and until
the French Administration are in better hands it would not be
safe to arm them with modern weapons . . .' Mr Eden again
urged that if we did not eliminate Darlan as soon as the military situation allowed, we should be committing a political error
which might have grave consequences not only for our good
name in Europe, but for the resistance of the oppressed peoples for whose liberation we were fighting.' "

Eden had made his own convictions plain, reiterating to
Churchill what he had earlier said to Hull: "Darlan is univer-
sally distrusted and despised throughout France and occupied
Europe. General de Gaulle has made it plain he cannot work
with him. We are pledged to de Gaulle." This argument had
only strengthened Hull's determination to bind Roosevelt even
more closely to Darlan. As we shall see, this further commitment was not made absolutely, brutally clear to the British
government until 12 December, but all its implications were
apparent to Eden when he turned, almost in despair, to Churchill.

Churchill differed from Eden in temperament, experience—and responsibility. Only Churchill had to bear the burden of both propitiating and opposing Roosevelt. But Churchill was not immune from British public opinion. Nor was Churchill, however much preoccupied with reasserting some degree of independence from Roosevelt, unaware that Darlan's pretensions, not merely his fascism, threatened Britain in several distinct yet related ways. On 24 November, Mack had strongly protested to Eisenhower at Darlan's arrogation of an imperial role, and his refusal to answer a carefully worded charge from the Conseilleurs d'Etat of Morocco, Algeria, and Tunisia that he was acting totally beyond any authority vested in French law.

Once aware of Mack's protest, and knowing also that Darlan continued to invoke the "Marshal" when it suited him, Churchill remarked: "If Darlan had to shoot Marshal Pétain, he would no doubt do it in Marshal Pétain's name." By 5 December Churchill, angered by Mack's communiqué of the preceding day that Darlan considered ". . . the High Commissioner to exercise the functions and prerogatives of the Chief of State . . ." had reverted to the counteroffensive against the 22 November agreement. More to the point, Churchill alerted his closest associate on intelligence matters, Desmond Morton, to the dangers posed by Darlan. From this moment protests about Darlan from Algiers to London, and from thence to Washington, were transmuted into a subversive operation, designed to ensure his elimination.

Overtly, the British government riposted to Darlan by providing the three North African Conseilleurs d'Etat with a platform from which their protest could be made: the BBC. Darlan's administration jammed the BBC whenever possible, but something got through to the 100,000 or so in North Africa whose radios could pick up the news from London to which so many in occupied France listened, nightly.

On 27 November, the French fleet at Toulon was scuttled, an act that not only was tragic in itself but also accelerated the momentum of North African events and increased the tensions among Darlan, a far from happy Eisenhower, and the British government. Admiral De La Borde's sacrifice ushered in "the final humiliation of Vichy," in Robert Aron's deliberate words, and gave to all that occurred in France thereafter a mood, both heroic and malignant, of a nation on the edge of civil war.

This final humiliation of Vichy produced a major paradox. As Henri Michel said in *The Shadow War*, France was totally occupied by Germany, "a vast concentration camp," where indeed "each man took his way alone." Yet within this stricken France, there were two countries: ". . . the Résistance was the real country which, little by little, grew up beside the legal country which was on its death bed." None, in North Africa, was more sharply aware of this truth than Darlan. He alone, in the confusion of North African events, was in a position to know, rather than to guess or fear, what would happen next in the France for which, in some measure, he was responsible. After De La Borde scuttled the Toulon fleet on 27 November 1942, Darlan knew that his return to France depended wholly on American support for his ambition.

Writing to Leahy on the day in question, Darlan makes but slight reference to the Toulon tragedy. But the letter unwittingly betrays certain fears. Darlan's long, rambling, confused letter is not only mendacious but contradictory. The letter, however, is mainly notable for Darlan's attempt to convince Leahy that he represents the "true" France; that de Gaulle and his "dissidents" are following a different road—by implication, one that was revolutionary, and hence inimical to American interests. This was a road that "true" Frenchmen could not follow. Darlan adds: "Besides, many Frenchmen were 'Gaullists' only from hatred of the Germans and not because they felt sympathetic to that movement's leader." Darlan urges Leahy to believe "I had the certainty of rallying Northern Africa and French West Africa which I certainly could not have done had I been a 'dissident.' "

We can see the cards that Darlan deals. He ignores the fact that some French territories had rallied to de Gaulle in

1940, just as Pétain, Laval, and he himself began their tortuous collaboration with Hitler. Darlan, bluffing, hopes to convince Leahy that, unlike Laval, he has "personal popularity in
France"; further, "the French Empire still stands"—by implication yet again, Darlan is its legitimate representative, indeed,
by his own rhetoric, its "Head of State." Thus—but only thus—
"France will totally revive." So much for the squeezed lemon.
Nevertheless, the letter, construed in its entirety, is that of a
man who is forced to even more extreme measures, not only
because of an innately authoritarian nature, but also because,
as in Vichy France, there was no solid foundation of genuinely
popular support or even orchestrated acclamation to sustain
what passed for policies.

Eisenhower believed he could deal with Darlan, propitiate him, let him play at imperial politics—provided, in doing
so he injured no American interest, foreswore further treachery, or did not change sides again. The message that Eisenhower sent to Marshall on 3 December, in which he summarizes
the intense opposition that Darlan and Boisson expressed to de
Gaulle and all his works—but primarily because he, too, nour-
ished imperial pretensions—was well received in Washington.
Provided Darlan maintained his virulent opposition to de Gaulle,
he was unlikely to double-cross Eisenhower. That, at all events,
was how Washington read the entrails.

Neither the British government, nor its advisers, could afford
detachment where Darlan was concerned. The necessity for
action against Darlan increased with every passing day. A copy
of Eisenhower's 3 December wire to Marshall was transmitted
to London—Cunningham again the agent—and therein the
advocates for Darlan's elimination read the former's version of
events:

> It is difficult to exaggerate the degree of suspicion with
> which these men [Darlan and Boisson] view British inten-

tions . . . All of us [they say] have every confidence in you and in the United States govt. But if the British are completely above board in this matter [acceptance of Darlan and Boisson as arbiters, with American collaboration, of French West Africa's adhesion to the "Imperial Federation"] why do they not cease their airplane flights over my [Boisson's] territory? Why do they not make de Gaulle stop these annoying raids by Central Africans on my borders? Why do they not stop this senseless de Gaulle propaganda in Central Africa [from Brazzaville Radio]?

Eisenhower was reduced to saying at the end of his communiqué, and much as before:

My point in all this is that it is necessary for us to preserve the attitude that we are treating with a friend rather than an enemy . . . we attempt to be magnanimous and ostentatiously trustful. Frequently some detail can be exchanged for a big advantage and that is what we are trying to get when we ask for the full use of French West Africa.

Neither the British government nor Whitehall swallowed Eisenhower's protestations. Eisenhower was trying to propitiate Darlan; the British government was committed to support of de Gaulle, and every message from Algiers, whatever the source, that indicated hostility and opposition to him only strengthened Whitehall's determination to eliminate Darlan by one means or another.

By early December, Whitehall collectively had begun to understand another, and most potent, factor in the great tangle of TORCH which also seems to have eluded Washington. Roosevelt, in his determination to collaborate with Darlan, had increased the risk of civil war in France. The Clark-Darlan Agreement was a surrender of American initiative to the ambitions and calculations of a political turncoat. Growing opposition to Darlan in late November and early December not only reflected backing for de Gaulle in the context of British support for French Résistance. The opposition was also based on the conviction that a fascist regime in North Africa, headed by a man pursuing his own ambitions, threatened Allied grand strategy as a whole. The British believed that the aim of that strategy was to liberate occupied and Western European countries with the active support of resistance movements. Darlan's advent in North Africa threatened that strategy; his seizure of power menaced it; his determination to crush all opposition could well destroy it. Given these factors, the British Chiefs of Staff joined forces with the Foreign Office in the evolution of an anti-Darlan policy.

British opposition to Darlan was further strengthened by the support that General Georges Catroux, de Gaulle's senior representative in the Middle East—and "High Commissioner in the Levant"—gave when he arrived in London from the Middle East in late November. On the 26th, Catroux told Eden: "Darlan is an utterly unreliable opportunist." Catroux then proceeded to elaborate on this accusation. Catroux was accepted by the British Chiefs of Staff as one of their own kind. Catroux was gifted not only with soldierly virtues and diplomatic talents but, in some indefinable way, was acceptable in a sense that de Gaulle, for all his greatness, could never be to men like Alan Brooke or Sir John Dill, Chief of the Imperial General Staff and head of British Joint Staff Mission in Washington. Catroux was the most senior French officer who, after a fleeting, understandable, but not wholly creditable hesitation, had rallied to de Gaulle. But once loyal to de Gaulle, Catroux stayed loyal. In the Middle East Catroux had been the one element that prevented relations between Churchill and de Gaulle from being strained almost to disruption.

Catroux, once he had made up his mind about de Gaulle, remained consistent in his acts, not only his convictions. "The senior man made it clear by every word, every gesture, by the turn he gave to every observation, that he accorded complete subservience to his junior and would take the maximum care to avoid crossing him. His innate tact and knowledge of men and things led him to realize he was dealing with a man who might conceivably break but would certainly not bend."

De Gaulle was, perhaps, more of a Roman than a Greek, but the comment is apt, and just. Catroux, in condemning Darlan for opportunism—a euphemism for treachery—reinforced all that the British Chiefs of Staff had come to fear about American strategic and political objectives. Catroux, moreover, knew something about the world that Darlan sought to conquer: "Catroux belonged to a comfortable world of good company and privilege. His family belonged to the rich colonial class of North African settlers . . ."

Thus, when such a Gaullist condemned Darlan, he struck a responsive chord in Eden. The latter immediately alerted Mack: Eisenhower should be given the gist of Catroux's views on Darlan. Eden also stressed to Mack: "De Gaulle is deeply depressed, but *not* yet exasperated. He wished to broadcast to Europe last weekend, and would have emphasized Darlan's treacherous character, but reluctantly accepted our ruling that such a statement could not be sent over the British Broadcasting Corporation at present." De Gaulle had achieved his *rapprochement* with Churchill—and the BBC—but Whitehall did not consider that the time was yet ripe for an outright Gaullist assault on Darlan, whether conducted by propaganda or conspiracy. On 4 December, de Gaulle "showed great emotion but made no comment" when told that the moment for his assault on Darlan had not yet arrived. But after meeting Eden, Catroux departed in some secrecy for Gibraltar. Catroux, and de Gaulle, were poised for conspiracy, but not yet involved in it.

British interests had first to be considered before Churchill's commitment to de Gaulle was put to the test of eliminating Darlan. By late 1942—"the end of the beginning"—the British nation in arms was united to an unprecedented degree behind Churchill. The business of war had been experienced by way of defeat and humiliation. The *purpose* of this particular war had been learned. The British, as a nation, were not going to allow Darlan to deflect them from the attainment of their objectives—preservation of the national interest *and* the liberation of Western Europe.

III

The French in North Africa were deeply divided among themselves and were no more capable of fomenting effective conspiracy, unaided by outside support, than was the Résistance in France able to wage war in the shadows, alone. This appreciation was conveyed to London by SIS and SOE in Algiers. Neither personal ambition, outraged emotion, nor the furtive distribution of *Combat* would eliminate Darlan.

Moreover, any purely French elimination of Darlan—either his political downfall or his assassination—posed the question of a successor. In North Africa, few saw de Gaulle as an obvious successor to Darlan; here was a reality accepted even by those who considered themselves Gaullist. Hence all French conspiracy was governed by the problem of succession. Giraud would doubtless offer himself. But who would rally to one whose descent on Algiers had been so humiliating?

British elimination of Darlan, in stark contrast, provided the opportunity for one ultimate if not necessarily immediate successor: de Gaulle, albeit after a decent interval. Such a successor, moreover, would set his sights on North Africa, as he had on the French Empire, only as a means of establishing a political role in France through leadership of Résistance. Darlan and de Gaulle shared the same ambition: to be "political leader in France."

There was, however, a vital distinction, fully recognized in London, ignored, when not rejected, in Washington: Darlan had no real following in France. Darlan's only effective support, in North Africa or France, was vested in Franklin Roosevelt and his subordinates. De Gaulle's claim to be symbol of Résistance might be disputed by assorted résistants, but it was one both accepted and proclaimed by a British government which, throughout 1942, had come to believe that the liberation of France depended in large measure on the "detonator" of sabotage and guerrilla war. Robin Brook recalls that "British strategic objectives for the liberation of France were inseparable from support for de Gaulle."

From Algiers, the British clandestine services' reaction to Darlan's advent and triumph was transmitted to London. The effect of this reaction was a continuation and an intensification of the British government's diplomatic counteroffensive against the Clark-Darlan Agreement and all that it implied, immediately and prospectively, for the assertion of Britain's strategic and political interests. That diplomatic counteroffensive nonetheless failed. On 24 November, Morton in London set in motion plans to use Gibraltar as a rendezvous at which to consider more deeply ways and means of eliminating Darlan. The fears expressed from Algeria traveled up to the top; reaction—and action—traveled down from the top.

Selborne and Eden were already in close communication. Eden quoted Selborne's "blasting and withering" letter of 20 November at a cabinet meeting on the 24th. Churchill personally, and no later than the 13th, had urged Selborne to "intensify the [SOE] operations in the newly-occupied regions of France." At this stage of events, Churchill and Eden were still mainly occupied with Roosevelt. Churchill, reviving an interest in SOE that was always violently affected by its successes and failures, had not yet grasped that the operations he urged on Selborne were dependent for success on a secure North African base. But Churchill was soon to be fully aware of this factor. As we have seen, on 18 November, and immediately after receiving MASSINGHAM's first signal, Gubbins wrote to Selborne, and for Eden's immediate attention, about "the extreme danger of the present situation" in Algiers. Morton was on the SOE "distribution"; Morton knew what to tell Churchill where "secret matters" were concerned.

Morton, personally, while retaining all his reservations

about de Gaulle, had decided that "the Darlan regime would not do." Morton made this assessment, in writing, to Churchill. Brook recalls: "It was well known amongst us all that Churchill was frustrated at the Darlan situation." That frustration had only to be endured for another month. On Christmas Eve 1941, Morton had written: "We shall have to hang some of our French [Vichy] 'friends' alongside Darlan and Pucheu [Vichy Minister of the Interior] when the war is over. Meanwhile let us use them." By Christmas Eve 1942, Darlan's fate, for one, had been settled. So: "Darlan would not do." *Ergo*, de Gaulle must "do."

Relations between de Gaulle and Morton were sufficiently rational for Churchill to use the latter as go-between when the former was in one of his very characteristic rages at what he considered were devious British actions. De Gaulle and Morton had met within the month of November. De Gaulle and Catroux had met, also in London. Catroux, en route to Gibraltar, should not be seen as an element in conspiracy fomented by the British government and de Gaulle. Catroux must be seen as an agent in place—in London, in Gibraltar, again in Cairo—held in readiness to play his persuasive role in North Africa once Darlan had been removed from the stage.

The Commander and second in command of MASSINGHAM, Colonels J. W. Munn and David Keswick, between them radioed three times to Baker Street on 27 November. Munn reported that "Keswick is very anxious about the political situation." Munn then repeated this phrase in a later wire, most of which was concerned with reporting that relations between MASSINGHAM and AFHQ were "satisfactory," but that no contact had been made with French forces. Keswick, by contrast, is explicit:

> We have not gained the adherence of our previous enemies and have forfeited the trust of our friends. Giraud has been sidetracked, Bethouard [sic] has been dismissed, and Darlan and the Vichyists are in complete power. Local

opinion is that we have utilised our friends and then double-crossed them. Algiers is mainly a British area; we will get the blame, although the political situation is certainly due to the Americans, especially Murphy. Mack and company have insisted that the position is temporary. [But] I believe that there is now very high tension to get rid of Darlan. The Vichyists are everywhere in power and all our friends have been cast out. Disillusionment is complete.

By the time Keswick sent this communiqué he had established himself as a formidable operator in the murky world of Algiers. Gubbins was the initial recipient in Baker Street of Keswick's warnings, the means by which their somber message was transmitted to higher authority. Among those on Gubbins's selective distribution list in the ensuing weeks were two brothers close to de Gaulle: General François and Baron Emmanuel d'Astier. Unlike their sibling Henri in Algiers, these brothers were convinced that, as the general put it, "Darlan must be liquidated." Method—and timing—were not wholly, however, within the province of Whitehall; there, the mandarins were determined primarily to support de Gaulle by disabusing him of the notion that his cause might be betrayed by British duplicity. Method—and timing—for such determined action depended on many factors, in the last resort on an agent willing and able to eliminate Darlan.

On 1 December de Monsabert was confirmed in his command of the Corps Franc by Giraud. An overt relationship between Giraud's headquarters and MASSINGHAM was a crucial element in Keswick's schemes. These schemes defy explicit definition, but were based on Keswick's absolute detestation of Vichy and his somewhat idiosyncratic Gaullism, strengthened by blood which was both Jewish and French. Keswick's first concern was SOE support for Résistance in France, anti-Vichy, not necessarily overtly Gaullist. An essential preliminary for such support was MASSINGHAM's credibility in North Africa—and its cover. Keswick duly contacted Giraud. The latter responded with every appearance of cordiality. Occasional crumbs of intelligence were acquired. Acquiring intelligence was not an SOE responsibility at all; Keswick established his own intelligence network in order to assess the capacity of his "friends" to take resolute action. Keswick quickly decided that "morale was poor," and that such friends as remained underground would be of little use in conducting a campaign to eliminate Darlan.

A premature Gaullist rising in North Africa, another abortive coup, would only entrench Darlan in power. Keswick was shrewd and imaginative enough to realize that actual and potential Gaullists in North Africa were prepared, even constrained, to wait. Failure of the 8 November coup and all that had followed since that ugly experience of double-cross and confusion imposed caution. But MASSINGHAM was no more able to wait on events than Churchill. Although the first operational instruction for MASSINGHAM was not issued until 1 December, its wording accurately reflected all the ideas about SOE and North Africa that the Chiefs of Staff had set in motion seven months earlier. The instruction stated that the main objectives were:

(i) To provide a forward base for the continuation and extension of SOE work in Europe.

(ii) To carry out such activities and operations as may be required by the Theatre Commander in connection with military operations.

There could be no "forward base"—in North Africa—while Darlan remained in power.

There is no doubt that Keswick's 27 November communiqué made a considerable impact in Baker Street. We may say the impact gained in force from the fact that neither Whitehall nor the British representatives in Algiers had produced an agreed or concerted plan for eliminating Darlan. Nor, despite the factors summarized here—above all, Morton's prospective presence in Gibraltar—was there ever to be the kind of concerted plan in which conspiracy-theory historians delight. "The urgency of elimination" was perceived with equal clarity in Algiers and London. Measures were taken in consequence. But fate played the major role. It is difficult to *arrange* an efficient assassination; one that depends on the personal—but deniable—act of an ardent soul meets all requirements. "There is a good deal of speculation that British Intelligence had been behind the removal of the embarrassing figure of Darlan." Let the historian's verdict stand.

Morton, all set for Gibraltar, had read Keswick's messages, receiving moreover on the 28th a letter from Hambro which referred to "this very distressing telegram" (Keswick's, of the 27th), and continued: "[What are we to do] regarding the treatment which has been meted out to our faithful friends in Algeria and Morocco who gave us such good service prior to the Anglo-American operations?"

Hambro pointed out to Morton that Eisenhower had been requested "to take steps to see that all these people are looked after." Hambro expressed doubts: "From what I hear, very little has been done. Would it not be possible for somebody to take the matter up so as to ensure that we do not again get the reputation of perfidious albion. I think the whole thing is a frightful scandal but I do not know how to set the ball rolling and so I appeal to your better nature."

On 1 December, shortly before leaving for Gibraltar, Morton replied to Hambro: "I do not quite know what to say, though I will bear the matter in mind . . . and if I get an opportunity will say something in certain quarters, but it is not too easy as the general situation is hardly satisfactory." Churchill was the certain quarter where Morton would say something, or repeat what was already known, feared, and opposed.

Morton arrived in Gibraltar on 4 December—where, for the moment we must leave him with his French compatriots. In London, Darlan's elimination continued to be the subject of anxious consideration; in Algiers, Darlan seemed irreplace-able. Eisenhower alternated between hopes and fears, illu-sions and moments of depressing realism. Bonnier, the instrument of fate, was instructed at Le Club des Pins in the limitations of that unsatisfactory weapon, the .38 Webley pis-tol. The war in Tunisia ground on. On 4 December, First Army and its American component were checked yet again in attempting to consolidate their positions in and about Tebourba.

Hitler's Tunisian bridgehead began to assume a political, not merely a strategic, dimension. French forces at Bizerta surrendered to Axis troops on 8 December. These portents were duly noted throughout Algiers. Giraud, from the first, had refused to put the few French troops who had opposed Axis forces under Anderson's command. Vanity and pride explain much in this decision; some excuse for Giraud may be found in his realization that if the Tunisian campaign continued to go so badly, French soldiers might be forced to change sides yet again.

Tunisia, that minor battlefield, was regarded in London, if not Washington, as a major element in Allied strategy. But with Eisenhower as commander-in-chief of Allied forces, Churchill and Whitehall perforce concentrated on the politics of a steadily deteriorating situation. On 2 December a Foreign Office assessment concluded:

> There has been an inclination in the United States to con-sider that with the now obvious collapse of the Marshal's Government, an alternative French Government should be recognized as existing at Algiers. Darlan is naturally doing his best to substantiate his position as head of such a government. He has indicated, for example, that he intends to administer French North Africa in accordance with the principles of the Third Republic. He proposes to set up a civil consultative assembly of some kind and has also created an administrative council which includes, among others, General Giraud, Admiral Michelier, and General Bergeret. "The Imperial Council" was stated by Radio Maroc on 1 December to have held two meetings,

after which Admiral Darlan's position was thus described: "The High Commission, representing French Sovereignty, assisted by the services of the High Commissariat, will exercise the functions and prerogatives of Head of State."

By the beginning of December, Churchill and Eden were fully aware that Eisenhower was as little able to prevent Darlan from usurping and arrogating power in North Africa as he was to check the assertion of the latter's ambition elsewhere in the world. Prime minister and foreign secretary sensed Eisenhower's growing concern about the true implications of the Clark-Darlan Agreement, but remained unconvinced that he would, or could, act decisively. British concern and further moves to action were given impetus by Eisenhower's broadcast from Algiers on 3 December in which he actually said that "all Frenchmen worthy of their great past had forgotten their small differences of ideas and were ready to fight hand in hand to vanquish the Axis."

This gratuitous, unintentional boost to Darlan aroused more concern in London than the unwitting insult to Fighting France and the Résistance. Eisenhower only compounded his verbal felony in London's eyes by hastily assuring Churchill and the Chiefs of Staff on 5 December that Darlan remained indispensable because of the difficult and dangerous situation that Allied forces faced in Tunisia. In the days immediately following the Allied landings in North Africa, the British government and Whitehall had reluctantly and unhappily accepted this argument. By early December Eisenhower's repeated protestations had been completely rejected.

Eisenhower's admission on 5 December that the "gamble" had failed aroused no sympathy in London. Another assertion—that Darlan's claims to be "a permanent authority" had been rebutted and that Eisenhower merely regarded him as "head of the local government"—was received with tired incredulity. Churchill sent "a friendly reply" to Eisenhower on 7 December, but the warmth of the words did not disguise his mounting anxieties. The time for excuses was over. Cadogan noted in his diary for the 5th: "There is every sort of flap [here] about Eisenhower's 'negotiations' with Boisson. These generally take the form of the Vichy French telling the Americans what they want and the Americans giving it to them regardless of our interests or feelings."

Cunningham attempted to assure London that Eisenhower was doing his best, but was worried "about the hesitations and hair splittings of [the] Foreign Office." For once, Cunningham's words were rejected: Eisenhower's best wasn't good enough. Nor was Murphy's. His assertion, also on 5 December, that Darlan had pledged the release of "twenty-seven communist deputies," was not only disbelieved, but was also further weakened by Darlan's continued, and on this occasion, explicit refusal to restore liberty and citizenship to Jews. The final move on this telegraphically active day was Eden's instruction to Halifax:

> . . . in spite of the President's statement of November 17, Admiral Darlan appeared to be digging himself in more and more firmly. He had assumed in his latest proclamation the office of Chief of State and the rights and responsibilities of the Government of France in the French Empire, and still regarded himself as holding his authority from Marshal Pétain. His administration was in fact a Vichy regime and some of our best friends—such as Generals Béthouart and Mast—were still without active employment.

Halifax was expressly instructed to see Roosevelt as soon as possible, not only so that "early effect should be given to the President's statement [of 17 November]," but also in order that action might be taken "in the internal political sphere." Halifax was to insist on Darlan's rescinding anti-democratic legislation, the restoration of the right of free association, for Trade Unions, the suppression of Fascist organizations, and the release of British and Allied internees and French and other sympathisers with the Allies. A start should be made with the dismissal of pro-Axis officials, and we should have ready a list of those whom we would wish to see in key positions in a new administration.

This was a strong program, made all the more verbally positive in being directed at Roosevelt. The time for reliance on Hull was over—if, indeed, it had ever existed. But, in retrospect, it is doubtful if either Churchill or Eden expected to get much change out of Roosevelt. The diplomatic counteroffensive would be sustained; one more attack on Roosevelt's Vichy policy would be made. But apart from Morton's mission to Gibraltar, Churchill and Eden were thinking ahead to a transformation of the North African—and French—political scene, and one to which Darlan's elimination was only an essential preliminary. Halifax was also instructed to discuss with Roosevelt the appointment of American and British "political representatives of high authority" who would not only relieve Eisenhower of burdens he could not, indeed should not, carry, but would also rid North Africa of Darlan and his version of Vichy. These American and British representatives, in short should

> ... try to bring about an agreement between General de Gaulle and a North African administration, and thus unite the French Empire once again in the war. *No united effort would be possible under Admiral Darlan* [writer's emphasis], but an agreement might well be made with a regime which had broken with Vichy and was pledged to administer the laws of France as they stood before the armistice until the people of France could elect a constitutional Government.

This explicit rejection of Darlan and all his objectives took the conflict between Roosevelt and Churchill to the stage summarized by Eden on 17 November: "It's a question of Darlan *or* de Gaulle." There were to be no third parties in this conflict, or none that the British government would actively—and covertly—support. The British government would introduce its own political Trojan horse into Algiers, from which would emerge Gaullist political shock troops, the vanguard of a new France.

By so instructing Halifax, Churchill and Eden made a declaration of great significance. But, on 5 December 1942, neither prime minister nor foreign secretary was sanguine of even ultimate success for their strategy of linking alliance with de Gaulle to the liberation of France. The immediate necessity was Darlan's elimination; a concomitant requirement was that Eisenhower receive an emissary of de Gaulle's whether he wanted to or not. On 6 December Eden again contacted Mack, instructing him to press Eisenhower to accept General d'Astier as de Gaulle's emissary. Eisenhower, by this time beginning to hedge his bets a little, agreed. A signal on 3 December from Admiral Stark in London may have influenced the harassed commander-in-chief. Stark described d'Astier as ". . . a gentleman and a soldier of the first caliber." Stark further sugared the pill by adding that d'Astier had expressed to him his sympathy with Eisenhower's problems regarding Darlan. D'Astier had apparently said to Stark: "No soldier could have acted differently."

Doubt is permissible whether this oblique remark was made, yet the fiction that "soldiers"—especially generals—detested politics and politicians was probably necessary. Eisenhower was not the strong silent type who kept his own counsel. He needed reassurance, and plenty of it. As we have seen, Eisenhower had poured out his woes to Marshall in a long summary of the situation—also of the 3rd—where, amidst the verbiage—". . . it is necessary for us here to preserve the attitude that we are treating with a friend rather than an enemy"—one detects a shift in Eisenhower's attitude to Darlan. Eisenhower recapitulates Darlan's (and Boisson's) Anglophobia but, in so doing, makes his first, tentative, gesture toward those French who had *not* forgotten "their small differences of ideas." Eisenhower tells Marshall: "Even the United States [has] certain commitments to de Gaulle which cannot be repudiated."

In Roosevelt's eyes, the United States had no commitments to de Gaulle whatsoever; Eisenhower's further statement in his 3 December summary that ". . . the British refusal to throw de Gaulle overboard when it might serve immediate expediency [to do so] is a guarantee to them [Darlan and Boisson] that England keeps her word . . ." was under the circumstances both courageous and prescient. True, these statements were made to Marshall—who was the strong, silent type. Eisenhower's fears, and speculations, would be safe with him.

Nevertheless, with this communiqué and in Eisenhower's assent to General d'Astier's visit, we may detect the first shift in the process whereby Darlan's elimination began to be perceived as a necessity by others than committed opponents of the Darlan regime. Roosevelt's ability to impose Darlan and Vichy on France had always been questionable. Beginning in early December, 1942, even Eisenhower, Roosevelt's most loyal lieutenant, began to doubt. Eisenhower's early December wires are full of contradictions and inconsistencies. He was shortly to renounce them. The slow dawning of the truth about Darlan can nevertheless be observed.

IV

Darlan, talking to Murphy a few hours before the assassination, repeated an earlier assertion that he knew of at least four conspiracies against him. This may have been so, but again it has to be said that in early December French conspirators remained disorganized and scattered. Darlan's distribution of favors had been particularly effective in neutralizing opposition. Although Achiary—possibly others—remained secretly anti-Vichy in sentiment and cautiously pro-Gaullist in covert action, Darlan's administration was well supplied with those who could spy on former comrades.

Keswick's wires to Baker Street of 27 November concentrate on lack of morale among anti-Darlan elements; in further communiqués thereafter, Keswick not only discounts the likelihood of a "Monarchist plot" against Darlan, but also continues his harsh assessment of what Brook on 4 December called "resisters." Brook's views appear rather more sanguine than Keswick's: ". . . the Darlan administration is a real chip off the old block, so that 'resisters' are clear out of favour. In terms of the President's statement [of 17 November] we have no grounds for intervention *yet*. But the tide will inevitably turn . . ."

The British in Algiers did not accept that there was anything inevitable about Darlan's elimination, in the sense that one could simply wait for the tide to turn. Action, if not this day, then in short order, was required. Keswick agreed with Churchill and Eden as to the necessity of eliminating Darlan. More to the point, Keswick would have agreed with the prime minister and the foreign secretary as to the urgency of elimination. But Keswick realized that London collectively still retained some hope Darlan could be eliminated without resort to the deniable violence so urbanely described in the SOE memorandum quoted on page 92.

Telegrams from Mack and the PWE team in Algiers have already been given in some detail. No apology is made for repetition. The reader may now perceive the force of what was jointly emphasized in a clear warning to Eden on 7 December: "Darlan is Vichy, and Vichy is the rule of the same wealthy and selfish interests which have ruined France. There may have to be civil war before the Darlan regime goes under. Darlan must go some time."

Eisenhower, brooding in his headquarters, was no longer immune from the atmosphere of Darlan's regime. Eisenhower had accepted that the Vichy gamble had failed. By the end of this first December week, Eisenhower had briefly removed himself from the corruption of Algiers to see what his soldiers were doing in the mud and slush of Tunisia. Eisenhower returned to Algiers enormously depressed by this second visit to the front. A member of Eisenhower's staff (Brigadier General Charles Saltzman) recalls: "Ike was always liable to go up and down. After visiting our positions behind Tebourba he sure went down. That day (8 December) I saw Ike more worried than at any time during the war." Admiral Louis Derrien's surrender to Axis forces at Bizerta deepened the volatile Eisenhower's belated conviction that Darlan could no longer be trusted. On the evening of the 8th Eisenhower radioed to Marshall: "Darlan continues to behave as Pétain's successor; if things continue to go badly for us here, he will change sides again."

But Eisenhower, ever mindful of the Washington conviction that Darlan was the president's protégé, referred in another wire of the 8th to Darlan being "in favor of a public announcement that aligns him definitely on the side of liberal government." This message was received in Washington after Halifax had been to see Roosevelt on the 8th, but even if the latter had read everything Eisenhower sent that day it would not have altered the course of an interview that was "not satisfactory" respecting British interests. Roosevelt made it plain that he "did not contemplate early action to get rid of Admiral Darlan."

Roosevelt went further. After ritual incantations about the restoration of civil liberties and a brief reference to "the appointment of qualified political representatives—subject always to the final authority of General Eisenhower" (which was precisely what Churchill and Eden did *not* want)—Roosevelt descended to abuse. Halifax, struggling as always to sound authoritative when confronted by Roosevelt the politician rather than the president as statesman, insisted that "public opinion in Great Britain, France, and elsewhere . . ." would not be satisfied unless the "temporary expedient" pledge of 17 November was honored. Roosevelt's reply is revealing: "Doubtless the Czechs would now ask him whether he intended, when we were liberating Czechoslovakia, to make terms with Czechoslovak 'quislings'; he would say 'not necessarily; everything will depend on circumstances, and whatever we have to do for military reasons will not prejudice your freedom of choice later.' "

Chamberlain's—and Halifax's—betrayal of Czechoslovakia in 1938 may not have been consciously in Roosevelt's mind when he so openly repudiated Churchill's anxiety and anger at the American deal with Darlan. But conscious or nor, Halifax knew what Roosevelt meant. On 9 December Halifax saw Hull as a matter of form—to be told "operations in North Africa were at a critical stage, and that with their long line of military communications, the United states could not afford to risk upsetting the arrangements with Admiral Darlan."

A robust ambassador could have pointed out that the operations in question were being conducted mostly by British troops—but Halifax was all for a quiet life. In any event, he knew that the diplomatic counteroffensive had failed. Not until 12 December did Leahy tell Dill, "We shall have Darlan with us for a very long time"—adding, gratuitously, "that is, at least until the end of the war in Europe"—but by then London knew what Algiers had known for weeks: Darlan's elimination would not be achieved by any attempt to put pressure on President Roosevelt.

In a wire to Gubbins of 4 December, Keswick's renewed criticisms of former conspirators were mingled with the conviction that one of them was insistent on Darlan's removal from the scene: "D'Astier de la Vigerie is very energetic and keen and the most active anticollaborationist. As Commissioner of the Interior he now controls propaganda and the police and is doing all he possibly can to help. He was the man behind the coup in Algiers. Although he is in Darlan's government, he opposes him as far as he can, and desires his elimination and the fusion of Giraud and de Gaulle."

From a very mixed bag, and ignoring d'Astier's eqivocations during the night of 8 November, Keswick selected one who seems to have been chosen by fate for war in the shadows. D'Astier had, however, another value in Keswick's—and MASSINGHAM's—eyes. He was, in early December, widely regarded as objective about de Gaulle. Collectively, the mission was seen by Eisenhower as all too Gaullist in its sympathies. Indeed, Douglas Dodds-Parker, another senior member of MASSINGHAM, recalls:

> We were not welcome in general, as a Special Service, British, with known Gaullist links. It was clear that little could be done operationally until the Darlan involvement, with all its consequences, was sorted out. General de Lattre [a former commander of the Department of the Puy-de-dôme] had set up resistance to the German occupation of the [formerly] non-occupied zone of France. He sent messages that as long as Darlan was known to hold any position in Algiers, French resistance would cease. De Lattre said "Darlan is as great an enemy to everything that France stands for as he is hostile to the Anglo-Saxons."

Keswick's further warning of 4 December concludes: "The problem of Darlan persists; I am convinced that he is going to be very difficult to shift." Thus, in something approaching acute frustration, did Keswick comment on Henri d'Astier as a suitable French instrument for Darlan's elimination. The choice was curious but, perhaps, inevitable. In 1941 and throughout 1942, Keswick had done much to develop British support for Résistance in France; his racial and cultural sympathies made him detest everything that Darlan represented; he had watched with mounting concern Eisenhower's and Murphy's connivance in Darlan's repressive regime and all that it portended for the future of France. Keswick had reported the situation and the dangers that it posed in a series of telegrams to London. These communications had caused decisions to be made—up to a point. There had been no word from the highest echelon calling for action this day, only Gubbins's authority to take such measures as seemed appropriate.

Morton's presence in Gibraltar might also be a portent. But Keswick needed more than portents. More than Fernand Bonnier, firing on the range—and at dummies of the human figure—at Le Club des Pins with a .38 pistol. Keswick needed a natural conspirator, reliable or otherwise, whose motives might be flawed, recent history dubious, and actions inconsistent, but whose talents might fit him for elimination. Elimination was necessary, quickly, before Darlan wrecked a strategy for the liberation of France that had been fashioned over so many arduous months.

7

Darlan's Death

I

Just before 1500 hours on Christmas Eve, a fortnight following the events narrated in the last chapter, Fernand Bonnier fired two shots into Darlan's stomach from a 7.65 pistol. Darlan had spent the morning with Murphy in further, futile discussion about internment of Jews. Darlan at luncheon with Cunningham and Royer Dick "had seemed in good form, rather tired." Dick recalls, "We finished with plum brandy. Darlan talked of the plots against him, as he had to Murphy the day before. I am told that on his deathbed he muttered, 'I knew the British would get me at last.' " Bonnier, when being trained by MASSINGHAM, had been armed with a .38 Webley. This weapon, issued from MASSINGHAM's armory, was initially replaced by the Colt for reasons that remain of interest only to those obsessed with minutiae. A Colt .45 makes less noise and emits less smoke than the old British service pistol. Just before Bonnier made his final confession to the Abbé Cordier, the Colt .45 was replaced by the 7.65. Neither a British nor an American weapon was deemed, at the end, appropriate.

The fortnight of plot and counterplot that culminated in the death of Churchill's "odious Quisling" is marked by several shifts of emphasis. Darlan, while continuing his policies of repression, his denial of outright support to the Allies, his covert relationship with Vichy, falls into a curiously immobile state. Darlan had staked all on the hazard. Now fate would decide whether his gamble would end in triumph, disaster, or death.

The Comte de Paris, Pretender to the French Throne, makes a brief appearance, then retires discreetly, not to the wings but from the scene. The comte, an essentially cautious, conciliatory Pretender, hoped for some role, however limited, in a North African administration which, in replacing or containing Darlan, would establish a sense of "unity." When, after ten days in Algiers (8 to 18 December) the Comte realized that his French supporters were divided, ineffectual, and that Murphy was adamantly opposed to him, he planned a return to his Moroccan farm, resuming the profitless but safe role of spectator and commentator.

Henri d'Astier and a young priest who has come to be known as l'Abbé Cordier (otherwise a lieutentant of the reserve) certainly plot and plan, although to what definable end remains obscure. General d'Astier arrives in Algiers on 19 November, but leaves in some haste to report to de Gaulle—and Churchill—on the fatal day of the 24th. Keswick meets Capitant, possibly with Henri d'Astier on 7 December, reports unfavorably to London, but nevertheless incurs Eisenhower's displeasure.

Bonnier, his two weeks' small arms and sabotage course completed, is neither "returned to unit" (BRANDON), nor tasked for other duties by MASSINGHAM, but loiters in Algiers. Bonnier, existing unhappily in a kind of spiritual limbo during weeks of alternating hope that he would not have to kill Darlan

and fear that he must, is supported—if that is the word—by
Cordier as his confessor, d'Astier as mentor. Several Frenchmen, later suspected of being British agents, enact a role that
is to provide the means of assassination, and escape.

The war in Tunisia ground on, in continued rain and mud.
By mid-December Eisenhower had concluded that no major
offensive was possible before the New Year, and that until then,
Allied forces must only seek to hold their own. British reinforcements from the United Kingdom began to arrive at the
front in some strength. On 13 December, Montgomery renewed
his offensive against Axis forces in Libya; by the end of the
year, the latter were still clinging to positions somewhat to the
east of the Tunisian frontier. American troops were also sent
to reinforce Anderson, but much of Eisenhower's disposable
military strength remained in Morocco, committed to deter an
Axis threat from Spain whose credibility did not increase with
the passage of time. Military stalemate set in; political activity
intensified.

Eden, and the Foreign Office, had been rebuffed by Roosevelt on 8 December, above all concerning the suggestion that
Eisenhower should be relieved of his political responsibilities.
Roosevelt's refusal to return Eisenhower to his proper sphere—
"Commander-in-Chief of the Allied Expeditionary Force"—
not only reflected determination to support Darlan but his
adamant opposition to de Gaulle. The British government, in
complete contrast, was being driven by the logic of its political
and strategic policies for the eventual liberation of France into
a position of total opposition to Roosevelt.

Not only was Darlan's elimination a necessity, but so was
his replacement by a North African administration not averse
from a Gaullist element. But, as advised by British representatives in Algiers, Eden was loath to thrust de Gaulle down
French North African throats. The time was not yet; premature action would be disastrous, above all if it was seen as
stemming from London. Another fiasco like that of 8 November—or Dakar in September 1940—would wreck not only

British policies but also de Gaulle's ambitions. Résistance in France, already gravely weakened by seeming British complicity in American collaboration with Darlan, would receive a blow from which it might never recover.

A protest by Eden to Roosevelt of 9 December may have gained strength from being nominally sent by Churchill, but its real purpose was to stress Darlan's contingent reversion to treachery. "If we had any serious military set backs in Tunisia we might get into grave difficulties from the hostile elements within the French administration." This warning expressed obliquely what Eisenhower had said simply, and in some anguish, to Marshall only a few hours before. Allied forces *had* suffered "serious military set backs" in Tunisia; Anderson, the neglected, inadequately supported commander of those forces, knew better than Eisenhower the kind of "grave difficulties" that the Allies faced, daily. Darlan's propensity for changing sides was, by mid-December, of more concern to Eisenhower and his colleagues than any other issue.

The tempo quickens. On 14 December Eisenhower asserted that the political situation in North Africa owed less to Darlan's actions than "Axis sympathizers *[agents provocateurs]* . . . disappointed office seekers . . . The de Gaulle element." Eisenhower compounded this odd catalogue of assertions by declaring that "the activities of Fascist organizations were being discontinued or kept under close observation. [I] can find no cases in which well-known German sympathizers have been reinstated." Yet on Eisenhower's own admission, Darlan was a potential traitor—to the Allied cause. Hence Darlan might again, and with a vengeance, become the best known of "German sympathizers."

Eisenhower artlessly concludes this communication nonetheless with a further assertion: "All officers and men imprisoned for aiding our landing have been released and reinstated." This was simply not the case, and Eden was not slow to tell him so: "General Eisenhower's answer was too optimistic . . . the facts in our [British] possession show, for example, that the reinstatement of German sympathisers and the victimisation of our friends continued." Thus Eden on 17 December was renewing the counterattack in local terms. Two days earlier, Laval had declared, "I hope Germany will win the war. Darlan had declared (almost) the opposite to Anderson over a month before—and with reason. But much had happened in that month, none of it good for prosecution of Allied strategy.

Eden then planted the goad: "It was impossible to change the whole basis of French administration within a few weeks, or transform a pro-Vichy regime without a long process of 'disinfection and re-education.' *The trouble was that with Darlan at the head of affairs, the process would not operate effectively"* [writer's emphasis]. Eden continued to show some sympathy for Eisenhower's dilemma but, having learned on the 15th that Roosevelt had reappointed Murphy as his personal representative in North Africa, with the rank of minister, decided that elimination must now be left to others, to use such means as they deemed appropriate.

Indeed, by the 15th, measures had already been taken to ensure that Darlan's elimination would take place without much further delay. SYMBOL—a long contemplated meeting in North Africa between Roosevelt and Churchill—was imminent; the prospect of a Vichy regime being approved by the presence of the two Allied leaders was, for Churchill, a denial of all his objectives, and principles. The "odious Quisling" had been given more than enough rope. The time had come when, if Darlan did not hang himself, other, equally fatal, measures must ensue.

On 15 December, Catroux, just returned to Cairo from Gibraltar, radioed de Gaulle: *"il m'a été affirmé à Gilbraltar que d'Astier de la Vigerie qui serait auprès de Darlan aurait à vous proposer une combinaison susceptible d'écarter l'Amiral et de réaliser une coordination. Un télégramme par voie anglaise aurait demandé une rencontre avec d'Astier à Gibraltar. Etes-vous au courant?"*

This telegram, graded *"Secret Le Plus Absolu,"* is not lacking in ambiguity. Morton was back in London; d'Astier was still on the Rock. What was there to propose that had not been contemplated already? The key phrase, of course, is *"une combinaison susceptible d'écarter l'Amiral,"* but even this requires interpretation. We know that Churchill and Eden were agreed not only on the necessity for elimination, but also on the requirement to replace a Vichy administration in North Africa by one that would allow Gaullism to establish a political base there. The Gibraltar meeting was expressly designed to consider the attainment of these related objectives. But the meeting as such did not concern itself with the specific methods by which either, or both, objectives could be attained. The primary objective of the Gibraltar meeting was to assemble those who had immediate or future roles to play in elimination and its aftermath. General d'Astier, representing *"une combinaison,"* had the immediate role to play.

On 12 December Giraud proposed that "the supreme command in Tunisia should pass to him." Eisenhower's rejection of this unreasonable claim did nothing to render Giraud tractable in other directions. The "Imperial Conseil," of which he was a member, was concerned with a successor to Darlan should the latter, for whatever reason, disappear from the scene. Giraud knew he had one qualification for the succession that, despite his humiliation of early November, gave him some grounds for optimism. Not only had he been an Allied nominee, of a kind but, unlike Boisson and Noguès, he was not actively associated with Darlan and all his works.

The only rational interpretation of Catroux's telegram is that General d'Astier was to operate covertly with the British during his forthcoming visit to Algiers. Baker Street wired Keswick on 14 December that d'Astier would arrive in Algiers a week later. D'Astier would have a reasonably free hand in deciding what to do, and with whom. D'Astier was also provided with funds ($38,000) sufficient to assist the elimination process. Darlan's elimination (*"écarter"* being a euphemism) could take place in any context that Henri d'Astier considered suitable. The one essential requirement was that neither the British government nor Fighting France should be implicated.

On 13 December, nevertheless, Mack stressed to Eisenhower that the British government was promoting General d'Astier's visit to Algiers in a last-ditch attempt to outflank Darlan. The agreed British and Gaullist objectives thus came to this: elimination of Darlan by one means or another, followed by an administration that would be a "Trojan horse" (in Harold Macmillan's words) for Gaullism, of a kind; elimination to be a French affair, so designed that neither de Gaulle and the French National Committee nor the British in North Africa would be directly implicated. The long-term objective was a Gaullist North Africa; Darlan's elimination, however urgent and necessary, was, in a sense, only the preliminary step.

Attainment of the objectives encapsulated in Catroux's telegram presented serious problems of timing and method, although they followed logically not only from the course of events but also the deliberations in Gibraltar. General d'Astier's visit to Algiers is, therefore, the key to much that developed immediately before and after 19 December, culminating in Bonnier's nervous hand gripping his pistol and the shots fired at point-blank range. Yet General d'Astier was no more the agent of assassination than his brother, or Cordier, or Morton, or Catroux, or Keswick, or Bonnier. There was no one agent for an act that was rendered inevitable by Darlan's intransigence. As in the days before the Allied landings in North Africa, French conspirators were driven by their own, individual motives, not by any sense of a grand design. New elements in conspiracy—above all the challenge posed by General d'Astier as a specifically Gaullist emissary—do not alter the fact that Darlan was assassinated because Bonnier represented what the British foreign office saw as the *urgency* of "elimination."

Whatever view one takes of de Gaulle's long-term political ambitions, he was regarded far and wide by the end of 1942 as the symbol of resistance to Nazi occupation and Vichy repression. The British government supported de Gaulle for many reasons, among which the national and imperial interest certainly predominated. But British support was not, in the final analysis, a matter of expediency. Churchill was never indifferent to British public opinion—by the end of 1942 he could not afford to be—and knew that de Gaulle's deep and genuine popularity in Britain reflected emotions that, indeed, Churchill shared.

Churchill and Eden had failed to budge Roosevelt but was there one, absolutely final, chance for pressure to be applied locally? If that final attempt failed, only one alternative would remain. During the week preceding General d'Astier's arrival in Algiers there seemed some hope that the reality of the situation in North Africa might, finally, dawn on Roosevelt—because it had begun to dawn on Eisenhower. D'Astier's imminent arrival produced a spate of telegrams between Algiers, London, and Washington, the analysis of which reveals that the hope was transient, and had vanished by 21 December.

Eisenhower wired Washington and London on 13 December. As usual, these telegrams are lengthy and diffuse, but these characteristics do accurately reflect the doubt and confusion in the mind of a commander-in-chief whose military operations were bogged down and whose enforced political role had passed from the invidious to the impossible. Eisenhower's communiqués, although indirectly reflecting his growing fears of Darlan, were specifically prompted by two factors: first, renewed doubts about the release of Jews from internment; second, a grandiloquent speech by Darlan, which, despite being ostensibly addressed to Muslims in North Africa, succeeded in revealing his nature and ambitions more clearly than on almost any previous occasion. Darlan had ceased to act decisively: his actions now lay in rhetoric, and incipient treachery.

Darlan stated:

I want to tell you how we shall meet the enemy. No sooner had the Americans and British landed when all of France was occupied in violation of the Armistice. An effort was made to seize the fleet, which was prevented by the heroic action of our sailors . . . Now by the side of the Allies and furnished with immense resources of which you see evidence every day we shall add Islam, Syria, and Egypt to the struggle. Tomorrow the Allies, Frenchmen and Mohammedans, closely united, will throw the Italians whom they scorn and their German masters into the sea. Then we shall carry the fire and sword to the soil of Italy.

In several senses this speech is nonsensical when it is not mendacious. There is no need for detailed textual analysis. It is the *tone* that matters. Here is the voice of a man whose sense of fate does not inhibit ambition. Darlan was known to be as reluctant to support the Muslim cause—essentially, political independence from French rule—as he was hostile to Jewry. Thus the "we" is the royal we, the voice of one whose seizure of power in North Africa was intended only as prelude to its further usurpation in the empire, and France. Throughout the first two weeks of December Eisenhower had striven to convince himself that Darlan could still be an asset to the Allied cause; Eisenhower had striven to convince his masters in Washington and his mentor Churchill in London that this was so. By 13 December, however, Eisenhower was driven, by sheer force of circumstance, to contemplate General d'Astier's visit as a possible alleviation, if no more, of an impossible situation.

Eisenhower confided doubts about Darlan and interned Jews to General Sir Hastings Ismay [in effect, Churchill's Chief of Staff]—thus to Churchill. Eisenhower attempted to make the best of Darlan's assurance that Jews in North Africa "would be recalled for military duty," but is clearly unconvinced that this statement had any more truth in it than Darlan's earlier protestations. In communicating with Stark on the 13th, Eisenhower makes no direct reference either to Darlan's latest speech or to the Jewish issue (an incompatible pair of problems in any event) but concentrates his attention on General d'Astier. Despite Mack's note of the same date, Eisenhower's comments to Stark disclose a certain lack of welcome for the visit. But they do indicate, if no more, that it might prove useful as a means of limiting Darlan's pretensions in some way. Eisenhower fails to grasp that General d'Astier's visit is essentially British in origin—not merely so in the backing that was necessary to make it possible—and is reluctant to concede that for a known Gaullist emissary to arrive openly in Darlan's camp is a politically motivated act.

Nevertheless, Eisenhower's contacts with Stark are revealing in detail. We should not make too much of references to brotherly connections, although they must be quoted:

> General d'Astier de la Vigerie has a brother here—Henri— who has proved a useful friend to us in the work preparatory to our arrival. Murphy depended on him. Darlan has taken d'Astier into his cabinet, where d'Astier is charged with police and propaganda matters and seems to be performing excellent service. He originally communicated with his brother, suggesting a meeting, but he and others do not agree that a delegation should come from the French National Committee at this time. If General d'Astier came alone for a quiet meeting and talked with his brother and other persons, it might be all right.

Eisenhower's problem is this: He distrusts—and fears— Darlan; he is aware of the need, if not for elimination, then for a brake on Darlan's actions; he is both ignorant and skeptical of Gaullist objectives; he knows, however, that he is faced with a major crisis—the prospect of Darlan's renewed treachery. But Eisenhower is unable, for reasons best known to himself, to say bluntly to Washington that Darlan has become a liability and is potentially a threat to the Allied cause. Thus Eisenhower's references to the Gibraltar meeting betray ignorance of the deeper issues.

We do learn, however, that Eisenhower knew Catroux had been in Gibraltar, and had indicated interest in a reconciliation between de Gaulle and Giraud. But Catroux had made absolutely clear that *"de Gaulle would have no dealing with Darlan under any circumstances."* Eisenhower should, therefore, have realized that whatever purpose was to be served by General d'Astier's visit to Algiers it was not to praise Darlan but to bury him. Yet Eisenhower, Roosevelt's viceroy—Murphy, despite promotion, little more than Darlan's boot boy—fails to alert Washington to the possibilities and the challenges posed by General d'Astier's visit.

We may say that if Eisenhower had tackled his problems head-on he could have told Washington: "General d'Astier's visit could be a breakthrough. Whatever you think of de Gaulle—the British here, let alone in London, think a great deal of him—we simply have to work with his movement at some time. We can't go on like this, as I implied to Marshall on the 8th. Give me break, will you, before something drastic happens." But Eisenhower sent no such appeal. He was caught in a trap unwittingly devised by Roosevelt. Eisenhower was thus a commander-in-chief unable to act decisively in the field, a viceroy incapable of settling political issues.

So, in the poker-playing terms that Murphy would have employed, Eisenhower was at this crucial moment a busted flush. But, in fairness to Eisenhower, the wires he received from Washington on the 16th were hardly calculated to persuade him that Roosevelt or Marshall would have listened to or acted on the views hypothetically expressed. On the 16th, Roosevelt gratuitously asserted that the "High Commission" in North Africa had granted amnesties to those interned or who were otherwise under surveillance. The same day Marshall, a soldier and a man of genuinely liberal conviction, warned Eisenhower to stop pressing for the release of Jews. In sum, and whatever Eisenhower might fear—and occasionally report—his masters were in no mood to curb Darlan, let alone abandon him. In this context, Darlan's statement of the 16th that he had "no personal ambition" can hardly be taken literally.

Keswick reviewed the increasingly complex situation between 13 and 18 December. Apart from communications with Baker Street—and hence Whitehall as a whole—links with Giraud's headquarters, and covert contacts elsewhere, Keswick had an open line to AFHQ. The British element in AFHQ predominated at the intelligence level. Keswick knew what Eisenhower had been sending, and receiving. Keswick was thus in a good position to appreciate that General d'Astier's visit was to be a make-or-break affair, a hinge on which Allied fortunes for the prosecution of the war in Tunisia and beyond might well turn. A hinge of fate for France also? We do not know, because although Keswick revealed his sympathies and antipathies, he avoided speculation about the widest issues. But in his communiqués to Baker Street before General d'Astier arrived in Algiers Keswick provides something more than an evaluation, or résumé, of impending events. We begin to see what is going to happen, as fate—and *"une combinaison"*— dictate.

On the 13th Keswick merely signals that Capitant wants to send a representative of *Combat* to London. Nothing in this, perhaps: who did what in the Algiers of December 1942, where so many people lived in other's pockets, blurred all normal lines of communication. Capitant's request is doubtless a straw in the Gaullist wind, but no more. Yet Capitant's request should have gone to AFHQ, thence to Mack, and no other British representative. Capitant approached MASSINGHAM for the simple, revealing reason that Keswick and his colleagues were, by mid-December, not merely Gaullist in persuasion but about to become so in practice.

On 17 December Gubbins had asked Selborne to review Keswick's earlier reports. The request was hardly necessary: events were moving to their culmination. Munn wanted Keswick to report personally to London, but before this suggestion could be implemented the latter had produced an assessment of the situation that lays bare all the factors narrated and analyzed in these pages. Dated 18 December, Keswick's assessment is a major contribution to the history of these times. Keswick makes no direct reference either to Eisenhower or

General d'Astier, but the harassed commander-in-chief and
the impending emissary of de Gaulle are present nonetheless.
The whole thrust of Keswick's review lies in this:

> We can work. We can get recruits in plenty, and the oper-
> ational side [in France, the Mediterranean, and Italy] can
> be expected to function, but the best recruits will be anti-
> Darlan, and if we take them we shall be accused of being
> pro-de Gaulle. We are specifically debarred from having
> any contact with Gaullism, and are threatened with expul-
> sion if we do so. The threat could be carried out at any
> moment by denouncing any of our agents as Gaullists, and
> the situation becomes farcical. We have naturally given
> assurance that we will not foment Gaullism here, and we
> are only concerned with overseas. But *Gaullism is being
> fomented by the Allied policy and it is indistinguishable here
> from real anti-Nazi activity* [writer's emphasis].

Keswick concludes ("What we want") on a sustained note
of moderation: "If possible, some understanding between (at
least), Giraud and de Gaulle." Moderation notwithstanding,
the whole evaluation is surely a remarkable indication of what
was actually at stake—couched, moreover, in language rather
more positive and sensitive than one normally finds in material
of this kind. The issues are laid bare: British strategic objectives are directly threatened by Darlan, and all his works; even
cautious attempts at a de Gaulle-Giraud reconciliation are
threatened. Crisis, in short. No help can be expected from
Eisenhower. Any last chance of Eisenhower's putting pressure
on Darlan had gone. Elimination by robust methods followed.

II

Eisenhower had been ordered to continue supporting Darlan.
He had been so ordered by Roosevelt and Marshall. On 18
December, six days before Darlan's assassination, Munn sent

another telegram to Baker Street which raised the ante to its
highest stakes: "We have today again received strongest warning that if we afford any assistance to anti Darlan and or Gaullist
elements General Eisenhower will order removal of MAS-
SINGHAM . . . Keswick will explain fully on arrival."

On the 18th, Hambro wrote to Cadogan, enclosing copies
of Eisenhower's warning about MASSINGHAM, and ensuring that Morton and Menzies were on the distribution. Eisenhower's warning to MASSINGHAM—in effect to Keswick—
forced a decision: elimination or *Darlan's* removal of the British presence. Hambro stressed: "We shall of course be careful
not to burn our fingers but this is pretty strong language considering that *His Majesty's Government are backing de Gaulle*
[writer's emphasis] and therefore I think you ought to know of
it."

Keswick's evaluation of 18 December was not, as such,
fully considered in London until after Darlan's assassination.
But the substance was known by 18 December, not least the
following:

> The French in becoming more and more Gaullist tend to
> look to the British for help to settle their political troubles;
> but although the British may feel willing, the French find
> them powerless to act, and they are thrown back on their
> own resources. In this atmosphere of bitter disappoint-
> ment and thwarted hopes a dangerous situation exists. I
> have heard three totally independent sources say that the
> assassination of Darlan is the only solution.

Certainly, by the time of General d'Astier's arrival "a dangerous situation" did exist in Algiers. The PWE reference of 7
December to prospective civil war is grimly relevant. But the
danger for Darlan lay in the fusion of British policy with the
mounting frustration of men who, whatever their real motives,
were convinced that his regime could not continue to repress
and intimidate indefinitely.

Thus, somewhere in the shadows of Algiers one can just

discern young Bonnier, tortured with doubt and wracked with fear. Cynicism is always inappropriate, but it is odd that those who love melodrama have made nothing of Bonnier's fiancée. She is that, no more, not even a figure in the shadows. Poor Bonnier—not even de la Chapelle, as he liked to call himself, (his mother's family name was Della Capella) but a simple, ardent bourgeois youth, trapped in a world in which he was no longer the agent but the victim, hardly even the instrument for assassination, merely the device for ensuring its success. Small wonder that Bonnier's short life and tragic death have been cheapened by absurd versions of conspiracy.

D'Astier's "stormy interview" with Darlan on the 21st remains important to history in the context of discord between Roosevelt and Churchill, and can best be understood by comparing what Eisenhower and Mack made of it. D'Astier was known by the time of his arrival to represent not only an agreed Anglo-Gaullist policy, but also agreement on its implementation. For what other reason had d'Astier met Catroux in Gibraltar, and then arrived in Algiers? Certainly not for "a quiet talk" with his brother. De Gaulle's emissary was, however, Eisenhower's nominal responsibility. Eisenhower treated his guest rather oddly. Eisenhower, a habitually courteous man, ensured that d'Astier was not met on arrival at Maison Blanche. The inference is obvious: despite d'Astier's acknowledged status—and strong personal recommendation from Stark, a close friend of Eisenhower's—his unacknowledged but known purpose in visiting Algiers had driven the latter back into an American bunker. Between 13 and 16 December Washington had recalled Eisenhower to order: it was a question of Darlan or de Gaulle. Indeed, when Eisenhower contacted Stark on the 13th, he revealed the truth of this simple fact.

In London Churchill was preparing to send his own emissary to Algiers as a riposte to Roosevelt's gratuitous promotion of Murphy. On 22 December Churchill briefed that "committed Gaullist," Harold Macmillan. On the 23rd Mack radioed Ismay—again, Churchill, in effect—about General d'Astier's "not unproductive visit." In Mack's opinion, d'Astier "has accomplished the major part of his mission." Eisenhower, by contrast, was convinced that d'Astier's visit had been a "fiasco." Eisenhower seems to have been convinced, doubtless by Darlan and Murphy, that d'Astier intended mischief. Even possibilities of some cooperation between Giraud and de Gaulle would have seemed mischievous to Darlan and Murphy.

Giraud accompanied d'Astier to the meeting with Darlan. No particular inference can be drawn, except that d'Astier wanted Giraud to witness his confrontation with Darlan. Nobody was about to assassinate Giraud, nor do more than shunt him aside at the appropriate moment. D'Astier had not come all the way to Algiers in order to be browbeaten by Giraud—or Darlan. But Eisenhower, wiring the Chiefs of Staff in London immediately after the "stormy interview," sought to convey the impression that d'Astier had been dismissed with a stinging rebuke.

Mack's assessment of d'Astier's visit can be interpreted in precisely the opposite sense: d'Astier had come to Algiers to orchestrate elimination, having been enabled to do so at British rather than Gaullist insistence. D'Astier's visit, in short, was designed to meet Mack's conviction that Darlan must be eliminated. Having tackled both the overt and covert requirements of his visit, d'Astier returned to London, to de Gaulle— and to Chequers. As Mack reported, d'Astier had "been able to tranquillise the local Gaullists who were, he considered, greater in number than people had thought and had increased since 8th November. (This is not intended to create the notion that there is a de Gaulle movement of large magnitude in the area.)" In short, d'Astier's message to prospective Gaullists in North Africa was clear: Wait upon events.

The event was imminent, but Mack's telegram is further quoted here because it conveys so perfectly not only the reality of the situation but also the lengths to which Anglo-Gaullists deemed it necessary to go in pursuit of a common objective.

> [Henri] d'Astier said his brother had left written instructions as follows: "With a view to avoiding an internal difficulty capable of harming the Allied war effort until the enemy menace has been definitely removed from French North Africa you will see that your campaigns while remaining firm on the Doctrinal Plan, suspend strictly personal attacks against the personalities who are at present in power." [General] d'Astier is sure that it [this directive] will have the effect of tranquillising impetuous spirits like Capitant whom it has been difficult to hold down and is having this circulated to local Gaullists.

The message requires little decoding. Darlan was to be eliminated *[écarter]* but no suspicion must attach to Gaullism in North Africa, which was still more of an idea rather than a movement, a "Doctrine" whose time for realization was not yet. Darlan was to be eliminated, nonetheless.

Christmas Eve in Algiers was a cold, sunny day. For the principals in the drama about to unfold, their actions were dictated by the roles that fate had allotted them. Darlan spends the morning with Murphy, who once more goes through the motions: questions about political prisoners and Jews. AFHQ had queried Darlan's assertion that amnesties had been granted, thus implicitly contesting Eisenhower's assurances on that score. The United States consulate at Casablanca had reported on 21 December that "the French authorities are making unnecessary difficulties to prevent the liberation of these persons." Darlan, his mind, and emotions, elsewhere, brushes these matters aside by referring to difficulties in maintaining an "equilibrium" between Arabs and Jews. Even to Murphy all this must have been specious. But did it matter? Darlan had five hours to live. Churchill is a Greek chorus: ". . . a cataract of amazing events fell upon him . . . Ambition stimulated his errors . . . there was not much left in life for him."

Fernand Bonnier, having received confession from Cordier and discarded both his British and American pistols, is armed with the 7.65. But assurances of reprieve weigh more with the assassin than spiritual comfort or possession of an effective weapon. Cordier, in any case, is in a highly nervous state: ". . . *semble tourmenté, perplexe.*" Bernard Pauphilet and Mario Faivre, *aspirants* in more senses than one, acquire a car, a Peugeot. Faivre and Pierre Raynaud will drive Bonnier to the Palais d'Été, wait for him, ensure escape from the consequences of a fatal act. Such, at least, is their intention.

Pauphilet and Faivre are joined by other members of the Algiers patriot group, Jean-Bernard d'Astier (Henri's son) and Roger Rosfelder. Sabatier is on the alert. Bonnier, whose courage had been high when he said *au revoir* to his compatriots after drawing the short straw on 18 November, who, according to Ragueneau, had been *"très tranquille"* then, needed the promise of rescue or, failing that, a stage-managed ordeal followed by reprieve, to bring him to the mark six weeks later. Yet Bonnier did not fail at the vital moment: ". . . *absolument calme et naturel . . .*" By a supreme effort of faith, an innocent forced himself to kill in cold blood.

We look at the young face, the boy who had rebelled against boarding school ten years before, the ardent patriot caught as cruelly in the hinge of fate as any soldier in the front line against fascism. *Dies Irae*—left now, to Bonnier, alone.

In London, Eden is about to read Keswick's report of 18 December. At Chequers, Churchill has two particular guests, de Gaulle and General d'Astier. In Washington, Harry Hopkins, Roosevelt's closest adviser, puts up a paper, "an admirable statement of Roosevelt's point of view in dealing with the French problem." Darlan would have derived comfort from Hopkins's conclusions; de Gaulle, none. These varied, con-

flicting arguments about the future of France are unknown to
Bonnier. By Christmas Eve his fate is sealed.

The atmosphere in Algiers is hard to define. "Darlan to
the gallows" had not been wholly effaced from the walls.
"Darlan is the worm in the fruit"—a refrain from Radio Brazzaville—was echoed by many. General d'Astier had come, and
gone, leaving others to eliminate. A Gaullist coup was impossible. Nor was "the street"—or the mob—a force, yet, to be
utilized. But no time is ripe: Darlan's time had come not because
Bonnier had been given $4,000 from General d'Astier's funds
but because neither requirement, nor circumstance, nor fate
could wait for the perfect moment. What finally pushed Bonnier over the edge will never be known: assassination is the
sum of many motives, fused into one overwhelming requirement. Bonnier was a martyr not so much to an idea as to the
motives of those who needed an instrument to serve their purpose.

Just before 1500, Bonnier is driven to the Palais d'Eté by
Mario Faivre and Pierre Raynaud. He is not in uniform, but is
furnished with a pass. Bonnier reaches Darlan's anteroom, is
questioned: within, an office from which ambition's stimulus
had brought TORCH to the level of a cheap conspiracy, Darlan sits, his luncheon over, his fate also now sealed. Bonnier
pushes through the door, fires the shots—*assassinates*, that most
singular fate for so many at all times, the good, the bad, the
indifferent. Bonnier attempts escape, shooting at random. He
is overpowered. The open window — a cold December day,
remember—the waiting car, the hero's return are not for him.
Bonnier is bundled off the stage, at this moment neither hero
nor martyr, merely a young man who has shot the high commissioner at his desk.

Darlan takes two hours to die. Some survive shots in the stomach at close range, but not this man. A surgeon at the Maillot

hospital called Tolstoy—odd touch—does his best, but Darlan had, indeed, been eliminated. No attempt is made to hide the fact; no surprise is expressed by those who had been Darlan's collaborators, dupes, or victims. Giraud and Murphy are active that eve of Christmas in their various, belatedly collaborative ways, but the latter, visiting Darlan on his deathbed, engages in mere ritual. In these final hours of Darlan's life, both Murphy and Eisenhower abrogate such authority as might have been retained, or regained, over the Vichy regime which had been reestablished in the guise of "liberation."

Giraud's account of these evening hours is marked by a strong sense that *his* time had come. There is a notable absence of regret for Darlan's elimination, an assurance that, as the latter's successor, fate was working in his favor. *"La ville est calme. Le général Bergeret a prévenu qu'aucune manifestation ne serait tolérée."* With Algiers quiet, Giraud indulges in speculation over the corpse of his rival: *"Hypothèse allemande? Non, aucune raison. Hypothèse Vichyiste? Peu probable. Hypothèse communiste? Peu probable. Hypothèse royaliste? Des présomptions troublantes. Hypothèse gaulliste? Egalement des présomptions troublantes."* It is a diverting (and mutually incompatible) catalogue of others' real or supposed actions.

But Giraud is not really interested in hypotheses or presumptions. He too has come to bury Caesar, neither to praise his life nor discuss his death. Giraud, whose prose is always lofty, adopts the tone of a man to whom neither Bonnier's motives nor his accomplices are of much account. *"La France vient de rentrer dans la guerre. Elle ne doit avoir qu'un souci, la guerre; un but, la Victoire."* Yet, not quite. Giraud wants not only Darlan buried, but his assassin also. *"Commandant en Chef d'un territoire en état de guerre, je prescris que la Cour Martiale se réunisse immédiatement. Elle jugera en toute impartialité. Son jugement, quel qu'il soit, sera appel."*

Giraud thus usurped authority, boldly and swiftly. Usurped it, moreover, while absent from Algiers, leaving to Bergeret the task of maintaining tranquillity in the city, asserting authority by force of opportunism. A characteristic proclamation was issued: *"Habitants de l'Afrique du Nord, l'Amiral Darlan vient de tomber à son poste, victime de ceux que ne lui pardonnaient pas d'avoir répondu aux voeux du peuple français, en reprenant, aux côtés des Alliés, le combat contre l'Allemagne. Les desseins de nos ennemis seraient déjoués"*. By defining assassination as unforgiveable, then coupling this assertion with a reminder that it now behooved his fellow citizens to join in the war, Giraud guaranteed Bonnier's fate while endeavoring to secure his own succession to Darlan's office—and power.

Murphy, as one would expect, says little to the point. Eisenhower was also absent from Algiers. Murphy and Clark, accompanied by Bergeret—a chief of staff with much on his mind—"called at the hospital to pay our respects to the deceased. I enquired of Darlan's assistant [*sic*] General Bergeret what immediate steps would be taken regarding maintenance of local authority. He is calling a council of local officials and requesting General Giraud to return from the Tunisian front for this purpose. [State] Department will be kept informed of developments. Assassin a young man, twenty-two years of age who in preliminary interview gives the name of Morand stated to be college instructor."

Roosevelt's personal representative to Vichy in North Africa can be forgiven for ignorance about Bonnier. But Murphy's inability to grasp that Darlan's assassination marked the final failure of the Vichy gamble is only equaled by Giraud's sanguine belief that his version of Vichy could be imposed on friend and foe alike. Yet the immediate aftermath of Darlan's assassination was to provide some warrant for that expectation.

III

"Good morning—and a very happy Christmas to you all. Last night Admiral Darlan was assassinated." The opening words of the BBC's first Home Service broadcast of Christmas Day 1942 were nothing if not brief and to the point. Among résistants the true dimension of Darlan's death was more deeply understood.

> In Algiers, a murder put paid to the Darlan scandal . . . an unknown young man walked into the victim's office without let or hindrance, waited there without anyone taking notice of him . . . his name could not be revealed for 'security reasons' . . . *Cui prodest?* Who profited by it? Giraud? de Gaulle? Pétain? One thing was certain: this was pure Shakespearian drama, where power was no longer delegated, but *seized*, as profit, intrigue, violence commanded.

Thus "Vercors" (the artist Jean Bruller), bicycling through gray Paris streets, past indifferent German soldiers and alert Gestapo, his parcel of clandestine, revolutionary books and pamphlets strapped none too securely behind him. Vercors knew, none better, that Darlan's death had saved Résistance. Disintegration from a sick sense of treachery; destruction by Vichy Milice and the Gestapo; this had been the shattering prospect as résistants accused, and betrayed, each other.

But Vercors and his like could not know that within hours of Darlan's death, the Cross of Lorraine was seen on the streets of Algiers. Members of the Corps Franc could walk openly in those streets, even to the Aletti Hotel, where Darlan's henchmen had distributed fear, and favors. Gaullism in Algiers was not yet; Giraud, with Rigault's knowledgeable assistance, was busy rounding up known Gaullists. The Aboulkers, with other former members of the Algiers patriot group, were arrested. But de Gaulle could no longer be dismissed as a rebel, a revolutionary.

At lunch on Christmas Day Bonnier was toasted in champagne by Robin Brook and "Passy," the enigmatic chief of de Gaulle's intelligence organization. In Baker Street, a member of Gubbins's staff noted: "Darlan has been bumped off. I was sure we had done it. We were pretty pleased." Reactions in Algiers were predictable. Mack was "unperturbed" at the news. Major General R.H. Barry, then a member of Eisenhower's staff, recalls "overwhelming relief" at hearing of Darlan's death. Indeed, the most striking aspect of the assassination was this prevailing lack of surprise, a sense that Darlan's time had come, and that his violent removal from the scene presaged a fundamental change in French fortunes. The era of Vichy had ended; that of Gaullism had begun. Churchill made the point to Roosevelt: "The French cannot wholly be denied some form of national political expression in their present phase." Darlan, alternately Hitler's creature and Roosevelt's surrogate—but better able to bargain with the latter than the former—had denied France essential political expression. De Gaulle, whatever his ultimate aim, was ambitious for France to recover political expression as a prelude to restoration of national liberation, and sovereignty.

Roosevelt and Churchill had differed fundamentally about Darlan during the six weeks of his triumph and power. The breach was not healed by Darlan's death. Roosevelt called the assassination "murder in the first degree." Churchill's view was that the assassination "relieved the allies of an embarrassment." Churchill was certainly relieved: between presidential hyperbole and prime ministerial understatement lies the issue: Darlan *or* de Gaulle. Churchill, in fact, echoed de Gaulle's reaction to the assassination when the latter was informed by Michael Saint-Denis ("Jacques Duchesal") on the evening of the 24th: *"Ça pour une nouvelle, c'est une nouvelle."*

De Gaulle's subsequent repudiation of direct, personal involvement in assassination—doubtless genuine enough, if somewhat beside the point—coupled with his immediate appeal to Giraud for a meeting and some form of joint "provisional administration" in North Africa herald his approaching triumphs. De Gaulle knew his time had come; Roosevelt's request that he delay a long-planned visit to the United States (a gesture designed to compensate for reiterated presidential rebuffs) worried him not at all. De Gaulle knew not only that his time had come, but also that he could take his time about strategy and tactics.

Darlan's assassination, in short, had transformed the situation not only in North Africa but in France as well. However much one can argue that de Gaulle would have preferred the blow to have been struck at a moment when "the street" had reacted violently to fascist rule, he knew that Giraud's succession could only be a temporary measure. De Gaulle's Christmas Eve broadcast, coupled with that of 28 December, reflects growing confidence; intransigence is tempered with assurance. "France sees her star rising again on the horizon." Darlan's assassination is ignored: the inevitable act already belongs to the past, to an era when "the defeatism of some leaders, treasonable intrigue and conspiracies by opponents of the sovereignty of the people . . . was only an episode which, frightful as it was, did not deter the will of the nation as it had been expressed while France was still free." A courteous reference to Giraud—"a renowned French military leader"—does nothing to dilute de Gaulle's declaration that "France is, and will remain, one and indivisible." Nor is one left in much doubt that de Gaulle intends that he, and no other, will be the unifying force.

De Gaulle could rhetorically strike while the iron was hot. In Algiers, the "Allies" whom he invoked on 28 December with a new touch of condescension had their hands full in dealing with the messy aftermath of assassination. Whatever Eisenhower's suspicions about the prime movers in Darlan's assassination, he acted quickly to confirm Giraud's appointment as high commissioner. Eisenhower also put up a smokescreen to cover any suggestion of British involvement in the assassination. On Christmas Day Berlin and Rome radio denounced the assassination as "engineered by the British Secret Service at Churchill's direction to get even with Roosevelt." An OSS report noted unctiously: "All German and German-dominated stations are unanimous in giving sole responsibility [for Darlan's assassination] to the British."

Cadogan in London insisted that Cunningham "deny charges that the Secret Service was in any way connected with the Darlan murder." Meanwhile, Eisenhower ordered his staff to put out stories to the effect that Darlan had met his death at the hand of "Axis agents." The large international press corps which, by Christmas 1942, was more or less resident in Algiers, duly obliged. In this flurry of charge and countercharge, "Monarchist plots" were reduced to the level of melodrama, while a Gaullist role was reserved for later speculation. The Comte de Paris touched his hat to Giraud. Henri d'Astier sought escape from arrest, and succeeded, by offering his services—to Giraud.

The "deafening silence" from London in the face of Axis propaganda—the BBC conspicuous by absence of comment— deluded none in Algiers that the assassination would simply blow over. French SOE agents in Algiers to whom suspicion might cling were promptly removed from the scene, bundled aboard a British warship, and told to make themselves scarce. Bonnier's court martial president was Chrétien, its moving spirit Bergeret. Giraud was inclined to leniency, but a court so composed, or directed, was unlikely to follow suit. Bonnier, with singular, touching, courage, maintained that he had acted alone, and from his own motives. The court was not, in fact, interested in Bonnier, or his motives. Darlan's assassination demanded a victim, Bergeret calculating accurately enough that Giraud stood a better chance of succeeding Darlan without opposition by offering a blood sacrifice than by propitiating "the street." Gaullists in Algiers were inclined to agree—to the extent that Bonnier as martyr also had a place in the scheme of things. By Henri d'Astier's insistence, no rescue was attempted. At 0730 on 26 December Bonnier was shot by firing squad in the courtyard of the police barracks at Hussein-Dey, in the environs of Algiers. Churchill noted: "He was surprised to be shot."

This valedictory leaves much unsaid. But what can be said of Bonnier's lonely death? To Henri Rosencher, fighting with BRANDON in Tunisia, falls the honor of one true epitaph: *"La mort de Bonnier est ressentie par nous tous, et par la Résistance française, comme un crime."* To many in the British camp *"Bonnier a rendu un grand service."* Yes, indeed. Bonnier's assassination of Darlan was of great service for the cause to which Churchill had been called in May 1940. We can only guess at Bonnier's final thoughts. There are letters and messages, last-minute appeals, fragmentary hopes. Perhaps all that can be said is this: *"Je ne meurs ni pour une faction, ni pour un homme. Je meurs pour Elle, pour mon idée à moi de la servir."*

Giraud was appointed high commissioner a few hours after Bonnier had fallen to the firing squad. Eisenhower approved the "Imperial Council's" nomination, one that had been made some days earlier. Pierre Flandin, a former Vichy minister, had arrived in Algiers during December, and was, reportedly, angling for the nomination. Boisson and Bergeret saw some future in Giraud, none in Flandin. Eisenhower had little choice but to accept Giraud; he rejected the remote possibility that Noguès, "that son of a bitch," might succeed Darlan. Giraud accepted both nomination and appointment with the dignified but misleading words "I am a soldier." Giraud certainly thought his hour had come at last, and was prepared to do Roosevelt's bidding—which, so far as both were concerned, meant continued rejection of de Gaulle.

On 27 December, Churchill gratuitously asked de Gaulle to exercise patience. The request was, in fact, not only gratuitous but disingenuous. On the 27th Churchill also told Roosevelt that he was not prepared to further delay the arrival of Harold Macmillan in Algiers as "Minister Resident at Allied Forces Headquarters." On the 29th, Roosevelt accepted this demand, stipulating nonetheless that Eisenhower "will continue to have full power over all civil officials in the area of operations." Churchill made no demur: he had his—and de Gaulle's—agent in place, at last. Churchill did not particularly care how Roosevelt reacted: London collectively had something more than a suspicion that the era of American ascendancy in North Africa had ended with Darlan's assassination, and that even Eisenhower had come to accept the fact. With Darlan's death, Roosevelt's Vichy policy was seen, at last, in its true colors.

Writing to Eden ("My dear Anthony"), on 24 December, Selborne had laid bare the bones of prospective change. Selborne argued:

> It has always been obvious to you and me in London that the inevitable political effect of re-instating Darlan in administrative control of North Africa would be further to divide and perplex Frenchmen in and outside France; and that over any but the shortest term the military effect would be to place an irredeemable pledge in the hands of this unscrupulous pawnbroker.

After some observations on Keswick's report, Selborne continued,

> It is increasingly evident that, if the use of such a two-edged weapon as Darlan ever was expedient, its expediency has entirely vanished. When news of the "affaire Darlan" first reached France, résistant opinion there reacted to the effect that it could only be comprehended if it was over within a fortnight. It is unfortunately only too clear that this instinctive and widespread reaction was correct. Expediency treated as an expedient might have served our turn, but entrenched and well watered it has become a major problem to uproot.

Three days later, Selborne, Hambro, and Gubbins were agreed that Darlan's assassination had uprooted the major problem. All in SOE were tasked to support French Résistance by every possible means. This task could again be executed.

When Selborne, in his letter of 24 December, referred to "preparing the ground in Europe for the next move forward" he knew well enough that Darlan's elimination would enable a North African base for this task to be established, at last. News of Darlan's death was greeted with enormous relief throughout the Résistance, but the sense of returning to the cause was probably felt most strongly among the SOE agents in France, whose tasks, dangerous enough at all times, had been rendered doubly so by Roosevelt's collaboration with Darlan.

Eisenhower was not fully aware of this intense feeling of relief, but he certainly made no very vigorous effort to lay any charges at British doors. An inquiry into Darlan's assassination was formally instituted by AFHQ; SOE, SIS, and British Security Service (MI5) officers in Algiers were put through a mild form of inquisition. But although Murphy and Bergeret were to consider retribution well into January, AFHQ was only too willing for SOE and its sister services to be exculpated. Eisenhower knew that OSS "had not been far behind SOE" in its collective detestation of Darlan. Eddy's request in late December to remove himself from Murphy's authority and place himself at Eisenhower's service is, perhaps, hardly more than straw in the wind, but indicates change nonetheless.

Eisenhower was anxious to return to his proper tasks. He condoled with Madame Darlan, and saw to it that she and her ailing son secured the sanctuary in the United States that the lately assassinated admiral had declared as his sole remaining ambition. Darlan's funeral on 30 December was conducted with suitable ceremony—but although a guard of honor was mounted, no British contingent was included among the troops detailed to line the route. By the year's end, this year that so dramatically marked "The end of the beginning," the hinge of fate had begun to swing toward a new arena of war, Axis Europe. Harold Macmillan arrived in Algiers on New Year's Eve. He traveled via Gibraltar, that center for so much designed to fuse the national interest with ideology. With Macmillan's advent, the curtain rises on the last act.

Epilogue

Algiers:
January to June 1943

O n 1 January 1943, H. Freeman Matthews, chargé d'affaires at the United States embassy in London, reported to the State Department:

> British policy requires that de Gaulle be maintained in a position of political primacy both during the war and in the early stages following the liberation of Continental France . . . if de Gaulle is a symbol to the people of France, he is also a symbol to the British Government, a symbol of justification for its whole French policy since June 1940 . . . British prestige requires that "the one Frenchman who stuck by us in the dark days of 1940" must be installed in France when the day of liberation comes, however fleeting his tenure may be and whatever the consequences for the people of France. It was this policy which lay behind

the Madagascar agreement. It was this policy which motivated the determination that Djibouti must join the Fighting French . . . It was this policy which made the Foreign
Office so insistent that Macmillan or some other political
officer [sic] of Cabinet rank be sent to Algiers without delay.
And it is this policy which is behind the present campaign
to emphasize Giraud as the military man and de Gaulle
as the political leader.

Matthews's meaning is clear: if the British Government
was pledged to de Gaulle's Free French before November 1942,
it was doubly committed to the man and the movement after
Darlan's assassination. Matthews intended that his words should
be heeded by his president, the secretary of state, and the State
Department as a whole. Matthews had served under Eisenhower in Algiers. Matthews knew what he was talking about.

On 3 June 1943 the French Committee of National Liberation was established in Algiers. This body, which included
the rudiments of a nonelective but quasi-parliamentary assembly, was endowed with two presidents, of equal status: Giraud
and de Gaulle. But, by the year's end, de Gaulle had painlessly
exercised that mastery of political maneuver and populist sentiment which, in France between 1944 and 1946, was to reveal
his natural vocation.

In the absence of a credible opponent some might think
that de Gaulle ran in a one-horse race. Giraud did not think
so. On succeeding Darlan, Giraud disposed of a formidable
security apparatus for hounding prospective Gaullists out of
North Africa or into prison. Roosevelt came to accept that
de Gaulle could no longer be ignored, but hoped to formulate
a scheme whereby the latter would be held in check by vari-
eties of pressure. Although Murphy was a back number by the
time of Darlan's assassination, and ceased utterly to be influential thereafter, he continued for some weeks to delude Roosevelt that Giraud could be run to suit American interests.
Murphy deluded himself that this process would shunt de Gaulle

into a corner. Macmillan's arrival in Algiers resulted in Giraud's being shunted—into obscurity.

Between January and June 1943 Harold Macmillan played a role in Algiers comparable to that of British representatives who were there before Darlan's assassination. Macmillan not only told London what was happening in North Africa; he recommended action. Macmillan, by his own confession, had been a committed Gaullist from June 1940. But, as a junior minister in departments somewhat removed from great affairs and stirring events, Macmillan had been forced to nurse rather than express his Gaullism. Promotion by Churchill, to cabinet rank and demanding responsibility, not only unlocked Macmillan's natural talent for intrigue. Promotion also released both an intellectual capacity and a practical gift that fused into one simple, basic decision within weeks of his arrival in Algiers: British support for de Gaulle meant support for his (undeclared) political ambition. Churchill, supporting the man and the movement, opposed the ambition. Macmillan's contribution to the history of these times was to convince Churchill that support for the man and the movement was inseparable from support for the political ambition.

We find in Macmillan's telegrams to London the story of de Gaulle's maneuvers in Algiers; he was not only supported by Churchill's man on the spot, but the British government was also provided with a running commentary so urbane yet so deft that de Gaulle's frequent sheer cussedness is put in a context where the central issue is never forgotten. Macmillan's American colleagues report these developments with the air of men who have put their money on the wrong horse. *Foreign Relations of the United States* is the only source that provides a day-to-day account of these events; two hundred pages of telegrams chart Murphy's decline from a player to a spectator. Murphy had been tasked by Roosevelt to foment a North African conspiracy—in the American long-term, post-war interest. Murphy had failed. Macmillan had been directed by Churchill to keep an eye on the Americans in North Africa. Macmillan exceeded his brief, but succeeded—brilliantly—in executing Churchill's undeclared intention: to prevent Roosevelt from arbitrating French affairs.

Macmillan was powerfully assisted in his policy of showing de Gaulle's ambition to be feasible—even if his method was well nigh intolerable—because of the role played by the always enigmatic but incontestably valuable figure of Catroux. The five-star general, the former governor of Indo-China, de Gaulle's "High Commissioner for the Levant," the elderly colon, descends intermittently on Algiers with the air of a man to whom the foibles of his leader are a matter of regret, nonetheless to be endured, explained, utilized. Macmillan appreciated Catroux: he was a kind of minor Catroux himself, sensitive to Churchill's moods, quick to seize the moment when de Gaulle was in favor, adroit at fielding the philippics that were regularly dispatched from Downing Street. Macmillan and Catroux in concert proved irresistible. De Gaulle's tantrums were (nearly always) ignored by one who was not only senior in rank but had proved his loyalty by an apparent subordination. De Gaulle also had the wit to perceive that Catroux could talk to Giraud as one five-star general to another. The hinge of fate was turning in de Gaulle's favor; it was Catroux's job to oil the machine.

II

Macmillan's one fear was that de Gaulle might bolt. Despite conviction about destiny, de Gaulle had this tendency. Catroux could admonish; Macmillan knew he must not do so. (He was not above admonishing Giraud, and did so roundly on at least one occasion, reminding him that de Gaulle had been fighting for France, as an exile, since June 1940.) The specific problems were relatively few, but they were basic; Macmillan could count himself fortunate that a mere month after his arrival in

Algiers he was able to trump Roosevelt's attempt to play the Giraud card. If Macmillan had not done this, thus reminding Churchill of basic issues, Giraud might well have consolidated his position as Roosevelt's satellite. The Giraud card was not exclusive to Roosevelt. Perhaps one should really say the Cordell Hull card, or even the State Department card, to be played with the express purpose of trumping de Gaulle.

Roosevelt and his subordinates wanted Giraud to accept a role in North Africa which, while granting him nominal status as high commissioner and commander-in-chief of the French armed forces, would make him little more than a spokesman for American policy. If Giraud accepted such a role, who was de Gaulle to bid for more? Setting aside the fact that Giraud sometimes chafed at this role, the card led on 6 February to a forcing bid from London. That bid was Churchill's renewed support for de Gaulle, expressed in the most significant terms possible; rejection by Churchill of Roosevelt's intentions *and* his methods.

Not for the first time, the United States embassy in London had its finger on the pulse of events; Washington, collectively, wanted Giraud as a satellite; the British government in general, Whitehall—to an increasing degree—and the Foreign Office specifically wanted a united French movement which, while expressing the aspirations of all who opposed Vichy, would rally behind de Gaulle. Just as Darlan and Bonnier had been laid to rest, and three days before Freeman Matthews spelled out for his masters the inner meaning of British support for de Gaulle, "The Embassy . . . warned Hull . . . that as far as the Fighting French were concerned, union with Giraud meant 'de Gaulle as supreme leader' . . ." This warning was timely. On 7 January the British embassy in Washington submitted, in an *aide memoire* for Hull, that

> The best solution would be the establishment in Algeria of a single authority in place of both the French National Committee in London and General Giraud's administra-

tion in Algiers . . . This authority would be treated as an
Allied power and formally admitted to the ranks of the
United Nations . . . it would be desirable that all links with
Vichy should be severed . . . The National Committee would
certainly press for [the] adoption [of these proposals] as
part of any agreement for fusion [with "General Giraud's
Administration"].

We should not be surprised to learn, therefore, that "This
[support for de Gaulle within the context of the French National
Committee] was to be British policy until June, when it was
consummated by the French Committee of National Liberation." The policy was powerfully assisted by the formation during May, and in *Paris*, of Moulin's Council of National
Resistance—which survived his capture, torture, and death. The
CNR brought together virtually all elements of French Résistance to Hitler, and Vichy. British support, not least from SOE
operating out of North Africa, enabled Moulin's version—and
vision—of Résistance to be realized.

Reports from Mack, from the OSS, and others, throughout
January and February, are a litany of protests against Giraud's
refusals, or inability, to curb anti-Semitism, release political
prisoners, grasp that Darlan was dead—and Pétain a mere
lackey in a wholly occupied France. Churchill's outburst to
Eden on 7 January provides counterpoint to the continuing
grisly North African scene. "There is a deep feeling of loathing
in this country, particularly amongst the working classes, against
anything which savours to them of intrigues with Darlan and
Vichy . . . You should tell Mr. Hull that there is almost a passion on the subject, and one which, if it broke loose, would
certainly cause differences of opinion and controversy in the
United States."

Giraud was, as one might say, incorrigible. An AFHQ report
of 5 January called Giraud's attempts to assert "command" in
Tunisia "a piece of unmitigated presumption." The report was

prompted by rejection not only of Giraud's asserted role in relation to Allied forces, but also of his political ambitions, disguised in lofty pronouncements. Giraud, from the moment of his succession to Darlan, had declared himself not only high commissioner but assumed also

> exclusive jurisdiction with reference to National Defence; French relations [*sic*]; approval of budgets where they exceed 50,000,000 francs; judicial and political status of individuals and foreigners; the organization of French justice and French penal legislation; the appointment of Governors-General, Residents-General . . . all French Magistrates . . . the Governors of Colonies . . .

This undoubted exercise in presumption was actually promulgated on 5 February, but was a dead letter. Eisenhower was not prepared to act as an occupying power in French North Africa—but he was certainly determined that Giraud should not become another Darlan.

Giraud's proclamation, in its timing as much as in its content, is the clearest possible indication that he saw himself invested with power because Roosevelt had made him sole "trustee" for the future of France. The all too revealing word *trustee* actually appears in the "Understanding" which Roosevelt and Giraud signed on 24 January—but which the alert Macmillan spotted once he perceived Murphy engaged in a revived attempt at conspiracy. SYMBOL had ended; Churchill had left for Adana in southeast Turkey, in yet another attempt to lug the Turkish government into the war. Roosevelt saw his chance—or so he thought.

SYMBOL was to be followed by TRIDENT during May, in Washington. There, Churchill might get his way over "Closing the Ring" from the Mediterranean, or he might not. Roosevelt decided that he could play the Giraud card as Churchill left for Adana, calculating that by the time the latter read the "Understanding" with Giraud he would accept it as the price for HUSKY—invasion of Sicily—and other, possible, concessions. Roosevelt's presumption may owe something to his observation of Churchill and de Gaulle during SYMBOL. De Gaulle was in his most stubborn mood; he "expressed no pleasure" at meeting Giraud, who returned the compliment by greeting him curtly with *"Bon jour de Gaulle."* The terrible inequalities of rank proved not less powerful a barrier to understanding than the tragic divide between two patriots, according to their lights.

Churchill was clearly fed up with de Gaulle. But Roosevelt might have reflected that Churchill had twice virtually begged de Gaulle to meet Giraud during SYMBOL, submitting to Eden's arguments because he realized that, if he broke with Fighting France, Roosevelt would revive the policy that Darlan's assassination was intended to destroy. Roosevelt consistently failed to grasp that Churchill's decisions, not merely his behavior, were based on emotion. Roosevelt may, or may not, have heard Churchill's SYMBOL valedictory on de Gaulle, as the latter stalked away from one more than usually difficult encounter. "His country has given up fighting, he himself is a refugee, and if we turn him down he's finished. Well, just look at him! Look at him! He might be Stalin with two hundred divisions behind his words!" Spears, a stern critic of de Gaulle commented: "How much of both men the scene conveys." But if Roosevelt did hear Churchill's words he failed to heed them.

Be that as it may, the alert Macmillan spotted Murphy passing around bits of paper on 23 January; confronted him with his behavior; extracted from that hopelessly miscast conspirator—"without judgment and without principles" is his interrogator's harsh verdict—the "Understanding" in question; and immediately transmitted it to Churchill. The latter, on 6 February, responded with verbal calm when he read Macmillan's telegram concerning the Roosevelt-Giraud "Understanding." Churchill merely noted that "he had been given no opportunity for consultation . . . but that he intended to deal with Giraud and de Gaulle on a basis of absolute equality." We now know exactly what those words were worth—to de Gaulle: British support, within the concept of "unity."

Roosevelt, by complete contrast, wanted "an anticommunist, pro-American French government under strong American influence composed of the kind of people who would be safe from their point of view." Giraud, in short, although one may wonder whether he would have accepted Roosevelt's insistence that the postwar France should lose Indochina; have Dakar and Bizerta put in commission for the defense of American hemispheric interests; and see the African colonial empire "disarmed from 'Casablanca to the Bight of Benin.' " Roosevelt, on 12 February, and presumably still sure of Giraud despite Churchill's rejoinders, repeated his insistence that "France should be totally disarmed after the war . . . a new state of Wallonia would be formed from the Walloon territory of Belgium and North-Eastern France."

The Foreign Office, in complete contrast, urged "a strong France that can play its part, with Russia, in containing Germany, firmly based on the French people as a whole and . . . generally speaking, left-wing rather than right-wing in character." De Gaulle, in short, despite the fact that he was as little an ally of the left as Churchill. That is not the point; after nearly half a century one must emphasize yet again that British public opinion in 1942 and 1943 was, in crude terms, pro-Russian, pro-de Gaulle. The Foreign Office, traditionally indifferent to such opinion, cashed in on this mood to develop its case. Churchill fumed—his "screams of rage" on one occasion reaching positively Bismarckian proportions—but, driven by the logic of his initial support for de Gaulle, accepted the choice: make with de Gaulle, or break with him.

The atmosphere in Algiers changed rapidly once Roosevelt's proposed deal with Giraud was exposed. By 18 February even Murphy realizes that the game is up. Radioing Washington,

Murphy reports—and implicitly recommends—". . . a political settlement between Giraud and de Gaulle." Murphy, as always, confuses the issue by declaring that SYMBOL "held out this promise" when, as we have seen, Roosevelt intended that it should do precisely the opposite. Murphy, possibly influenced by Eisenhower rather than Macmillan, begins from late February to shift his ground at accelerating speed. This shift certainly owed much to Roosevelt's reaction to exposure. On 20 February Giraud received a philippic from Roosevelt which must have chastened him considerably: the French armies in North Africa would be rearmed and reequipped from the arsenal of democracy—but only after more urgent matters had been attended to. In the meantime, would Giraud please shut up—and get on with his job, whatever that might be.

De Gaulle had his cares—the French National Committee in London by no means gave him the nod to do as he pleased—but Giraud's dilemma lay in the truth that he lacked a following. When declaring to Macmillan on 26 April that he could disregard "politicians," the latter was constrained to remind him that he could not do so. By 2 March, with Churchill hinting that "a central provisional authority of the French Empire . . ." should be established, Giraud came under direct attack. The following day—admittedly by coincidence—a delegation from the FNC arrived in Algiers. From 3 March until the end of April, this delegation concentrated its energies on compelling Giraud to repudiate the Compiègne Armistice as preliminary to stripping him of his claim to "legitimacy"—as heir to Pétain. It is a matter of fact that Giraud never did explicitly repudiate, but on 14 March he made a public statement repudiating "the legality of any acts taken since the Armistice . . ."

The FNC delegates at once raised the ante, as Murphy ruefully reported to Washington on 18 March. The men of Vichy were next on the FNC hit list. Matthews, in London, commented hyperbolically on the 22nd: " . . . suffering France demands the leadership of de Gaulle the man, not merely de Gaulle the symbol." Suffering France demanded nothing of the kind: de Gaulle as leader of Résistance was distinguished in many French minds—left, right, and center—from de Gaulle with his eye on the main chance. That is not the point. Matthews in London understood what Murphy in Algiers had for so long failed to grasp: just as in November it had been "Darlan or de Gaulle" so, by March, it was a case of Giraud or de Gaulle. Eden, who had drawn the crude distinction in November, was more careful when he met Hull on the very day of Matthews's comment. A long, inconclusive discussion at the State Department suggests that Eden had the impending TRIDENT Conference more on his mind than the fate of de Gaulle.

Nevertheless, Eden proposed that discussions between Frenchmen in Algiers should lead to "a rather larger French National Committee." This version of a Trojan horse was mirrored, supreme irony, by a meeting between Murphy and Noguès on 14 April. Noguès's arrogance was undiminished. He demanded from Murphy an end to the "hostile attitude of American consular and civilian officials in French Morocco." Noguès asserted that the officials in question were supporting "a minority of Frenchmen who stood for a return of the Popular Front." This version of de Gaulle's "Jewish and left-wing" supporters would once have met with Murphy's sympathetic response.

On the day in question, Murphy finally went over to the other side: "I suggested to General Noguès that as it had been long since he had been in contact with active public opinion that possibly he exaggerated the importance of the present mild manifestations of a critical minority." Murphy added, in his wire to Hull: "There is understandable rancor on the part of French and Americans over General Noguès's activities and attitudes at the time of the American landing. I said that I was confidant that some of my compatriots would never understand why he had acted as he had; that they and I considered that he bore a great responsibility which resulted in the loss of the lives of both Americans and Frenchmen . . . these things are not easily forgotten . . . His reaction to this was that any American who felt that way should be removed."

Murphy, in April 1943, could not accept rebuke from such a source. His riposte was excessive. As he reported to Hull:

> My conversation with General Noguès confirms the conviction which I have had for a long time that he is unreliable, insincere, and an obstructionist. It is obvious that for some time past he has made a desperate effort to placate American sentiment and so ingratiate himself with us by the shopworn method of social attentions. In my opinion, General Noguès's heart is not in this war; he lives in constant fear of the bogey of communism and the return of the Popular Front in France, and he has completely lost any idea of liberation and a reasonable play of public opinion.

Poor Noguès! Murphy's recantation was doubtless complete—if hardly sincere—but there is something distinctly odd about biting the hand you have attempted to feed. Nor was Murphy accurate in his rebuttal of Noguès's complaints. The Gaullist campaign against Giraud was not a series of "mild manifestations." René Capitant and *Combat* saw to that. Noguès doubtless deserved his dismissal, but his otherwise pointless exchange with Murphy is only given so that the implications for de Gaulle and the FNC delegation in Algiers of a further swing in the hinge of fate can be sufficiently appreciated.

By mid-April Catroux, more closely in touch with Eden than de Gaulle, has sensed that the latter might bolt. Catroux knew that he must convince de Gaulle that Giraud would lose providing the FNC also rode a waiting race. De Gaulle was hard to hold; he wanted, naturally enough, to be in Algiers. Plans were made to send de Gaulle to North Africa, but they were hedged about with qualifications. Stark backed de Gaulle's demand that he would only meet Giraud "on French soil"— namely, in Algiers. Others in London, while strong in de Gaulle's support, were less responsive to French pride. While de Gaulle alternately raged and sulked in London, Catroux and Eden edged the FNC toward a position that could only result in Giraud accepting that an enlarged FNC would not be packed with his supporters. The position is best summarized in the FNC's statement of 17 April, in which one can detect more than a touch of Jean Moulin's October 1941 report:

(1) The abolition of Vichy legislation should be complete, and this implies that the principal posts of direction should not be confided to men who have had a general responsibility in capitulation to or collaboration with the enemy.
(2) When the liberation of France comes, departmental administrators should not be designated by the military authority; this would not be acceptable to the organizations of resistance in France.
(3) The central authority will have to act not only for the Empire, but for the nation, including the internal forces of resistance; administrative personnel, such as colonial governors, resident-generals, etc., should normally be subordinated to the central authority.
(4) The commander-in-chief should be subordinated to the central authority.
(5) A legal council should be formed to prevent abuse of powers and to decide on the legality of decrees and administrative decisions; the national council should, as far as possible, allow the people of France to express their views.
(6) The central authority should be constituted in such a way as to correspond as closely as possible to traditional French governmental organization.

De Gaulle's outstandingly difficult behavior during May and early June was only endured by Catroux and Macmillan because they were determined not to lose the race. On 6 May Macmillan admitted to his diary that de Gaulle appeared bent on "a personal drive for power." This, in fact, was true. It was also irrelevant. Two days before, de Gaulle had publicly

denounced Giraud's "North African regime as a mere continuation of 'L'Expédient temporaire' of Darlan." Capitant ensured
widespread coverage for this unhelpful—although accurate—
denunciation.

TRIDENT, which ran a far from harmonious course from
early to late May, further complicated an already confused situation in Algiers. A geographical gulf of some three thousand
miles served only to widen and deepen differences. Churchill,
pressing for the invasion of Italy, returned to criticism of
de Gaulle as the best—or the only—means of propitiating
Roosevelt. The latter proved obdurate over Italy; on 21 May
Churchill told Eden "to break off negotiations with
de Gaulle." But, yet again, Roosevelt overplayed his hand.
Churchill could bear with comparative indifference Roosevelt's attacks on de Gaulle. By May 1943 this was an old story.
But when, on 8 May, Roosevelt asserted that "I am inclined to
think that when we get in to France we will have to regard it
as a military occupation run by British and American generals
. . ." Churchill balked. He balked even more at Roosevelt's
notion of an "Allied Commander-in-Chief" exercising a
potentate's role in France.

Churchill knew that, yet again, he was being forced to
choose. Roosevelt assumed that the "Commander-in-Chief"
would be American; he made plain that this potentate's creature should be Giraud. Italian ambitions and agitated telegrams to Eden were one thing; *renouncing* de Gaulle was
another. Churchill fired off a further series of telegrams to Eden,
painting de Gaulle in the blackest of colors, resorting to assertions that only convinced the recipient and his advisers that
they were intended for rejection.

On 23 May, the Cabinet in London did so reject. Ernest
Bevin, "the one indispensable man" in the War Cabinet, spoke
for more than his colleagues in emphasizing that any break
with de Gaulle would be attributed to American pressure—a
pressure that he, Bevin, intended to resist. The Chiefs of Staff,
whose views hardly mirrored Bevin's, and whose attitude to

de Gaulle personally never eased into warmth, were nevertheless equally solid for rejection of Churchill's assertions. Given
the Chiefs' importance in supporting those who fought the
common enemy, their conclusions on this point are worthy of
recapitulation:

> ... There were 80,000 Fighting French troops in various
> parts of the world and fifty-seven ships which played a
> valuable part in the Allied war effort ... the political
> repercussions, both in terms of British public opinion and
> of the effect on the morale of the French resistance and
> the Allied governments in exile, were likely to be damag-
> ing to the war effort.
> We do not consider your policy practicable.

No Cabinet meeting would have dared to tell Churchill that in
1940, 1941, or 1942. By May 1943, Churchill was no longer
omnipotent. He may even have welcomed this change: declin-
ing health and strength is reflected in a greater readiness to
share burdens. The War Cabinet in general and Eden in particular could not be unaware of this shift in the balance of
domestic political power. Despite Bevin's resistance to American pressure—widely reflected in British public opinion, particularly among those "working classes" to which Churchill
himself had somewhat deliberately referred in earlier exchanges
with Eden—there was little the British government collectively
could do to oppose the emerging super-power relationship
between the United States and the Soviet Union.

But, over a seemingly less fundamental issue, the future
of France, government, cabinet, British public opinion—and
one may add, the King—were solidly united: the France in
question would be led by de Gaulle, not because, as Bevin
declared, he had rallied the "workers" of France—although he
had—but because he and his Fighting French had stood by
Britain on the edge of the abyss. It is in that context, and that
only, that the cabinet recorded and expressed its united opposition to Churchill's apparent submission regarding Roose-

velt's detestation of de Gaulle. By May 1943 it was not practicable British politics to abandon the cause for which ordinary British subjects were fighting and enduring.

Given these truths it may seem odd that de Gaulle should have given his myriad champions such a hard time. Gladwyn Jebb's views are extremely relevant at this point. Jebb had been an early champion; had advocated anti-Vichy—and hence prospectively Gaullist—operations when seconded to SOE; and had written, in November 1942, one of the most savage attacks on the "temporary expedient" that ever found its way onto Eden's desk. Jebb knew de Gaulle as one who:

> . . . had dreadful faults . . . He was vindictive, arrogant, proud, unscrupulous, self-centered, merciless and, in a queer way, out of date . . . he had no humility, little compassion, and he by no means loved his neighbour as himself . . . *But:* . . . The fact was he was possessed by an all-consuming and uncontrollable passion, transcending all other cravings, for France.

Jebb, something of a hard case himself and certainly a very considerable cynic, then reminds us of de Gaulle's own allegiance to France: "I instinctively feel that Providence has decreed that she must either be completely successful or utterly unsuccessful. For France, mediocrity is an absurd anomaly."

Churchill's accurate suspicion about de Gaulle's political ambitions are subsumed by these words: in May 1943, de Gaulle stood on the brink of a triumph which would transcend ambition, and survive the savageries of liberation. But de Gaulle could not move: he was forced to watch while his delegates bickered with Giraud, the whole process being supervised by the Americans he despised and the British whom he doubted. No excuses need be made for de Gaulle: if he had bolted or gone the wrong side of the posts during May 1943, it is probable that the hinge of fate would have continued to swing in his favor. But that de Gaulle did give his champions a hard time, and that he neither eased their burdens nor acknowledged their role is a fact that, belatedly, should be recorded. Jean Monnet, René Massigli, and others have told their tale; Murphy we can forget; Eisenhower had other cares; Catroux remains inscrutably elliptical; Churchill—arriving, rather inopportunely, in Algiers on 28 May—is idiosyncratic, to say the least; Macmillian spills few beans for public consumption. The truth lies embedded in telegrams.

The issues dividing the FNC from Giraud were both profound and trivial. Therein lay the problem. The FNC strategy was to establish an outright political power base for de Gaulle in North Africa. The committee's members differed in their views about de Gaulle, but were united on the central issue: He represented Résistance, and it was there, in France, that the future would be decided. The FNC's tactics were to give Giraud what he appeared to want more than anything else— namely the "High Command"—while denying him effective power in any other direction.

Even Murphy could work all this out. By May 1943, he was reduced to making background noises. Thus, the FNC delegates could reckon on positive or tacit support from the British and American camp in Algiers. Indeed, negotiations appeared to be making progress when de Gaulle issued a statement that, while essentially a recapitulation of the issues, was as grandiloquent in tone as anything penned by Darlan or Giraud.

> The National Committee is of the same opinion as you that preliminary discussion should be brought to an end, and that it is necessary immediately to establish in Algiers the body which will exercise the common central power. You and I will alternately assume the presidency. We are in agreement that the responsibility of this body is collective and that the length [duration] of its functions shall be limited at the latest to the date which the law of February 25/15 1872 will permit the nation to obtain a provisional representation that constitutes the government. With regard to the composition of this body to be created which from

now will exercise the central power and with regard to other questions which remain to be settled it is understood that we will discuss them in Algiers, you and I, as well as two persons proposed by you, and two by the National Committee. I expect to arrive in Algiers by the end of this week and I am pleased that shortly I shall collaborate directly with you in the service of France.

De Gaulle had not forgotten *"Bonjour de Gaulle."* In one sense, de Gaulle had arrived, and he knew it. But when de Gaulle actually did appear in Algiers on 27 May—the day his statement was made public—tantrums, and worse, immediately became the order of the day. Giraud was prepared, just, to suffer the indignity of a temporary brigadier general addressing him like a newly joined second lieutenant. But Churchill's proposal on arriving in Algiers that the British government should end its "subsidy" to the FNC—in effect to Fighting France—appears to have convinced him that he was still the preferred Anglo-American candidate for leadership in the new Committee.

Giraud posed; de Gaulle raged. He was perfectly well aware that his movement owed much to Britain; he was revolted at being reminded of this fact at the moment of his imminent triumph. Threats to leave Algiers were made—even to Murphy. The latter reported on 1 June: ". . . de Gaulle would give no assurance that he intended to surrender his freedom of action." But Murphy added with weary, belated insight: "At the same time I do not believe de Gaulle has any intention of departing. He is convinced of his own ability eventually to prevail."

Fortunately Eden accompanied Churchill to Algiers. One proud and lonely man came to the support of another, enduring the absurdities of Giraud's insistence that "posters of living persons" should be removed from the lampposts of Algiers and his demand that de Gaulle—the "living person" in question—must publicly repudiate any intention "to establish a totalitarian political system in France under his personal leadership."

Absurdity lay in the fact that Giraud's portrait adorned many an Algiers office wall—superseding Pétain's—and in supposing that de Gaulle intended anything else but reaffirmation of that personal leadership that had led him to defy a France of collaborators and *attentistes*. De Gaulle's riposte was directed solely at this point; on 31 May he demanded *"Le nettoyage administratif"*—a clean sweep, in which the men of Vichy would be sacked, or put up against a wall.

Yet, in a way, Giraud's demand cleared the air. A tremendous row, a good deal of panic even from Catroux, culminated on 3 June with just such a repudiation from de Gaulle which Giraud demanded. This immensely useful but utterly facile climb-down enabled patriots of ill will to compose a committee whose principals reflected not so much allegiance to this or that as an enforced acceptance of the need to show serious intent. The committee's terms of reference accorded in all material respects with de Gaulle's 27 May démarche. For de Gaulle, Massigli and Philip; for Giraud, Monnet, General Alphonse-Joseph Georges (an elderly makeweight, lately smuggled out of France at Churchill's insistence), and Catroux.

A brilliant balancing act enabled de Gaulle in due time to riposte with men more than able to tilt the committee's balance decisively in his favor. Monnet shifted his ground; Georges cut no ice; Catroux was essentially de Gaulle's man. Giraud was given a consolation prize: Roosevelt invited him to visit the United States. The invitation was gratefully accepted, but displays Giraud's political naïveté as no other act could have; de Gaulle used his absence for purposes of committee consolidation.

A long road for France lay ahead, made much harder by Roosevelt's reluctance to accord any authority to a committee dominated by de Gaulle. Not until 22 October 1944, with Paris at de Gaulle's feet, did Roosevelt concede defeat. But the seeds of that defeat lay in factors that, even today, we can only discern: one man's will; another's imagination; the refusal of Frenchmen, everywhere—if often so late—to accept dictatorship. De Gaulle no more spoke for France than did his enemies and opponents, but he represented an idea of France that struck response from men who needed to know for what purpose they fought, and died.

Glossary

AFHQ   Allied Forces Headquarters

ARCADIA   Anglo-American Washington Conference, December 1941

ATTILA   German occupation of French Unoccupied Zone, November 1942

BARBAROSSA   German invasion of Soviet Union, June 1941

BBC   British Broadcasting Corporation

BRANDON   SOE Mission in French North Africa

CATAPULT   British attack on French warships at Mers-el-Kébir, July 1940

CNL   (French) Committee of National Liberation

CNR   (French) Council of National Résistance

DYNAMO   Evacuation of British and French forces from Dunkirk, May and June 1940

ENIGMA   Cyphering system used by German commands, etc., as intercepted and read by British Intelligence

EXPORTER   Anglo-Free French invasion of Syria, June 1941

FNC   French National Committee

GYMNAST/SUPER GYMNAST   British code name for invasion of French North Africa; predecessors of TORCH

HUSKY   Projected Anglo-American invasion of Sicily

IRONCLAD   British attack on Madagascar, May 1942

LEOPARD   SOE weapons supply to Algiers Patriot Group

LONMAY   SOE role in TORCH

MASSINGHAM   SOE Mission in French North Africa

MENACE   Anglo–Free French attack on Dakar, September 1940

MI5   (British) Security Services

OSS   (American) Office of Strategic Services

OWI   (American) Office of War Information

PWE   (British) Political Warfare Executive

RYGOR   Polish Intelligence circuit in French North Africa

SIS   (British) Secret Intelligence Service

SLEDGEHAMMER   Projected   Anglo-American   cross-Channel operation, 1942

SOE   (British) Special Operations Executive

SOL   (French) Service d'Ordre Legionnaire

SYMBOL   Anglo-American Casablanca Conference, January 1943

TORCH   Anglo-American invasion of French North Africa, November 1942

TRIDENT   Anglo-American Washington Conference, May 1943

YANKEE   Robert Murphy's signals net

Sources

Text references and quotations are mainly from unpublished primary sources, namely interviews and archives. In most cases the source will be clear from the text, but note, particularly for Part Two:

1. SOE Archive in London and OSS material in the National Archives, Washington (including reports from North Africa before the establishment of OSS): subversive operations concerning TORCH and its antecedents; reactions in Algiers and elsewhere in North Africa to Darlan's appointment as high commissioner.

2. Foreign Office File 660 and War Office File 204 in the Public Record Office, Kew: FO 660 includes telegrams from Foreign Office and Political Warfare Executive representatives in Algiers, together with replies and instructions from Eden. WO 204 is the AFHQ record of events and military operations from early August 1942, but is remarkably comprehensive on *political* aspects of TORCH. The file not only includes the Combined Chiefs of Staff's directives, but Clark's signals to Eisenhower during the former's negotiations with Darlan, and what transpired thereafter. Eisenhower's increasing concern at the course of events after his initial support for the Clark-Darlan Agreement is fully revealed, as is the collective Washington response. The file also includes signals from Eisenhower to Ismay, and expressions of the British Chiefs of Staff of objections to Darlan's arrogation of power.

Appropriately enough, the file contains the quoted examples of Darlan's proclamations and speeches, together with examples of the equivocal relationship between Eisenhower and Giraud, plus the latter's attempt, on succeeding Darlan as high commissioner, to assert a largely spurious authority. The file also contains several SIS and MI5 reports, the former cited in the text at p. 163. Infrequent citation of SIS reports from North Africa (as distinct from the ENIGMA) are also to be found in F. H. Hinsley et al., *British Intelligence in the Second World War* (London: 1981), vol. 2.

3. A Report dated 4 February 1944, sent to the Admiralty from "the Office of the Commander-in-Chief, Mediterranean, Algiers," namely: "Record of Negotiations with French During Period 9th–16th November 1942."

Where published primary sources are quoted, note that, except as otherwise indicated:

1. Warren F. Kimball, ed., *Churchill & Roosevelt: The Complete Correspondence*, 3 vols. (Princeton: 1984).

2. R. T. Thomas, *Britain and Vichy: The Dilemma of Anglo-French Relations, 1940–42* (London: 1979): British views on United States policy toward Vichy.

3. Sir Llewellyn Woodward, *British Foreign Policy in the Second World War* (London: 1971), vol. 2: Communications between Churchill, Eden, and Halifax, particularly for the period between 8 November and 24 December 1942; Foreign Office minutes during this period.

4. Arthur J. Marder, *From the Dardanelles to Oran: Studies of the Royal Navy in War and Peace, 1915–1940* (London: 1974): Background to and narrative of Mers el-Kébir, 3 July 1940.

5. Robert L. Melka, "Darlan Between Britain and Germany, 1940–41," *Journal of Contemporary History* 8 (1973): Darlan's collaboration with Hitler in 1940 and 1941, particularly relating to Syria.

6. *Foreign Relations of the United States, Washington.* (vol. 2 for 1942 and 1943): Communications between Robert Murphy and Washington, together with reports from U.S. consuls in North Africa.

7. Alfred D. Chandler, Jr., ed., *The Papers of Dwight David Eisenhower*, vols. 1 and 2, *The War Years* (Baltimore: 1970): AFHQ developments in London between August and October 1942; communications between Eisenhower and Churchill, Marshall, Stark, etc., particularly for the period between 8 November and 24 December 1942, thus complementing WO 204.

8. John D. Charmley, "British Policy Towards General de Gaulle, 1942–44" (Ph.D. diss., 1982): Events between January and June 1943, above all as expressed in Harold Macmillan's telegrams to Churchill and Eden, and their replies. This source also constitutes a valuable record of Roosevelt's views and actions during the earlier part of this period.

Notes

Page

17. Francois Kersaudy, *Churchill and de Gaulle* (London: 1981), 427–29.

19. The assassination weapon has been variously thought to be an (American) Colt Woodsman .45, and a pistol described by Mario Faivre to Pierre Raynaud in a letter of 26 September 1988, and made available to the writer, thanks to Henri Rosencher, as a 7.65, "fabriqué à Hendaye." As Faivre and Raynaud were with Bonnier up to the point of the latter entering the Palais d'Eté, Faivre's version is likely to be correct. Bonnier had been issued a .38 during his training course with the SOE Mission, MASSINGHAM; the Colt is claimed by some who are not averse from seeing an OSS role somewhere along the line. Faivre has some interesting comments on the effectiveness, or otherwise, of these various weapons, how, and when they were acquired. Of the 7.65, Faivre says all that need be said: *"Elle fonctionnait parfaitement"*. This is hardly surprising. A pistol with the caliber of a rifle would give the target, at close range, no chance at all.

20. See p. 253 for the interpretation given by the embassy to "political primacy."

20–21. Robert Sherwood, *The White House Papers of Harry L. Hopkins: An Intimate History* (New York; 1948), vol. 1, 259. Sherwood is, in fact, quoting Roosevelt's main apologist, William Langer. Thomas, 175.

22. Thomas, 110.

23. J.M.A. Gwyer and J.R.M. Butler, *History of the Second World War* (London, 1964), vol. 3, *Grand Strategy*, 671.

23. Much controversy remains concerning Stalin and the "Second Front." Churchill's account of his first meeting with Stalin in August 1942 suggests that the latter wel-

comed TORCH in almost effusive terms. Thanks to the writer's friend Robin Edmonds, the verbatim record has been produced, and is given below. It would seem that Stalin swallowed the fact that there was not going to be a full-scale "Second Front" in 1942—or 1943—and made the best of a bad job. As Churchill concealed his real intentions concerning TORCH—which was not only to "strengthen this ring" but to open a Balkan front as a deterrent to Soviet ambitions in southeast Europe—Stalin apparently concentrated on Anglo-American objectives concerning Western Europe. Stalin clearly had no inkling of *Roosevelt's* intentions, or of the conflict between him and Churchill over the future of France. TORCH, incidentally, took some German pressure off the Russian fronts. Luftwaffe units, for example, were transferred to southern Italy and Tunisia.

The Soviet account of the August 1942 meetings between Churchill and Stalin is in Sovetsko-Anglüskie Otnosheniya vo vremya velikoi otcchestvennoi voiny, 1941–1945: dokumenty i materialy, Politizdat, Moscow; 1983; Vol. I.

12 August (p. 270)

"Stalin states that from his military point of view, he fully understands the operation for the seizure of the North African seaboard. In his opinion, it possesses four advantages: opening Mediterranean communications; bases for aerial bombardment of Italy; threatening Rommel's rear; and barring the Axis' way to Dakar." Stalin then said: "He would consider that it would be advantageous to carry out this operation with the participation of de Gaulle or one of the French generals."

13 August (p. 272)

Stalin reverted to TORCH, along the lines of the previous day, but added: "... the operation is politically not well enough founded. But it can be done."

15 August (pp. 280–81)

"In connection with this operation Stalin would like to ask Churchill whether it is not necessary to occupy France. He supposes that this would not be a bad thing."

24.   The economic implications of Roosevelt's Vichy policy, especially in relation to Britain, its Empire, and British oil interests in the Middle East, are beyond the scope of this

book. But that Roosevelt was determined to penetrate
British markets on the basis of his Vichy policy is clear
enough from evidence of conflict between London and
Washington on commercial matters. The conflict was particularly acute concerning West Africa, and intensified
when an emissary of Roosevelt's, Admiral Glasspool, was
sent to Dakar at the end of 1942—but while Darlan's
henchman Boisson was still in authority there.

27. WO 204/303.

27. Major-General Sir Edward Spears, *Two Mén Who Saved
France: Pétain and de Gaulle* (London: 1966), 209.
Nigel Nicolson, *Harold Nicolson: Diaries and Letters, 1939–
1945* (London, 1967), 263.

36. Major-General Sir Edward Spears, *Assignment to Catastrophe* (London: 1954), vol. 2, 323. Kersaudy, 73. A fuller
account of the meeting between Churchill and de Gaulle
in London on 16 June 1940 is in the Spears papers.

44. Kersaudy, 85.

44. Thomas, 52. The formation of the French National Committee at the end of July 1940 secured recognition by the
British government of de Gaulle as "the leader of all Free
Frenchmen, wherever they may be, who rally to the support of the Allied cause."

46. J.R.M. Butler, *History of the Second World War: Grand
Strategy* (London: 1957), vol. 2, 245.

46. Winston S. Churchill, *The Second World War* (London:
1949), vol. 2, *Their Finest Hour*, 357.

47. Thomas, 71.
Thomas, 71. Churchill added: ". . . these men have committed acts of baseness which have earned them the last-
ing contempt of the world . . ."

53. Brian Crozier, *De Gaulle: The Warrior* (London: 1973),
149.

59. Nicolson, 156.

59–60. Woodward, 80.
Thomas, 123.
A verbatim printed account of the 12 September meeting
is in the Spears papers. One should remember that the
June 1940 "recognition" of de Gaulle and the Free French
by the British government deliberately avoided any commitment to the restoration of French overseas territories,

Page

including the mandates of Syria and Lebanon. This British escape clause always fueled the deepest suspicions in de Gaulle.

61. Thomas, 123.

61. Foreign Office Weekly Intelligence Summary: 30 November 1941.

62. Moulin's report is given in full in M.R.D. Foot, *SOE in France: An Account of the Work of the British Special Operations Executive in France, 1940–1944* (London: 1966), 489–95.

63. David Stafford, *Britain and European Resistance, 1940–1945: A Survey of the Special Operations Executive, with Documents* (London: 1980), 72–73.

66. Thomas, 101, representing assorted British views on Murphy.

66–67. Robert Murphy, *Diplomat Among Warriors* (New York: 1964), 70.

Thomas, 117.

67. Thomas, 108.

67. Robert O. Paxton, *Politics and Parades at Vichy: The French Officer Corps under Marshal Pétain* (Princeton: 1966), 251.

68. Thomas, 139.

Thomas, 108.

69–71. Gwyer and Butler, 325–29.

74. Thomas, 130.

Thomas, 133.

76. Woodward, 358.

77–78. Kersaudy, 187–89.

79. Thomas, 127.

80. Woodward, pp. 340–42, revealing that change in terminology was equated, at least by the Foreign Office, with change in status.

81. Sheila Mathieu and W. G. Corap, trans., *Speeches of General de Gaulle* (London: 1943), vol. 2, *1942*, 40.

84. The directives are summarized in Hinsley, 14. The directives were, in fact, written by the Joint Planning Staff, and the originals, in the Public Record Office, provide essential background to the gradual evolution of SOE's role in support of Churchill's "closing the ring" strategy. (Chief of Staff Papers: 79/20.) SOE was thus tasked—but responsibility for execution was given to F Section, not

Page

RF. The former operated independently of de Gaulle; the latter in cooperation with him—an oversimplification of a complex relationship, but giving the essential element. The point is of importance in the context of a situation where the Chiefs of Staff, in the spring of 1942, were not prepared to support Gaullism. Ostensibly, this policy obtained well into 1943, so far as SOE's operating from North Africa into France was concerned. Thereafter, RF influence predominated. Nevertheless, Robin Brook, head of all SOE French sections from November 1942, has commented: "It always seemed to me that SOE and even more OSS had a much freer hand in North Africa [than in France]. The thread that was common to both was attitudes to de Gaulle. In this respect, we had a fairly steady task of persuading departments that, whatever one thought of de Gaulle, he was indispensable." (Letter to the writer of 12 June 1986.)

84. M.R.D. Foot, "British Aid to Armed French Resistance: 1940–44 and the Secret Services," *Journal of the British Institute in Paris* 2 (Autumn 1986), 19.

85. Forrest C. Pogue, *George C. Marshall: Ordeal and Hope* (London: 1968), 403.

85–86. George Frederick Howe, *The United States Army in World War II: North-West Africa: Seizing the Initiative in the West* (Washington: 1957), 29.
Hinsley, 475.

88. Major-General I.S.O. Playfair et al., *History of the Second World War* (London: 1966), vol. 4, *The Mediterranean and Middle East*, 115.

92. Bickham Sweet-Escott, *Baker Street Irregular* (London: 1965), 17.

93. Quoted in *The Observer* of 15 March 1987.

94. Thomas, 122.

96. Hinsley, 463.

97–98. The writer has had the privilege of reading the original typescript of General Rygor Slowikowski's *In the Secret Service: The Lighting of the Torch* (London: 1988), from which the report quoted and the description of Eddy are taken.

109. Murphy, 97–98.

110. On Giraud's pledge of loyalty to Pétain: Michael Howard,

Page

    History of the Second World War (London: 1972), vol. 4, *Grand Strategy*, 148. Howard reveals, more clearly than Woodward, Playfair, or Howe that at this stage in planning TORCH, neither Churchill nor the British Chiefs of Staff was heeded by Roosevelt. SOE played an essential role in Giraud's escape. A Section F officer (operating independently of de Gaulle and his affiliates), John Goldsmith, was in touch with him via an intermediary, General Chambe. This Section F involvement with Giraud has some bearing on subsequent events in Algiers.

110–11. Paxton, 325.

112. The original of this letter, in Darlan's handwriting, is most oddly in WO 204.

114. *Foreign Office Weekly Intelligence Summary* 2 May 1943, giving a retrospective account of Mast's role in conspiracy.

116. Jacques Soustelle, *Envers et Contre Tout; De Londres à Alger: Souvenirs et documents sur La France Libre, 1940–1942* (Paris: 1947), 425.

121. Murphy, 118.

123. Henri Rosencher: *Le Sel, La Cendre Et La Flamme*, 113. (privately printed, Paris, 1985).

124. Murphy, 109.

138–39. Foreign Office Weekly Intelligence Summary for 7 November 1942.

    The order on the following page from Jousse to the Algiers Patriot Group reveals that he, at least among the senior officers ostensibly conspiring with Murphy, was capable of decision. The objective is clear: to seize Juin at his headquarters.

141–42. Howe, 230.

143. Foot, 4.

147–48. Woodward, 360.

    The writer is indebted to General Lemnitzer for an account of Patton's attitude—and of his always fractious relationship with Eisenhower.

158–59. Arthur Layton Funk, *The Politics of TORCH: The Allied Landings and the Algiers* Putsch *1942* (University of Kansas Press, 1974), 220. Putsch in the subtitle refers to OSS usage for the events of 8 November 1942. But the OSS Report in question—of 28 January 1943—makes quite clear that such a putsch was intended to install an *anti*-Vichy administration in North Africa.

Page

XIX° Région,
Division Territoriale d'Alger,   Alger, le 7 Novembre I942.
Place d'Alger,
N°/8●8.

ORDRE DE MISSION.

En application des dispositions du Plan de Protection
de la Place d'Alger, le Groupe de Volontaires EI assurera la
garde de la Villa des Oliviers, résidence du Général Commandant
en Chef les Forces en A.F.N.

Il relèvera le poste de garde dont le personnel re-
joindra immédiatement son corps.

Le Général Commandant d'armes Délégué
de la Place d'Alger,
P.O. Le Major de Garnison,

162–63.   Kersaudy, 219.
          Woodward, 391. See also Crozier, 201.
  169.   Unpublished Anderson dispatch of 22 October 1951, Public
          Record Office, Cab/106/708.
173–74.   Cunningham Papers, British Library.
180–82.   For exchanges between Churchill and de Gaulle, and
          Roosevelt's Press Conference, Kersaudy, 222–25. Chur-
          chill was undoubtedly increasingly influenced by the Brit-
          ish Cabinet, no longer prepared to accept all he did without
          demur, especially in relation to Roosevelt. Leo Amery,
          Secretary of State for India, and an old but outspoken friend
          of Churchill, noted in his diary: "16 November 1942:
          Cabinet at which we discussed at some length the curious
          situation created by Eisenhower's adoption of Darlan as
          his Chief Collaborator. Apparently he and our own Ser-
          vice authorities on the spot were convinced that it was only
          by use of Pétain's name that the French authorities in
          North Africa could be induced to cease resistance and
          Darlan as Pétain's emissary has been able to use the sacred

name effectively in spite of the old dodderer's indignant protests from Vichy. The result in enabling us to get quickly to Tunis and even in securing French resistance to the German landings at Tunis is indeed worthwhile. But there is a danger of the situation continuing and of the Americans committing themselves to men who are passionately hated by all the French who have loyally stood out in France and outside. This morning our Consul in Tangier [Alvary Gascoigne] sent in a passionate protest, in this respect voicing the views of his American colleagues as well."

182–83. Ronald Steel, *Walter Lippmann and the American Century* (London: 1980), 401. A Gallup Poll in July 1942 showed overwhelming American public support for Fighting France, minimal support for Vichy. (Thomas; 214, n. 33.) British public opinion was similarly clear cut; the British press was extremely critical of Darlan. (Philip Bell; "British Public Opinion and the Darlan Deal" (November–December 1942), *Journal of British Institute in Paris*, 7 (Spring 1989), 71–79.)

184–85. Anderson's views also reflect his worries, and prejudices. BRANDON was well received by French citizens when it moved into Tunisia. But Anderson's criticisms remain valid in the context of Darlan's refusal positively to support Allied efforts to reach Tunis as quickly as possible.

188. "Squeezed lemon" is given in full by Funk, 259.

190. David Dilks, ed., *The Diaries of Sir Alexander Cadogan* (London: 1971), 493. Professor Dilks comments: "This is not, of course, to be read literally." Is it not? And if not, why not?

191. The following orders etc., indicate the scale of British support. Some former members of the Algiers Patriot Group have suggested to the writer that whether or not one accepts or discounts a "Gaullist plot" to assassinate Darlan, members of the Corps Franc, including Bonnier, were approached by Gaullist emissaries in early December 1942. But these approaches were both overt and widespread, extending to French Navy, Army, and Air Force personnel stationed near or in North Africa. Such approaches—and recruitment—are not evidence of a "Gaullist plot";

COMMANDEMENT EN CHEF
DES FORCES FRANÇAISES
TERRESTRES ET AÉRIENNES
EN AFRIQUE
————

CORPS FRANC D'AFRIQUE

Etat-Major

O R D R E de M I S S I O N
- - - - - - - - - - - - - - - -

Le sous lieutenant PAUPHILET officier de
liaison du général de Monsabert commandant le
Corps Franc d'Afrique, se mettra en liaison av
ec les autorités alliées pour r gler les
questions relatives à l'armement et à l'équi-
pement des unités du Corps Franc , conformé-
ment à l'accord de principe réalisé auprès
du commandant de la Ière armée britannique .

Alger le 7 décembre 1942

Le général Commandant le CFA

Page
they do reveal that de Gaulle was determined to under-
mine *Giraud*.
192. Funk, 258.

Page
194. Chandler, vol. 2, 795.
195–96. OSS Archive. Mack's telegram to London is to be found
in CAB66/WP42/565—sufficient evidence that the cabinet, not only the Foreign Office, got the message.
198. *Annual Register*, 1942: 91–92. Amery's diary notes: "27
November 1942 ... to a Cabinet at which we first of all
discussed the Darlan situation, and decided that if the
House wanted a debate it would have to be in secret session ..." The House of Commons certainly wanted to
debate the "situation," and on a motion condemning Darlan and all that he was believed to represent. The Secret
Session debate of 10 December—in which Churchill, on
his own admission, "took refuge"—unreported in Han-
sard, enabled him to defend his equivocal relationship with
Roosevelt. But much unease remained, as Harold Nicolson's diary reveals, despite, or because of, Churchill's
misleading account of events. We should also note that
although the BBC gave de Gaulle much assistance—and
was a crucial factor in British support of French Résistance in terms of broadcasting coded messages—it was
censored regarding outright criticism of Darlan. In this
connection see: W. J. West, ed., *George Orwell: The War
Commentaries* (London: 1985).
200. *Foreign Relations of the United States*, vol. 2, *1942*, 546–
47.
203. D. Barlone, *A French Officer's Diary* (Cambridge: 1942),
110.
203. See p. 112 for location of Darlan's letter.
206–7. WO204/303.
Major-General Sir Edward Spears, *Fulfilment of a Mission: Syria and Lebanon, 1941–1944*, 8.
207. See also Woodward, 395–98, for further discussions among
Eden, de Gaulle, and Catroux on 8 December. From this
account it is clear that despite Churchill's Secret Session
speech of only two days later, not only was Darlan's
"elimination" virtually agreed upon, but de Gaulle's role
as the only major French leader worthy of sustained British support acknowledged.
210. Morton Papers in the Public Record Office (PREM/3).
Thomas, 143. Pierre Puchau was Vichy Minister of the
Interior at the time, a much hated figure.

O/C. Ordenance Depôt.—

'Please Supply the bearer with The following Stores in accordance with 1st Army Orders.

Sten Guns.	1,000.
9 m/m Ammo.	800,000
303 Rifles.	500
303 S.A.A.	200,000
? Mills grenades.	2,000.
(No 75) Hawkins grenades.	2,000

J. Lawrence Maj
JH.

13 Nov. 1942.

Page
211–12. Keswick was well aware of the fact that as at the time
MASSINGHAM was a Section F operation, *liaison* with
Giraud and his intelligence and operations subordinates
was a specific requirement. That is not the point: Keswick

knew, and reported to Baker Street—hence to higher authority—that no SOE operation could succeed until Darlan was eliminated.

213. H. R. Kedward, *Occupied France; Collaboration and Resistance, 1940–1944* (Oxford: 1985), 68.

216. Dilks, 498.

Murphy, as usual, is slack. On 20 June 1940, twenty-nine members of the National Assembly opposed to capitulation sailed for Casablanca. All were promptly interned by Noguès. Among the party was Georges Mandel, Reynaud's Minister of the Interior, a Jew and a committed enemy of Hitler. Mandel was Churchill's original choice as leader of a France which would refuse capitulation. Vichy in France and North Africa turned Mandel over to the Germans in November 1942; he was returned to Vichy and murdered by its agents in Paris on 7 July 1944.

223. Sir Douglas Dodds-Parker, *Setting Europe Ablaze: Some Account of Ungentlemanly Warfare* (Springwood Books; 1984), 113.

226. Chequers guest list for 21–28 December 1942, a copy of which has come into the writer's possession.

229. Thomas, 154, describes Laval's continued importance to Noguès and others in North Africa.

229–30. A copy of this telegram is in the writer's possession, having been kindly provided by a former member of the Algiers Patriot Group. There is, today, no particular confidentiality about the telegram, which has been quite widely cited by French writers as evidence of an entirely Gaullist plot against Darlan.

235. "Under any circumstances . . .": See Chandler, vol. 2, 835, editorial note.

239. Bonnier's Italian mother bore the family name of Della Capella. Bonnier, for some reason, adapted this name, that of another family.

242. Winston S. Churchill, *The Second World War* (London, 1951), vol. 4, *The Hinge of Fate*, 580.

242. Cordier "seemed tormented, perplexed," and Bonnier "absolutely calm": Pierre Raynaud to the writer, 2 August 1989.

245. Général [Henri] Giraud, *Un Seul But, La Victoire: Alger, 1942–1944* (Paris: 1949), 75–81. The Appendices to this

Page

self-congratulatory autobiography contain examples of Giraud's demands to Murphy.

245.   Murphy's account is in the OSS Archive. Bonnier had been provided with a passport in the name of Morand. Provision of a passport was part of the process whereby Bonnier was led to believe that assassination would be followed by rescue, and sanctuary abroad.

245–46.   Asa Briggs, *The History of Broadcasting in the United Kingdom* (London, 1970), vol. 3, *The War of Words*, 455, note 2. An internal BBC directive of 25 December instructed that Darlan's assassination should not elicit "any discernable delight."

248–49.   Eisenhower ordered a Committee of Inquiry into the assassination, but this was intended to exculpate, not accuse. The Colt .45 aroused momentary concern—in being an American weapon—but speculation as to how Bonnier acquired it produced no conclusions. The Inquiry findings specifically exculpated British secret and special services. The OSS Archive contains a detailed account of Berlin and Rome Radio broadcasts.
Dilks, 501.

250.   C. V. Wedgwood, *Velvet Studies* (London: 1946), 150—quoting a letter written by a young résistant in Paris shortly before his death. The "idea" of France thus expressed may seem close to de Gaulle's. But Veronica Wedgwood put Bonnier's death in a wider perspective: "The idea is still an idea uncorrupted by practice, unconfined by definition. Over what gulfs of misunderstanding, what differences of heritage and outlook this one luminous idea cast a cloak of heroic sameness; over the Left and Right, the Monarchist and the Communist, the disreputable and the respectable." Résistance was not a political need but a necessity.

253.   *Foreign Relations of the United States: 1943*, vol. 2, 24.

260.   Kersaudy, 249.

267.   Chandler, 80.

268.   A privately printed memoir of de Gaulle, kindly made available to the writer by Lord Gladwyn.

Translations

Page

244. "The city is quiet. General Bergeret has seen to that."

244–45. "How did all this come about? Was it the Germans? No, they had no reason to kill Darlan. Vichy? Perhaps. Communists? Perhaps. Royalists? They certainly like to make trouble. Gaullists? They also are troublemakers."

"France has returned to the war. We must have no doubts. There is only one aim—victory."

"As commander-in-chief of a territory at war, I order an immediate court martial. Judgment will be impartial—but from that judgment there will be no appeal."

"People of North Africa—Admiral Darlan has fallen at his post, victim of a crime which cannot be forgiven in the sight of French citizens who have, once again, by the side of their Allies, taken up arms against Germany. Thus will our enemies be frustrated."

247. "That's something, that's new."

250. "Bonnier's death is considered by all of us, and by the French Résistance, to be a crime."

"Bonnier has performed a great service."

"I have not died for a faction, or an individual. I have died for France, for an idea, to which I have given all."

Index

With a few unavoidable or obvious exceptions, individuals' titles and ranks are given as held at the time of the events described, not necessarily as given in the text.

For abbreviations used, see glossary.